W9-CFS-756

PRAISE FOR *HOLLYWOOD EDEN*

"*Hollywood Eden* brings the lost humanity of the record business vividly back to life... [Selvin's] style is blunt, unpretentious and brisk; he knows how to move things along entertainingly... Songs about surfboards and convertibles had turned quaint, but in this book, their coolness is restored." — *New York Times*

"A jukebox musical of a book... If Altamont marked the premature end of the 1960s, *Hollywood Eden* is the decade's origin story, capturing the lingering 1950s and the transition in Southern California music from surfing and hot rods to the singer-songwriters of the canyons." — *San Francisco Chronicle*

"For a tale of dreams, there's a lot of hustle going on in *Hollywood Eden*... For every sonic visionary, be it [Brian] Wilson or Phil Spector, there are a dozen people scraping by... What Selvin does so well is focus on a specific community and what made it work... Selvin took a similar approach in his '60s Bay Area pop book, *Summer of Love*. Here he zooms in tighter on less trodden ground, with more revelatory results." — *Los Angeles Times*

"Selvin tells this inside story as if he were right there... *Hollywood Eden* is a lively and well-researched book." — *Winnipeg Free Press*

"Forget the subtitle, which is its own myth. The book is in stray facts no one else would dig up, yet alone think of publishing... and, in this ten-years-on-the-strip tale of white people coming out of University High in Los Angeles and making records, the way Selvin can cut right down to what really matters, over and over again." — Greil Marcus, *Los Angeles Review of Books*

"My life back in those days was truly 'fun fun fun' and *Hollywood Eden* beautifully captures our Fifties and Sixties California music scene. Please don't change a word!" —Bruce Johnston of the Beach Boys

"*Hollywood Eden* is a keeper! Startlingly moving, it features a cast of somehow sympathetic characters who are all looking for a fast buck, some luck of the draw, or intimations of immortality. I knew full well most of the subjects of this tumultuous time; I was also there in a hedge-row cameo. So I read the book through and through. I warrant every word of it is true." —Van Dyke Parks, composer, songwriter, and lyricist of Brian Wilson's renowned *Smile* album

"*Hollywood Eden* is a detailed look at the hugely influential California music scene just before the arrival of folk rock and psychedelic music—a vital link in the chronicles of the American popular song. I found it fascinating; I love the book." —Linda Ronstadt, vocalist, songwriter, and bestselling author of *Simple Dreams*

"Those of us who grew up in the Darwinian slaughterhouse of New Jersey couldn't have imagined the paradise so accurately described in *Hollywood Eden*. Through the years I became familiar with most of the characters in this book, yet I learned something new on every page. Joel Selvin's special gift is putting you in the room to witness these unlikely events that became essential Rock History." —Stevie Van Zandt, musician, actor, and syndicated radio host of *Little Steven's Underground Garage*

"There's a panoramic sweep to Joel Selvin's *Hollywood Eden*. It's a story told not as a history, but as a dramatic tale, an adventure, with scenes described so vividly, they become cinematic." —*Rock & Roll Globe*

"*Hollywood Eden* doesn't shy away from the darkness that often boiled under the sun-flecked harmonies, but it ultimately celebrates these audacious young people and the enduring art they created... *Hollywood Eden* is a vivid and engaging snapshot of California in the 1960s—both the harsh reality and the fantasy world of song."
— *The Second Disc*

"Behind the scenes it wasn't always fun, fun, fun, but fans of late '50s and '60s pop will feel like they've caught the perfect wave."
—*School Library Journal*

ALSO BY JOEL SELVIN

Ricky Nelson: Idol for a Generation

Monterey Pop (with Jim Marshall)

Summer of Love

San Francisco: The Musical History Tour

Photo Pass: The Rock and Roll Photography of Randy Bachman

Mid-Life Confidential (with Stephen King, Dave Barry,
Amy Tan, and others)

Sly and the Family Stone: An Oral History

The Treasures of the Hard Rock Café (with Paul Grushkin)

Smart Ass: The Music Journalism of Joel Selvin

Red: My Uncensored Life in Rock (with Sammy Hagar)

Peppermint Twist (with John Johnson Jr. and Dick Cami)

Wear Your Dreams: My Life in Tattoos (with Ed Hardy)

*Here Comes the Night: The Dark Soul of Bert Berns and the Dirty
Business of Rhythm and Blues*

The Haight: Love, Rock, and Revolution (with Jim Marshall)

Sing to Me (with L. A. Reid)

Altamont

Fare Thee Well (with Pamela Turley)

Electric Guitars, Fast Cars, and the
Myth of the California Paradise

HOLLYWOOD EDEN

JOEL SELVIN

ANANSI

Copyright © 2021 Joel Selvin

First published in Canada in 2021 in hardcover and the USA in 2021 by House of Anansi Press Inc.
www.houseofanansi.com

This edition published in Canada in 2022 and in the USA in 2022 by House of Anansi Press Inc.

All rights reserved. No part of this publication may be reproduced or transmitted in any
form or by any means, electronic or mechanical, including photocopying, recording, or
any information storage and retrieval system, without permission in writing from the
publisher.

House of Anansi Press is committed to protecting our natural environment.
This book is made of material from well-managed FSC®-certified forests,
recycled materials, and other controlled sources.

House of Anansi Press is a Global Certified Accessible™ (GCA by Benetech) publisher.
The ebook version of this book meets stringent accessibility standards and is available
to students and readers with print disabilities.

26 25 24 23 22   1 2 3 4 5

Library and Archives Canada Cataloguing in Publication

Title: Hollywood Eden : electric guitars, fast cars, and the myth of the
California paradise / Joel Selvin.
Other titles: Electric guitars, fast cars, and the myth of the California paradise
Names: Selvin, Joel, author.
Description: Includes bibliographical references and index.
Identifiers: Canadiana 20210389338 | ISBN 9781487011376 (softcover)
Subjects: LCSH: Rock musicians—California—Biography. | LCSH: Rock music—
California—History and criticism. | LCGFT: Biographies.
Classification: LCC ML394 .S469 2022 | DDC 782.42166092/2794—dc23

Book design: Alysia Shewchuk

*House of Anansi Press respectfully acknowledges that the land on which we operate
is the Traditional Territory of many Nations, including the Anishinabeg, the Wendat,
and the Haudenosaunee. It is also the Treaty Lands of the Mississaugas of the Credit.*

 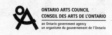

Canada Council   Conseil des Arts
for the Arts   du Canada

ONTARIO ARTS COUNCIL
CONSEIL DES ARTS DE L'ONTARIO
an Ontario government agency
un organisme du gouvernement de l'Ontario

With the participation of the Government of Canada | Canadä
Avec la participation du gouvernement du Canada

*We acknowledge for their financial support of our publishing program
the Canada Council for the Arts, the Ontario Arts Council, and the Government of Canada.*

Printed and bound in Canada

To Charlie Winton.
You made this one possible.

CONTENTS

PART 3: DUSK

THE CAST

UNIVERSITY HIGH SCHOOL

Jan Berry — vocalist, producer
Dean Torrence — vocalist
Nancy Sinatra — vocalist
Kim Fowley — producer, publisher, provocateur
Jill Gibson — songwriter, model, vocalist
Sandy Nelson — drummer, recording artist
Bruce Johnston — vocalist, keyboardist, producer
Arnie Ginsburg — vocalist
Barry Keenan — kidnapper
Kathy Kohner — surfer, diarist, "Gidget"

FAIRFAX HIGH SCHOOL

Herb Alpert — songwriter, producer, trumpeter
Phil Spector — guitarist, songwriter, producer
Steve Douglas — saxophonist
Steve Barri — songwriter, vocalist
Phil Sloan — songwriter, vocalist

BEVERLY HILLS HIGH SCHOOL

Terry Melcher — vocalist, producer

ROOSEVELT HIGH SCHOOL

Lou Adler — songwriter, producer

HAWTHORNE HIGH SCHOOL

Brian Wilson — vocalist, songwriter, producer

ALSO FEATURING

Gary S. Paxton — vocalist, songwriter, producer, troublemaker
Nick (Nik) Venet — songwriter, producer
Richard Allen Podolor — guitarist, songwriter
James (Kip) Tyler — vocalist, bandleader
Lee Hazlewood — producer, songwriter, curmudgeon

MUSICAL APPEARANCES BY

Jan and Dean
Beach Boys
The Mama's and the Papa's
The Byrds
Ike and Tina Turner
Barry McGuire
Johnny Rivers
Nancy Sinatra
...and many others

THE STUDIO BAND

Arranger/conductor: Jack Nitzsche | Guitars: Glen Campbell, Billy Strange, Tommy Tedesco, Barney Kessel | Keyboards: Al De Lory, Russell Bridges (Leon Russell), Larry Knechtel, Don Randi | Bass: Carol Kaye, Ray Pohlman, Lyle Ritz | Drums: Hal Blaine, Earl Palmer | Saxophones: Steve Douglas, Plas Johnson, Jay Migliori

PROLOGUE

THERE WAS A time when California was a quiet corner of the country and Hollywood was a small town. Outside of the people who lived there, few Americans gave much thought to the sunshine and beaches of the West Coast. The people who did live there knew what kind of sunny skies and palm tree paradise they had found. The city of Los Angeles doubled in size during the Forties and added half again in the Fifties, but it was still a scrawny, sprawling collection of villages spread over five hundred square miles and connected by long, straight, handsome boulevards built for the automobile, all leading inexorably to the shore. The crystalline beaches were never crowded, although they were always an attraction, an essential element of life in Southern California.

To young people growing up in Los Angeles after the Second World War, this was their birthright. Their parents had largely come to California before or during the war to secure a piece of the American dream out West. Those growing up in Los Angeles knew nothing of icy winters or steam bath summers. They lived a life immune from the hardships of the elements. Their world was different. Even the scourge of poverty and the rigid divisions of class were blunted by the warm California sun.

Life like this couldn't remain a secret. In fact, in its midst were the makings of modern mythology—a vision of youth, beauty, poetry, and music unique to the inspirations and aspirations of California, out there on the faraway coast, distant from the centers of established power and culture in those days before jet travel. There was a promise of freedom, a sense of infinite possibilities, the prospect of fresh life without limits. This time and place felt like it had been made for teenagers. The youth of California grew up in a world of their own, innocent and fearless, bold and open. They were born to live this life, and they never questioned the way they lived. California was a land of dreams and the future was as wide and clear as the blue sky over the Pacific Ocean.

PART I

DAWN

There rise her timeless capitals of
   Empires daily born,
Whose plinths are laid at midnight, and
   whose streets are packed at morn;
And here come hired youths and maids
   that feign to love or sin
In tones like rusty razor-blades to
   tunes like smitten tin.

— Rudyard Kipling

UNIVERSITY HIGH

Fall 1957

THE WATER RICOCHETED off the walls and floor of the locker room shower like BBs in a barrel. A couple of dozen high school football players heckled and joked around with each other after practice as they washed up and showered off. Their youthful naked bodies glistened with soap and water. The clamor they raised rattled around the shower room and mixed with the sizzle of the streams bouncing off the floor. This was the varsity squad, the athletic elite of University High School.

Built in the Twenties, University High stood in Olympian splendor across three terraced and landscaped levels at the east end of Santa Monica, a public school that served the wealthy residents of Bel Air and Brentwood in west Los Angeles. The varnished floors of the old buildings smelled of fresh wax every morning as the students crowded the hallways. Carrying armloads of books and chattering noisily, seven hundred of them made their way to class each day. They did not know they lived in paradise, even if they drove themselves to school in their own cars, or took the ten-minute drive after school to the beach. Life on the Westside was idyllic for these patrician youths, living the good life in the Promised Land among the sunshine and palms.

Into this steaming, blindingly white shower room walked Jan Berry, a striking blonde boy, movie star handsome, more than six feet tall. He smoked cigars and was something of a petty thief. He was also a rich kid who lived on top of the hill with a father who was right-hand man to millionaire industrialist Howard Hughes. Young Berry carried himself with the kind of confidence that showed in his stride as he walked across the showers after pausing at the entrance and spying his best friend. Stark naked, he approached his locker mate Dean Torrence, already under the shower. Berry had known Dean Torrence since junior high school, but they had only recently struck up a close friendship, after Berry went out for football. Berry had just returned to school that fall, after he'd been expelled as a troublemaker in his junior year. He'd spent the last year living in San Francisco under an assumed name.

Torrence was an easy-going, tall and lanky blonde who came from a more middle-class home than most of his classmates, though he still drove himself to school in a gleaming white '32 Ford pickup truck that he used to ferry surfboards to the beach for weekends of volleyball and sun. He smiled as he saw his friend approach. Berry leaned under the shower into Torrence's ear. In an exaggerated bass voice that boomed over the showers, he started singing.

> *Yip yip yip yip yip yip yip yip*
> *Sha na na na, sha na na na*
> *Sha na na na, sha na na na*
> *Sha na na na, sha na na na*
> *Mum mum mum mum mum mum*
> *Get a job*

Not only did Torrence jump in at the chorus, half the other football players in the showers started shouting along to the song, a current hit on the radio by a New York vocal group called the Silhouettes. Their voices banged off the tiles with a satisfying echo that made it sound like there were hundreds of them singing. The reverberations made it feel like a record. Their glee filled the room.

This senior class of 1958 was the original rock and roll class. They entered University High in fall 1955, just as James Dean died in a car crash and "Rock Around the Clock" by Bill Haley and his Comets hit the charts. The excitement of music struck the student body like lightning, a fascination for many, an obsession for some. While many of the white Southerners who made rock and roll records were popular — Elvis Presley, Buddy Holly, the Everly Brothers — it was the sound of New York street corners that had the cool kids at Uni High buzzing. These dreamy melodic songs sung by Black vocal groups often named after birds, like the Orioles or the Crows — leading them to be called "bird groups" — had found an unlikely audience among the sun-kissed Southern California teens.

The music had been hidden in plain sight, and all the teens knew where to find it on the radio. Hunter Hancock was a white deejay who had been playing Black music for a largely Black audience on Los Angeles radio since the Forties. Originally, he played jazz on his *Harlem Holiday* show on KFVD, but he began to court a broader audience by playing jukebox favorites, dance records known as "race music" at the time. In 1954, a few exceptional records seeped through to mainstream success — "Gee" by the Crows, "Earth Angel" by the Penguins, "Sh-Boom" by the Chords — and suddenly these Black vocal group records were the rage among white California teens who heard three and a half hours of the music every night on Hancock's radio show.

The songs could be chaotic and irreverent or silken and romantic, but they were a million miles from the "Canadian Sunset" pop music of the day. Somehow these sounds from Harlem and the outer boroughs struck home with kids in the white-bread Hollywood hills. As different as they may have been from their own lives, these privileged teens found a common thread in the songs. Even amidst all their abundance, they still yearned for freedom from restraint. They knew their parents did not understand them, and sometimes they felt like strangers in a strange land. The songs spoke of simple aspirations, touched on universal topics of their tender age, often with sly humor, and most important of all, they were easy to sing.

As the football players laughed and splashed in the showers, the joy of singing together hung in the air. Something deep inside rock-and-roll-crazy Jan Berry started to bloom. Football was fine, but rock and roll...now that was a heroic, mythical kingdom, far removed from the chlorinated gymnasium locker room. This raucous sound, this melee of voices, sparked a hidden desire in Berry. These were thoughts he never before dared to think, little seeds poking their way to the air and sunlight. He had glimpsed his destiny, even if the farthest into the future he could see was the school talent show.

EVERYBODY AT UNI HIGH knew they went to school with Nancy Sinatra. Her father, Frank Sinatra, was the number one entertainer in the business. She was his darling daughter and oldest child, who drove herself to school every morning in the first pink '57 Thunderbird made by Ford—a seventeenth-birthday present from dad (for her sweet sixteen, he gave her a mink coat). Nancy lived in a seven-bedroom Spanish mansion with a cobblestone courtyard and swimming pool on Carolwood Drive in the Holmby Hills with her mother, Nancy— invariably known as "Big Nancy" or "Nancy Sr." in the Nancy-centric household. Her mother bought the house for a princely $250,000 after divorcing Frank when Nancy was ten years old. Of the Sinatra children, the divorce hit Nancy the hardest. Her brother, Frank Jr., and sister, Christina, were younger, so she took the emotional brunt of the family split. Her father, perhaps from guilt, paid her a lot of special attention and was a constant presence around the Carolwood house.

Nancy, in turn, idolized her father. When he flew to Los Angeles to attend the 1954 Academy Awards, where he was nominated for Best Supporting Actor for his career-reviving role in *From Here to Eternity*, Sinatra went straight from the Van Nuys Airport to Carolwood, where his ex-wife made a spaghetti dinner and Nancy presented him with a medallion from his children—*Dad, all our love from here to eternity* inscribed on the back. The next evening, Nancy, nearly fourteen years old and wearing an ermine cape, and ten-year-old Frank Jr., sporting a bow-tie strongly reminiscent of his father's old trademark, accompanied Sinatra to the ceremony, where he did indeed take home a statuette.

In January 1955, Nancy went with her father on a triumphant ten-night run of shows in Australia, where he brought along some American jazz musicians, including vocalist Ann McCormack. Nancy had suspected her father was seeing someone in the show, but she was shocked to discover a pair of silky panties in the desk drawer of his suite when she went looking for stationery. She felt betrayed, like he was cheating on her, and couldn't bring herself to write about the remainder of the trip in her diary. Her circumspect mother had never allowed her so much as a glimpse beyond the veil of her private life, but her father forced Nancy to confront his sexuality just as she was on the cusp of discovering her own. She would never be daddy's little girl so completely again.

Unlike her volatile, emotional father, Nancy's mother was a serene and stable Italian lady who did her own hair and nails—the mark of a true *paisan* in Beverly Hills. She made Nancy's school lunches herself, which Nancy often traded with her best friend Val Romoff, who eagerly ate the homemade meatball sandwiches or eggplant parmesan. Nancy was an active and popular student at University High, a ranking member of the Hi-Y social club the Tierres, an elite enclave in the school's social order. She was highly musical and took charge of the club's annual appearance in the intraclub song contest, a highpoint of social calendars for all the girls' clubs. Nancy not only picked the material, she wrote the arrangements, conducted the harmonies, and rehearsed the singers. The Tierres won, of course.

Dad couldn't help but get involved. Nancy and two other Tierres singers—Belinda Burrell and Jane Ross—called themselves the Tri-Tones and appeared on her father's television show, *The Frank Sinatra Show*, in November 1957, singing "Side By Side," reprising the same song Sinatra and his daughter sang together the year before in a special appearance in the school auditorium at the annual University High PTA Awards show.

Nancy was a teen queen—cute, brunette, cheerful, and approachable. She dated a succession of good-looking guys, one at a time, careful never to get too attached. Sensitive to her elevated social status, Nancy deliberately left her good clothes at home; the cashmere sweaters stayed in the drawer. In her senior year, among other student activities, she served on the Appropriate Dress Board, a student council that enforced the school dress code (no slacks for girls, etc.). On

Saturday mornings, she joined the crowd at the movies at the Bruin or Westwood Theater in Westwood Village, a tiny adjunct of the UCLA campus, and then ate cheeseburgers across the street at Crumpler's Diner, often with classmate and fellow Tierres sister Lynn Crumpler, daughter of the proprietor. She had friends overnight at Carolwood practically every weekend.

♪

KATHY KOHNER DIDN'T care for University High School. The pint-sized, freckle-faced tomboy liked her literature teacher, but thought the rest of high school was a drag. She would rather be at the beach. Her parents used to make her accompany them on trips to visit friends at the Malibu Colony, where the bored teenager would wander off to watch the surfers at Malibu Pier. She had known about surfing since older neighbors threw their surfboards in the rumble seat of her mother's Model A Ford to hitch a ride to the beach from their Brentwood home, but standing on the sand and watching the surfers ride the waves during the summer of her tenth grade in June 1956, Kathy was determined to try surfing herself.

At the time, surfing was relegated to a few hardy souls on scattered beaches along the Southern California coast. At Malibu Point, Kathy encountered a group of determined outcasts who lived in a palm-frond-and-driftwood shack on the beach and called each other by nicknames like Moondoggie, Bubblehead, Beetle, Fencer, and the Cat. They did not immediately embrace the young girl.

"I'm not bothering you," she told one of the surfers.

"You're still breathing," he said.

Finally, Kathy traded a peanut butter sandwich to one of the guys to borrow his board. She spent the rest of the summer learning to surf and working her way into the mostly male crew that hung around the pier. She knew she had gained their reluctant acceptance when they gave her a nickname of her own; they called her the girl midget—Gidget.

Kathy breathlessly recorded her summer adventures in a diary. When she showed the diary to her screenwriter father Frederick Kohner and confessed that she wanted to write a book based on her experiences, he told her he would do it for her. Kohner had grown up in a Czechoslovakian spa town where his father ran the movie theater. After graduating with a Ph.D. in psychology from the University of Vienna, he worked as a screenwriter in Berlin before escaping the Nazis in 1936 and emigrating to Hollywood, where his older brother, already working as an agent, had landed him a deal writing scripts. He turned out nearly twenty movie scripts, in addition to a handful of Broadway plays, but he had never before written a novel.

After reading his daughter's diary, Kohner found himself fascinated by the language and lifestyle of the beach. Though his first language was German, Kohner proved to have an aptitude for capturing the fresh slang these weirdo kids had invented. He caught some of the maverick appeal of this bunch of social outriders and hinted at the immense romance of their sport. In just six weeks, he spat out *Gidget: The Little Girl with Big Ideas*, and introduced the world to the California paradise and the nascent surf culture developing like spots of mold along the coastline. When it was published in October 1957, *Gidget* hit the bestseller lists in Los Angeles above *On the Road* by Jack Kerouac. Columbia Pictures snapped up the film rights for a hefty $50,000, and *Life* magazine featured photos over several pages of the real-life Gidget at the beach in Malibu. Predictably, the beach boys were not impressed—"If I had a couple of bucks to buy a book," one told *Life*, "I wouldn't buy a book—I'd buy a bottle of beer." Even Gidget herself couldn't muster all that much enthusiasm. "The book's all right," Kathy said, "but it didn't have enough surfing in it to suit me."

The kids from University High frequented State Beach, a short drive down Sunset Boulevard to Chautauqua Boulevard, where they could scrounge parking on the street. They drove barefoot with their convertible tops down. The beach was a remote village in those days. There were no traffic lights on Sunset, only a few stop signs, and the tree-lined road wound past acres of vacant lots. Sunset and Sepulveda was a four-way stop with crops growing on every corner. At the intersection with the Pacific Coast Highway, there was a gas station and hamburger stand, Roy's Cabana, across the street from the beach.

Kathy went to State Beach from time to time, but nobody surfed. The kids played volleyball on the sand, cards on the seawall, and sometimes got in the water and rode the breakers at the shore. They smoked cigarettes and necked with their boyfriends. Not many kids at University High surfed, and certainly no girls other than Kathy. She appeared on the cover of her father's book, fresh-faced, wading through surf in her bathing suit, carrying her board. She won $500 as a contestant on the Groucho Marx TV quiz show, *You Bet Your Life*, but her high school life, such as it was, went uninterrupted by any fleeting celebrity the book could have brought her. There were a lot of show business kids at Uni High.

2

THE BARONS

THE SINGING IN the showers continued all football season. They sang "At the Hop" by Danny and the Juniors and "Tell Me Why" by Norman Fox and the Rob-Roys. The University High Warriors football team finished the season undefeated, although they lost the 1957 city championship to Banning High (who they had thrashed during the regular season).

Jan Berry began to assemble and polish his vocal group. After first moving the sessions to the boys' bathroom on campus, a select group of the singing football players began meeting after school at Berry's house to plot the next stage of their musical careers — the school talent show. Jan found a lead vocalist by simply introducing himself to one of the only Black guys in school, Chuck Steele, and inviting him to join the group.

The four-bedroom ranch-style home at 1111 Linda Flora Drive was perched on the edge of the Bel Air hills down a steep driveway, where a small parking area held several cars. Jan's new turquoise '57 Chevy was parked next to his father's sailboat and trailer. The Berry family had converted the two-car garage into a bedroom for

Jan and one of his brothers, but Jan turned the garage into his own private music studio. His electrical-engineer father had purchased two used Ampex tape recorders, rare and precious equipment that had originally belonged to his boss, Howard Hughes, and the family owned a poorly tuned upright piano.

The garage also housed Jan's immense and growing record collection; shelves groaned under boxes of heavy vinyl records. Tired of shoplifting the new releases, Jan printed up letterhead at school for "KJAN —Voice of the Bel Air Hills," and solicited promotional records from distributors and record companies for his imaginary disc jockeys—all five of them. Packages containing five copies of every new record soon began showing up at his home, often more than fifty a day, his imaginary radio station building an enormous actual record library.

At first, Jan called his group the Internationals, but soon changed the name to the Barons, after the Hi-Y boys' club that many of the players belonged to. Club members wore letterman-style jackets with insignias on the sleeves and their names embroidered on the chest. They were one of many officially sanctioned Hi-Y clubs sponsored by the YMCA, although with the Barons' incessant pranks and hijinks, the club bordered on a street gang. Their misbehavior caused school officials to pull the official photograph of the Barons from the yearbook.

Jan was a ringleader of many Barons misadventures and a pack of trouble all on his own. He liked to stage fake fistfights in public with other members of the Barons, but also got involved in more than a few authentic brawls. He was a fearless driver who recklessly raced his Chevy on city streets; Sepulveda Boulevard was his nighttime dragstrip. He nearly sank his father's racing sloop when he stole the boat for a night run to Catalina Island with some of the Barons. He was arrested at the beach for indecent exposure, although he was merely hanging a BA (for "bare ass"), a ritual teen insult. He was busted at Pacific Ocean Park amusement park after getting into a beef with a ticket-seller and decking two cops, although charges were dropped. Jan had a long list of youthful indiscretions, the most serious of which involved the theft of an M16 rifle from ROTC headquarters—this was the final straw that got him expelled in his junior year. He also earned surprisingly good grades without any apparent effort, even though he attended class only sporadically. Jan Berry was not some-one you could tell what to do.

Don Altfeld met Jan Berry in the tenth grade after the Altfeld family moved from Cleveland, Ohio, to Brentwood, so his father could seek treatment for his leukemia at UCLA. Altfeld, who wrote a record review column for the school newspaper, kept noticing that the pick hits he included at the end of his column had been changed. He traced the unsolicited editing back to the high school printshop, where the guilty Linotype operator introduced himself. "Hi, I'm Jan Berry," he said.

The two quickly became fast friends, adjourning to Jan's house every afternoon to listen to records, talk about music, and make tape-recorded radio shows they would later play at school over the PA system during rainy day lunchtimes. They traded tapes with a friend of Altfeld's from Ohio, who in turn kept them up to date on the wild, untamed rock and roll played by Pete "Mad Daddy" Myers, who was burning up the Cleveland airwaves with a mouthful of rhyming jive and red-hot rhythm and blues records. Myers had taken over from Alan Freed, the inventor of rock and roll radio, after Freed left Cleveland for New York.

Berry and Altfeld would often cut school and go to South Central Los Angeles to hang out with rhythm and blues musicians like

Johnny Otis and Richard Berry (no relation to Jan). They would visit radio stations and stare at the disc jockeys through the studio glass. They went to rhythm and blues concerts at the El Monte Legion Stadium in East Los Angeles. Altfeld accompanied Berry to the one-stop record distributors on Pico Boulevard, where Jan tried to convince the distributors to give him free copies of the records to play at his school. When that didn't work, he shoplifted them, stuffing his Barons jacket's sleeves full while Altfeld acted as lookout.

At Wallichs Music City, the big Hollywood record store at the corner of Sunset Boulevard and Vine Street, they spied Ricky Nelson shopping for records. A senior at nearby Hollywood High, seventeen-year-old Nelson already had hit records on the charts, courtesy of his role in his father's TV program, *The Adventures of Ozzie and Harriet*. Altfeld saw the intense look on his friend's face as Jan gazed across the room at the teenage TV star, and knew instantly what he was thinking: *I can do this too.*

The Barons' after-school rehearsals soon thinned down to a select few guys. Chuck Steele remained the group's lead vocalist and sole Black member. Arnie Ginsburg, one of the Hi-Y Barons, sang first tenor. A Japanese American named Wally Yagi sang second tenor, but so did John "Sagi" Seligman because Yagi didn't sing that loud. Jan sang bass, and Dean Torrence handled falsetto because he was the only one who could. By linking the tape recorders and delaying the signal, Jan could achieve the kind of reverb echo that was a critical component of the vocal group records he loved. He would connect the recorders to a speaker so the vocalists could hear themselves sing, their voices drenched in echo, lending a kind of heightened realism to their performances that could be quite entrancing. Jan was an exacting perfectionist in the studio, but there was still plenty of horsing around.

The spring school talent show came and went in a blur. The Barons sang "Get a Job" and two other numbers. The whole act lasted about five minutes and didn't bring the house down or anything. Some of the guys figured that would be the end of this musical interlude, but Jan continued to pour himself into the after-school sessions. He wrote a ballad, "There in the Night," that he arranged in five-part harmony with a falsetto on top that sounded straight out of Brooklyn. Although Jan would frequently bang away on the piano at these sessions, he decided to bring in other musicians to round out the sound. Dean enlisted his neighbor, Sammy Nelson, another University High kid, to play piano, but when Nelson showed up at Jan's house, he had a set of drums in the back of Dean's hot rod pickup. Jan drafted Bruce Johnston, a friend who lived around the corner, to play piano.

Jan had met Johnston waiting for the bus in the neighborhood. At the time, Johnston was still attending junior high at the exclusive Bel Air Town and Country School and had studied classical piano. He lived a couple of doors down the street from movie star Burt Lancaster and grew up watching movies as a guest at the actor's home. Jan had been thrown out of Johnston's house many times for his rambunctious piano-playing mornings before going to school with Johnston, who was two years younger than the other Barons and stayed mostly in the background playing piano. Nelson brought another school friend named Dave Shostac, who played saxophone. You couldn't make R&B records without a sax break in the middle. After six weeks of rehearsing and recording, the Barons finally finished an acceptable version of "There in the Night." Jan was ecstatic, but for some of the other Barons, music was more of a passing interest.

Arnie Ginsburg met a roller-skating waitress at the Frostee Freeze and started spending his afternoons hanging out in the parking lot waiting for her to get off work. Wally Yagi bought a new '57 Chevy and had to spend every day after school working on it. John Seligman's mother wanted him to be an accountant like his father and refused to let him borrow her car to drive to the Berry house. Lead vocalist Chuck Steele lowered his Buick and could no longer drive down Berry's steep driveway. Also, he had a better offer from another group. Before long, it was down to Jan and Dean.

♪

SAMMY NELSON, WHO was mad for drums, had dropped out of University High the year before, after he turned eighteen. His mother's boyfriend, a sound man at 20th Century Fox studios, landed him a job as a temporary laborer on a movie shoot. One early morning, he found himself in a skiff on the Century City backlot amidst the swamps and beanfields, keeping ducks out of the shot while they made a war movie. At one point, he was asked to row actor Dean Martin across the swamp, and Nelson fumbled the oars. Martin, who was sipping bourbon from a brown paper bag, rolled his eyes.

"Jesus Christ," he said, "I'm out here on this fucking lake with a kid that can't row a boat."

Before fooling around with his pals in Jan's garage, Nelson had picked back up playing drums after he rediscovered his childhood love of the instrument while serving on stage crew at Uni High. When he was a child of around eight, Nelson's parents took him to see swing drum king Gene Krupa at the Orpheum Theatre in downtown Los Angeles. Krupa had floodlights under the floor toms of his sparkling silver kit, and when he played his solo, they threw giant shadows of him and his drums on the curtain behind him. The sights and sounds deeply impressed young Nelson, although his enthusiasm for pounding drums wouldn't bloom fully until high school, when he set up three kits as a member of the stage crew for a drum battle. Alone in the auditorium, Nelson sat at the middle kit and, using wooden coat hangers for drumsticks, reacquainted himself with his childhood passion. Suddenly he was back watching Gene Krupa playing his solo again. Nelson would sneak into the band room at lunch hour and bash away, his playing drawing a crowd of students who broke out dancing. The experience stuck with him, rattling around in his head—people dancing to nothing but drums.

After meeting in Jan's garage, Nelson, saxophonist Dave Shostac, and pianist Bruce Johnston started the Sleepwalkers, the first rock and roll band at Uni High. Johnston, despite being only fifteen, was more than capable on the piano, up to speed on the whole rhythm and blues scene, could sing like a birdie, and even wrote his own songs. Johnston was ambitious and talented, and he looked like a choirboy. Guitar players were harder to find; the Sleepwalkers occasionally used a Fairfax High musician named Phil Spector, who had a habit of playing too loud. He was not an especially agreeable character. "You come back here and complain one more time," Spector told someone at a party who dared voice objections, "and I'll stick this guitar up your ass."

Bruce Johnston was all about music. He was a smart, good-looking, and presentable young man with a quirky smile that he slipped into easily. He had been adopted by a wealthy Chicago couple who moved to Los Angeles in 1946, when his father started the Rexall Drug chain, but his father had died the year before, and he now lived at home with his widowed mother. Despite his youth, Johnston saw the Sleepwalkers as a thoroughly professional enterprise that he wanted to record.

On Saturday morning, February 1, 1958, Johnston and the other

Sleepwalkers, Nelson and Shostac, assembled at Radio Recorders, a relic from the days of live Hollywood radio broadcasts, with seats for the audience still in the room. Guitarist Arthur "Sleepy" Wright was waiting around the studio. He was a Black musician a few years older than Nelson and the others, who had played around the L.A. rhythm and blues scene for a few years and was currently working with bandleader Roy Milton. Wright joined the band for the session. The shiny linoleum tile and the polished wood baffles hanging on the tall walls of the enormous room lent the proceedings the properly serious atmosphere for their first professional recording session. They sounded more than adequately adept and made short work of the three-song session. Without their noticing, other people made note of their work.

Wright came to the studio with John Dolphin, who was there on business of his own. Dolphin was a towering figure of the Los Angeles rhythm and blues scene. He was the owner and operator of Dolphin's of Hollywood, a twenty-four-hour, seven-day-a-week record store at the corner of Vernon and Central Avenues, deep in South Central L.A., a pulsing heart for the city's Black community. He named his store Dolphin's *of Hollywood* insolently; the store was many miles from Hollywood, where a Black man wouldn't have been allowed to own a record store.

Since 1948, Dolphin's had been a gathering place for Black musicians, a cultural salon open all night. Dolphin held concerts in the shop and hosted disc jockeys doing their broadcasts from his store window. Huggy Boy, another key figure in breaking the East Coast vocal group sound on Los Angeles radio, was broadcasting from the Dolphin's front window when he made a hit record out of the 1954 landmark "Earth Angel" by the Penguins, after Dolphin suggested he turn the record over and play the B-side. Another key R&B deejay,

Magnificent Montague, grabbed the first copy of the new single by a then-unknown singer named Sam Cooke, a slight ballad titled "You Send Me," and camped out on the record, playing it over and over all night from the Dolphin's window, drawing massive crowds to the store until, around four in the morning, Cooke himself showed up to sing the song live over the air. They kept that jam session rolling until dawn.

As rhythm and blues music spread beyond the confines of the Black community, Dolphin's experienced an unexpected turn of events. Almost half the store's sales the past year went to young whites who drove down to Dolphin's to buy R&B records; the year before that, the store had approximately no white customers. All this reached a climax in 1956, when Elvis Presley visited the store.

John Dolphin also produced R&B records for various labels that he ran personally. He started the Recorded In Hollywood label shortly after opening the store and scored his first hit with Percy Mayfield's "Two Years of Torture" in 1950. Dolphin dabbled in jazz, blues, vocal groups, anything he thought might sell. It was no accident he named his next label Cash Records. Dolphin's records were thoroughly professional productions, featuring top-flight players on the sessions, often run by pianist Ernie Freeman, who'd had a Top Five R&B instrumental hit, "Jivin' Around," with Cash Records in 1955. When John Dolphin took an interest in your case, you were circulating in the highest realms of the Los Angeles rhythm and blues world.

The record business in Hollywood had grown up largely as the poor relation of the film industry. Outside of Capitol Records, no major labels had established headquarters in Los Angeles. The West Coast was a remote outpost of the music power center in New York City. A handful of scrappy independent labels like Dolphin's accounted for the small but thriving rhythm and blues business, many operated literally out of storefronts.

A large, forty-two-year-old man with a pencil-thin mustache and an inevitable cigar in his mouth, John Dolphin was married with three children, and enjoyed whiskey, card games, and other women— not necessarily in that order. He was a big man in every regard. At Radio Recorders that morning, he liked what he heard from the young white boys. Mindful of the new audience for rhythm and blues records he had watched grow in his own store, Dolphin thought there might be something there for him. He introduced himself to the musicians and told them to bring the dub to his office so they could talk about making records together.

The three teenagers, Nelson, Shostac, and Johnston, along with their new guitarist, Arthur Wright, drove to downtown Los Angeles and rang the bell to Dolphin's office at 1252 South Berendo Street. They were about to get into the record business, as simple as that. While they waited outside on the sidewalk in front of the block-long storefronts, a large, agitated Black man joined them. His name was Percy Ivy, a twenty-six-year-old aspiring singer and songwriter who worked as a shipping clerk at the Alcoa plant in Hollywood. Ivy was upset about money he claimed was owed him by Dolphin. "Watch out for John Dolphin," he told the Sleepwalkers. "He'll cheat you."

When there was no answer, Wright went down to the phone booth at a gas station on the corner of Pico Boulevard and called the office. Dolphin told Wright he would let them in, but to keep the other guy out on the sidewalk.

But when Wright returned and Dolphin opened the door, Ivy pushed past everyone and made his way inside. Dolphin knew Ivy well; he was a frequent customer at the store, and Dolphin had recorded four songs with him—more as a favor to Ivy than anything.

The songs were mediocre, and Ivy wasn't much of a singer despite his delusions of grandeur. The R&B world was tough. Royalties were rarely paid fairly, and many record labels gave their artists less money than they deserved. But given the relative morality in the rhythm and blues world, Dolphin was what passed for an honest record man — slow to pay, perhaps, but not a thief.

Dolphin sat down behind his desk, a cigar clenched between his teeth, and Ivy took the chair across from him. The guys in the Sleepwalkers took seats against the wall. Ivy declared that Dolphin owed him a rather grand $250 per song, and he wanted his money. Now. He also accused Dolphin of sending men to threaten him.

"I don't need to send out any guys to do you in," Dolphin told him. "I can do it myself."

Ivy stood up and produced a .32 Italian automatic. "Give me my money, John," he said, pointing the gun at Dolphin.

Dolphin pulled out a switchblade and reached over the desk for the gun. The two men struggled briefly, and the gun went off. Twice. Three times. Four...five. Everyone scattered, some bursting out of the office door onto the sidewalk. The Coca-Cola that Nelson had been drinking fizzed out of the bottle. Dave Shostac slipped and fell on the floor and a ricochet grazed his leg. Dolphin collapsed over a floor heater. Bruce Johnston carefully moved Dolphin off the heater and lowered him to the floor. "Are you all right, Mr. Dolphin?" he asked.

There was no reply.

When the police arrived, they found John Dolphin dead on his office floor and Percy Ivy seated behind the desk, the gun and knife laid out in front of him. The incident had taken place so quickly, the shaken teens could scarcely believe what had happened. Ivy was sobbing while Johnston asked him about his songs, trying to figure out what this was all about. The teens went home and didn't say a word to their parents. Dave Shostac's mother would never have known anything if he hadn't had to get a tetanus shot. After the story came out, she stopped giving her son the phone messages the guys left when they had gigs for him. Clearly, this record business was more complicated than they had imagined.

3

GRADUATION

KIM FOWLEY ARRIVED as a freshman at University High already seething with resentments. Life had been cruel to him, and he saw no reason not to return the favor. All through high school, no matter how much he may have yearned for acceptance, to be recognized for his cool, he was treated as a misfit. At six-foot-four, Fowley towered over the other students, his gawky frame bent by childhood polio. His face looked like a squashed muffin. He was not one of the good-looking, popular, athletic guys that the girls in the Hi-Y clubs went for, but he was true Hollywood spawn with a middling B-movie pedigree.

His father, Douglas Fowley, was experiencing the highpoint of a twenty-five-year acting career that spanned about a hundred Hollywood movies, by playing Doc Holliday in the TV series *The Life and Legend of Wyatt Earp*. In her most prominent part, Kim's mother, Shelby Payne, had played a cigarette girl next to Humphrey Bogart in *The Big Sleep*, but settled for marrying well after ditching Douglas Fowley while he was serving in the Navy during the Second World War. She shuttled baby Kim off to foster care, where the crippled kid battled for food and space with a couple of dozen older, bigger boys for several years. She married William Friml, wealthy son of the composer Rudolf Friml, who wrote treacly operettas for Nelson Eddy and Jeanette MacDonald.

When father Fowley returned from the war, marginally more interested in parenthood than his ex-wife, he retrieved young Kim from foster care, and then proceeded to run through a succession of wives and stepmothers. In the eighth grade, Kim was living in a garage in Pacific Beach with his father and his fifth wife, and a baby stepbrother, when his mother reappeared in his life. She whisked Fowley away to the Frimls' Beverly Hills mansion, where he fell asleep every night in his basement bedroom listening through the wall as his stepfather worked on musical arrangements. Kim spent his summers during junior high visiting his father's family in the Bronx, where he first encountered rhythm and blues music and the fabulous sound of the vocal groups.

At Uni High, Fowley was an indifferent if gifted student who attended accelerated classes at UCLA. He always worked odd jobs and had his own money, so he bought his own clothes and wore Ivy League sports clothes to school, thinking he was dressed like Troy Donahue. He aspired to date the private school girls from Marlborough School, but he had no chance of that. He was also something of a juvenile delinquent, associated not with one of the candy-ass social clubs that were so popular at Uni, but with a proper Westside gang that operated out of more than a dozen high school campuses: the Pagans of West L.A.

The Pagans were said to be behind the massive disruption of the October 1957 UCLA Homecoming Parade, where more than a hundred hoodlums swarmed the streets of Westwood Village and bombarded the eighty or so official floats with eggs, spoiled vegetables, beer cans, and bottles. One policeman was sent to the hospital with severe burns after a cherry bomb exploded in the front seat of his police car. It was violent enough to make the *CBS Evening News with Douglas Edwards*—not exactly Walter Cronkite, but close.

The summer before his senior year, Fowley contracted polio again and went back in the hospital. When he was released, his father wanted nothing to do with a crippled kid, so Fowley bunked up with a Uni High classmate and fellow Pagan, Kit Marshal, and his mother, a thirty-seven-year-old Carnation Milk heiress with Rhonda Fleming red hair named Mary Grace Marshal. Her ex-husband was Alan Marshal, a B-movie version of Errol Flynn past his prime. She soon began sleeping with her son's ungainly but extravagantly verbal and oddly charming, offbeat friend. She drove him to school in her pink Jaguar.

To make ends meet, Fowley was running a profitable hustle throwing illegal parties every weekend for Westside teens at homes where somebody's parents were out of town. He would sell liquor and sometimes reefer. Accomplices would rifle the girls' purses and break into the cars outside. Fowley paid older toughs to act as muscle. He started booking the only rock and roll band at Uni High, the Sleepwalkers. Fowley quickly attached himself to the band as a kind of booking agent and manager.

The Sleepwalkers represented an opportunity for Fowley. Drawn powerfully to music, Fowley wasn't a musician, but he could put stuff together. He was fiercely intelligent, wickedly witty, and driven by deeply secret personal forces, and he would make things happen any way he could. He found the Sleepwalkers jobs at Catholic high school dances and nightclubs in the San Fernando Valley. He and Bruce Johnston even began writing songs together. Under his tough, jaded exterior, Fowley was a beatnik poet who scribbled bad rhymes in notebooks. Johnston was always eager for musical opportunity.

They became a team and made plans to move forward together in the music business.

It all came crashing to a stop not long before the end of the school year, when the cops busted Fowley for selling wine to minors—and for stealing the wine he was selling in the first place. The judge, noting that Fowley had recently celebrated his eighteenth birthday, gave him the choice between hard time and the National Guard. The cops took him to the recruitment office to enlist and waited outside until he returned with his papers signed. Days later, he was off to Fort Ord in Monterey for basic training. For Kim Fowley, there would be no senior prom.

♪

ARNIE GINSBURG BROKE up with his girlfriend at the Frostee Freeze and started hanging out again after school at Jan Berry's garage with the other guys. Dark-haired, olive-skinned Ginsburg was a stark contrast to the blonde gentiles that composed most of his crowd. Not only was he a jacket-wearing member of the Barons, but Ginsburg was also one of the KJAN disc jockeys. A good-natured guy, easy to get along with, he looked muscled and built with his shirt off at the beach—another young Adonis. He showed up at the garage one night while Jan and a few friends were trying to work out the lyrics to a new record by the Diamonds. Ginsburg was bubbling over with a fresh enthusiasm—a stripper named Jennie Lee, who was appearing in the New Follies Burlesk. They all piled into a car and headed downtown to catch the show.

The New Follies had seen better days. Opened in 1893 on a block full of theaters in downtown Los Angeles, the old Burbank Theater had presented burlesque shows since the Twenties. In 1952, the company from the Follies Theatre two blocks down Main Street moved into the decrepit building in the rundown neighborhood. Since the Forties, a buxom, bossy older woman named Lillian Hunt had found, trained, and produced burlesque dancers for the company. She presented such attractions as Patti Waggin (since she went to college, she was billed as the "Co-ed with the Educated Torso"); blonde bombshell Dixie Evans, the "Marilyn Monroe of Burlesque"; former *Our Gang* child star Shirley Jean Rickert dancing as "Gilda and her Crowning Glory," a reference to her long blonde hair; and Virginia Lee Hicks — Jennie Lee, "The Bazoom Girl" — a thirty-year-old, five-foot-two dyed blonde with a cheerleader smile and a 42-28-40 figure.

The fellows settled into threadbare seats in a middle row of the darkened theater. Dean Torrence was excited to see naked breasts for the first time. Sammy Nelson, who recognized the drumbeat of the five-piece pit band from Duke Ellington's "Caravan," was captivated by the old man behind the trap drum set, putting beats in the bumps and grinds. The first couple of dancers left something to be desired, but they were just the warm-up acts. Everybody was waiting for the star — Jennie Lee.

She did not disappoint. Jennie Lee skipped out to center stage amidst the clatter of the band in a slight costume that, after prancing back and forth to each side of the stage, she quickly started to remove. Her silvery blonde hair sparkled in the spotlight, and her ample breasts poked out from under their cantilevered constraints. Cheerful and cherubic, Jennie Lee bounced more than danced, swirling and bending over to display her prodigious backside through filmy underwear. She finally doffed her brassiere to reveal shiny, colored tassels. As she swung her hips, the tassels spun in opposite directions like tiny propellers. With little effort, they gained speed until they were whirring around her chest. The older men in the front rows picked up the beat, chanting along with her gyrations, "bomp...bomp...bomp."

For this gaggle of teenage boys, the performance was a smash. They spilled out of the theater into the car for the ride home, laughing and jabbering excitedly. In the car, they began singing "bomp...bomp...bomp" and occasionally shouting "Jennie Lee!" By the time they turned off Sunset Boulevard and headed back up the hill to Jan's home on Linda Flora, they had the makings of a song.

For the next week, the boys beavered away in Jan's garage, singing and re-singing the song to tape, Jan pounding out the melody on piano, Don Altfeld beating on the back of a metal high chair with a stick he picked up off the garage floor. They used a professional Electro-Voice microphone Jan had appropriated from the high school auditorium. Jan managed crude overdubs by bouncing parts from one tape recorder to another. By reading the instruction manual, he had learned how to create an even more effective echo on his recordings.

They caught a whiff of daylight on tape, a burst of boyish joy and teen madness, a little over two minutes long. Far from polished, with only a bare-bones instrumental backing, the heavy reverb nevertheless made the garage recording sound almost like a real record. Jan couldn't resist adding "Jennie Lee" and his other garage original, the dreamy ballad "There in the Night," to the KJAN playlist. He lugged his father's tape recorder to school to play disc jockey during lunchtimes and took it to parties, where he played his own records alongside hits of the day. Jan even tucked it into one of the taped radio programs he sent back to Altfeld's friend in Cleveland.

"I want to play you a record by a group called the Barons," Jan announced on the tape. "I just received this a couple of days ago. I'll play both sides. First, you'll hear 'There in the Night'...Well, there they go, the Barons. And that's entitled, 'There in the Night.' Tell ya what I'll do, I'll just flip this one over, set it down here. This side's called 'Jennie Lee.' C'mon, Jennie!"

"Jennie Lee" received good reactions when Jan played it for his friends, and he certainly enjoyed the distinction of having made his own record. He wanted to take the record to a party at fellow Barons member Jim Bruderlin's house, but his father was getting tired of him dragging the tape deck around. Altfeld suggested Jan see about making an acetate. When Altfeld was taking piano lessons as a young boy in Cleveland, his piano teacher had taken him to a studio and recorded him playing. They cut an acetate for him at the studio so he could take the recording home and play it on a phonograph. Jan had never heard of acetates and had never seen the inside of a recording studio. He opened the Yellow Pages and found a studio that would make him an acetate for three dollars.

Dean Torrence had graduated early at the midterm in January 1958 and signed up for the Army Reserves, figuring to get his duty out of the way rather than face the draft. He was scheduled to leave for basic training at Fort Ord that Sunday. Jan asked if he wanted to go with him to the recording studio on Saturday and cut an acetate of "Jennie Lee." It was his last day of freedom, so Dean opted to spend the day frolicking in the snow with his new girlfriend and some other buddies who were also headed to Fort Ord the next day. It would be several weeks before he found out what he'd missed.

IN HOLLYWOOD THINGS were still possible. Jan Berry walked into a recording studio for the first time in his life at United Studios on

Sunset Boulevard. He and Arnie Ginsburg brought their homemade tape of "Jennie Lee" and pushed open the door into the dark, cool, sacred chamber where records were created. The engineer was working on a Doris Day track—heady stuff for a couple of teenage amateur musicians, since she was one of the biggest stars in Hollywood. They asked if they could watch him work, and the engineer agreed, but first he wanted to hear their tape. They handed him the reel, and he spooled it onto the tape deck and pressed play. "Jennie Lee" pounded out of the studio monitors.

The thick swinging door to the control room opened again and a burly man wearing black horn-rims and speaking in a working-class English accent poked his head through. "What's that you're playing?" he asked.

"It's theirs," said the engineer, indicating the pair of youths slouching on the couch in the corner.

Joe Lubin was the songwriter behind three songs on the new Doris Day movie, *Teacher's Pet*. He had come by the studio on this Saturday morning to drop off a tape of vocalist Gordon MacRae to be edited. He heard about four bars of "Jennie Lee" through the door, and that was enough to pique his interest. At forty-two, Lubin had been around. He'd begun his musical career in the post-war era on Denmark Street, London's answer to the Brill Building, writing pop songs for British singers virtually unknown across the Atlantic, like Vera Lynn and Anne Shelton. In the late Forties, he had moved to New York, where he composed special material for Danny Kaye, Bob Hope, and others, before venturing to Los Angeles to pursue a romance with a costume designer who worked for Cecil B. DeMille. He soon married the costume designer and started a family. Lubin received a co-writer credit when the publishing company asked him to "clean up" the lyrics on Little Richard's rock and roll hit "Tutti Frutti" for Pat Boone, whose sanitized rendition wound up outscoring the Little Richard original on the charts.

Lubin had recently gone into business with Marty Melcher, Doris Day's husband and manager. Melcher long before negotiated an agreement with his wife's film studio that he would retain publishing rights to any music Doris Day sang in their movies for his Daywin Music. In early 1958, as an offshoot of his music publishing operation, Melcher opened Arwin Records and installed Lubin as vice-president and artist and repertoire (A&R) director. The label had released only a few records, without any success yet. Lubin listened intently. There was something to the untamed energy and the raw sound of "Jennie Lee" that caught his ear.

"Where did you record this?" he asked.

When Jan told him that it had been recorded in his garage, Lubin decided this he wanted to see for himself. He hopped in his car and followed Jan's Chevy convertible, swerving up the winding road to the top of the hills high above Bel Air. Lubin caught the fever. He spent the next several nights in the garage with Jan and Arnie, cutting the song over and over again, trying to get that same garage sound he'd heard on the first tape. Lubin loved the out-of-tune piano. It took a while to duplicate the hypnotic percussion sound of the original recording that first attracted Lubin, but Jan's mother, while serving snacks, reminded them that it was Don Altfeld beating on the back of the high chair. Jan's parents and the other Berry children could hear the music through the walls late into the night. Professional songwriter that he was, Lubin came up with a title for a flip side, "Gotta Get a Date on a Saturday Night," that seemed ripe with teen appeal, and the three of them hammered out the tune and recorded it in the garage.

Lubin took the garage recordings into a genuine recording studio with a group of studio musicians that included drummer Earl Palmer, guitarist René Hall, and saxophonist Plas Johnson — an elite cadre behind rhythm and blues records by the likes of Sam Cooke and Little Richard. Lubin wanted the Jan and Arnie record to sound Black. There were issues with the somewhat fluid tempo, but the assembled musicians were able to navigate the flow. Lubin convinced Melcher to release the record, and he cut a deal for distribution with an established independent label, Dot Records.

Earl Palmer and Plas Johnson also played on another session for Lubin, accompanying a young guitarist named Richard Podolor. A teenage guitar prodigy, Podolor served as house guitarist for a country label called Fabor Records, where he played on the 1956 Bonnie Guitar hit "Dark Moon." Podolor led the session musicians through an instrumental written by Lubin with Arwin music director Adam Ross called "Cha-Hua-Hua." The two singles, "Jennie Lee" by Jan and Arnie and "Cha-Hua-Hua" by the Pets, were released the same week in April 1958 by the little label with offices in a building owned by Doris Day on Canon Drive in Beverly Hills.

The Barons went to work. They arranged parties with the girls' club the Flairs to phone radio stations and request the Jan and Arnie record. Jan handed out lists of radio station phone numbers and rolls of dimes. He also organized an assault on Wallichs Music City in Hollywood, buying and stealing as many copies as he could, until he eventually simply took to hiding the Jan and Arnie records elsewhere in the store and alerting staff to their absence.

In May, the duo lip-synched their record on the ABC-TV primetime-hour *Dick Clark Saturday Night Beechnut Show*, and "Jennie Lee" started to climb the charts. Jan and Arnie walked the halls of University High with a bounce in their steps; everybody in the school knew they had a record on the radio. In June, the week school let out, the record rose into the nationwide Top Ten, a certified hit. They were living a teenage dream.

♪

BALMY JUNE BREEZES blew warm ocean air and the sounds of the surf across the street to the stately seaside Santa Monica landmark the Miramar Hotel, which had once been the mansion of razor blade magnate King Gillette, and where Greta Garbo lived in the Twenties and Jean Harlow stayed in a poolside bungalow during the Thirties. The elegant Starlight Ballroom, twenty-five thousand square feet grand, overlooked the hundred-year-old Moreton Bay Fig Tree in front of the hotel and the Pacific Ocean beyond. The University High class of '58 came here to celebrate their graduation — one last sweet kiss of youth.

The Nelson Riddle Orchestra played for dancers, and with the celebrated arranger of lush pop hits by Frank Sinatra and Nat King Cole on the bandstand, this was clearly no ordinary high school prom. But University High students had long been comfortable around the trappings of show business. Many of their parents worked for the movie studios as accountants, lawyers, and other functional occupations associated with the business called show. Some of them were the children of well-known actors, like Jim Mitchum and Johnny Weissmuller Jr., son of the most famous Tarzan. The kid who played Jeff Miller in the TV series *Lassie,* Tommy Rettig, was in the junior class at Uni, struggling to find acting work now that he had grown out of his best part.

They showed up dressed for the ball, the girls rustling in chiffon over layers of petticoats, the boys sleek and serious in tuxedos, their crew-cuts glistening with Butch Wax. A crowd of seven hundred filled the ballroom, dancing to the elegant orchestra under the massive crystal chandeliers. Kathy Kohner came, not with one of her beach-bum buddies, but with a fellow who rented a room from her mother. The orchestra played at the rear of a large stage, and everybody was thrilled, if not too terribly surprised, when KFWB disc jockey B. Mitchel Reed—who had himself been invited by their celebrated classmate, Nancy Sinatra—introduced Nancy's father, Frank Sinatra, who walked out beaming and took charge of center stage.

Only a few days before, Sinatra had called his darling daughter on her eighteenth birthday from Monaco, where he was attending the world premiere of his new film, *Kings Go Forth*, and giving a benefit concert for Princess Grace in Monte Carlo with the fifty-five-piece Barclay Disques house band led by Quincy Jones—with Noel Coward, Yul Brynner, and Cary Grant in the audience. On his way back to California, the night before his daughter's grad party in Santa Monica, Sinatra sang "Moonlight in Vermont" with Ella Fitzgerald during her encore at the Copa in New York City.

Sinatra, warm and relaxed, sang a few songs, joked with the kids, lit a cigarette, and brought out Sammy Davis Jr. Now that *was* a surprise; nobody expected Sammy. They kidded around and sang a couple of duets, before Sinatra left the stage to Sammy, who dazzled the kids with his singing and dancing but knocked everybody dead on their feet with his spot-on impression of Elvis Presley. The crowd went ape.

Sinatra also brought out Keely Smith, and the two of them sang a couple of songs together. With her husband Louis Prima, Keely Smith was one of the favorite nightclub acts of show business insiders like Sinatra and Ed Sullivan, who frequently booked the pair on his popular Sunday night TV show. She could sing, make sly bawdy jokes, and easily entertained the graduates on this star-studded evening.

The class of '58 danced into the wee hours to the Dick Stabile Orchestra, another top-flight dance band, having been feted by the greatest entertainers and the finest musicians in the business. This celestial evening belonged to the new generation of old Hollywood. They did not celebrate the end of anything so much as the prospects of what lay ahead for these anointed ones, poised on the brink of exciting, promising futures. Whatever misfortunes and adversities were yet to come in their lives, on this evening the world paused for these young people who had grown up breathing the sea-swept air of the Westside, where shadows were short and sunny days were long. These young people grew up assured of their place in life, without fear, confident of the possibilities that lay ahead. Life came with a promise to them; they all believed that. The American dream was their California birthright.

The party ended late, but even as dawn creaked over the rim of the Hollywood hills behind them, there were couples in their party dresses and formal wear walking arm in arm on the beach across the street. School was out.

4

KIP TYLER AND THE FLIPS

SUMMER IN SOUTHERN California meant the kids lived outdoors for three months—days at the beach, nights at the drive-in. Some ambitious souls picked up part-time summer jobs, like taking a shift as lifeguard at the beach or delivering for a liquor store. The end of school signaled the start of vacation, when these teens could take full advantage of life in paradise. Even Uni High's rock and roll band, the Sleepwalkers, were ready to graduate.

When the thunderous instrumental by guitarist Duane Eddy "Rebel-'Rouser" blasted off on *American Bandstand* and the hit parade in June 1958, he needed to find a band. Eddy and his producer Lee Hazlewood were based in Phoenix, Arizona, but they used a Los Angeles rhythm and blues vocal group called the Sharps to shout on their records. It was the Sharps who recommended Steve Douglas, the saxophonist who played with Kip Tyler and the Flips, the house band at the El Monte Legion Stadium. Along with Douglas, fresh out of Fairfax High, the ascendant Eddy plundered from the band Douglas's high school friends, drummer Mike Bermani and keyboardist

Larry Knechtel. Duane Eddy obviously couldn't use guitarist Mike Deasy, but Kip Tyler suddenly needed a whole new set of Flips.

With Deasy still on board, Sleepwalkers drummer Sammy Nelson, who had substituted with the Flips on occasion, brought his bandmates, Bruce Johnston on keyboards and Dave Shostac on sax. They became the new Kip Tyler and the Flips, who were at the absolute center of Los Angeles rock and roll in the summer of 1958.

Kip Tyler was a hulking barbarian, a hustler and a self-promoter, a real Hollywood kind of guy. At twenty-nine, he was a few years older than the young guys in the band. Tyler was an ex-cab driver from Miami who looked a little like Kirk Douglas and came to Hollywood to make it in the movies, but ended up playing the greasy rock and roll wild man in black leather. He sang the ghost vocals for movie star John Saxon as rock and roll singer Jimmy Daley in the 1957 film *Rock, Pretty Baby!* There were even a couple of singles by the movie's fictional character with Tyler on vocals, and a second film whose failure at the box office ended the Jimmy Daley franchise.

Disc jockey Art Laboe discovered Kip Tyler and the Flips and not only signed the band to his fledgling record label but installed them as the house band at his regular concerts at the El Monte Legion Stadium. Laboe had been holding these dances since 1955 in the city of El Monte, just outside the city limits of Los Angeles, where rock and roll dances were illegal. On his KPOP radio show, Laboe fanned the flames of rock and roll with after-school remote broadcasts from Scrivner's Drive-In at Sunset and Cahuenga, a few short blocks from Hollywood High, where he was mobbed daily. Along with Hunter Hancock and Dick "Huggy Boy" Hugg, Art Laboe broke the raucous new music on the radio in Los Angeles. He was a cool, with-it guy whose secretary was married to one of the Platters.

At El Monte, the wilder the show, the bigger the sensation you were. Saxophonist Big Jay McNeely was a star at El Monte, his squeal-ing, shrieking high notes piercing the din of his band as he rolled around the stage on his back. Any local group that landed a record on the radio would be booked to play the dances at El Monte, or, if not the actual group that made the record, at least a reasonable facsimile. Touring acts would come through on the rhythm and blues circuit. They would perform their three songs, then another group would do three songs, all backed by the house band, Kip Tyler and the Flips.

The Kip Tyler records never really clicked. His best shot was "Jungle Hop" in April 1958, just before Steve Douglas and the rest of the Flips left for Duane Eddy, but even that rough and rowdy outing failed to elicit much interest, and the band was still backing other acts for Art Laboe and the El Monte Legion Stadium when the Sleepwalkers took over the franchise.

That summer, one of the most popular acts at El Monte was a young Mexican-American singer named Ritchie Valens, who had his first record on the radio, "Come On, Let's Go," and was making a name for himself as a guitarist (even though session guitarist René Hall played the solo on the record). Valens was perfect for El Monte, which drew a crowd that was almost half Latin, and at age seventeen he wasn't much older than the audience. Or the Flips.

Rock and roll was teen music, and Southern California teens were a breed apart. They existed in a land whose myth was only beginning to grow. In 1955, Disneyland opened among the strawberry fields of Orange County. The Mattel toy company in industrial Hawthorne in South Central Los Angeles made a small fortune turning out hats with mouse ears. Every kid in the country tuned in to the Sunday night TV program *Walt Disney's Disneyland* and stared goggle-eyed at the exotic worlds they glimpsed. Young eyes all over the nation began turning in wonder to Southern California.

There was no real established music business in Los Angeles to speak of, just a handful of small labels that put out records for a mostly regional audience. Imperial Records was owned by the utterly humorless Lew Chudd, a relic of the swing era who started the label aiming to focus on the growing market in Black and Latin communities in Southern California. When rock and roll broke nationwide in the Fifties, he sold millions of records by New Orleans rhythm and blues singer Fats Domino and Hollywood TV star Ricky Nelson, more by fortune than design.

Liberty Records was founded in 1955 by Simon Waronker and Al Bennett, who hit a home run out of the box with Julie London's "Cry Me a River." The label had subsequently managed incidental lightweight pop hits by acts like Patience and Prudence or Margie Rayburn, but currently had one of the bestselling records of the year with the number one novelty hit "Witch Doctor" by David Seville.

Herb Newman had worked at Liberty for his cousin Si Waronker before he and Lew Bedell began Era Records in 1955, where they scored a major hit with pop vocalist Gogi Grant, "The Wayward Wind." Bedell was an egg-shaped, balding former Catskills comic and New York television host who never held a firm opinion on anything and knew next to nothing about music. He would dance with the doorknob in his office when he auditioned songs, announcing happily, "It's got that little beat the kids like." He and Newman had recently started a new label called Doré Records (named after Newman's son) specifically for rock and roll records when they were introduced to a recent Fairfax High School graduate with a demo tape: Phil Spector, the sometime guitarist with the Sleepwalkers.

Spector had spent long after-school hours with three classmates in a friend's living room, polishing his original song "Don't You Worry My Little Pet." He pooled funds from the classmates to raise the forty dollars for a two-hour session at Gold Star Studios on Santa Monica Boulevard. At the Era Records offices on Sunset and Vine, Bedell played the acetate of "Don't You Worry My Little Pet" over and over, calling in his partner to listen. Spector showed them a second original song, "Wonderful Loveable You," on guitar, and the record company signed the group, who hastily came up with the name "the Teddy Bears."

Before the group could enter the studio, bass vocalist Harvey Goldstein left for summer duty in the Army Reserves and missed the sessions. Spector, who had become quite taken with the voice of sixteen-year-old Annette Kleinbard, his girlfriend's best friend and one of the Teddy Bears, wrote a song specifically for her light, clear soprano, taking the title from the gravestone of his father, whose suicide forced teenage Spector's move from the Bronx to Los Angeles: "To Know Him Is to Love Him." As emotionally damaged as the young Spector was, he channeled a ceaseless dedication into his musical ambitions. At the session, Spector and his fellow Teddy Bear and Fairfax High classmate Marshall Leib took over from Newman and Bedell as they experimented with tricky guitar overdubs on the intended A-side, "Don't You Worry My Little Pet," that were beyond the label owners, using a lot of studio time in the process. By the end of the Friday morning session at Gold Star, "Wonderful Loveable You" was still not finished, and another session was booked for Monday.

On the Monday, having decided the record needed a stronger backbeat, Spector returned with the only drummer he knew, Sammy Nelson. The tempo of the track fluctuated, and Nelson had trouble overdubbing the drum part. Bedell ended up waving his arms like a kind of deranged symphony conductor from the other side of the glass in the control room. Bedell and Newman grew impatient with Spector and left the session, telling the studio owner to cut them off after two hours. They finished "Wonderful Loveable You" and asked the engineer if they had enough time for one more song. Feeling charitable, he gave them an extra half hour and they recorded "To Know Him Is to Love Him," with Nelson playing snare drum with steel brushes.

The single came out in August with "Don't You Worry My Little Pet" on the A-side. Nothing happened. A month later, after near total radio silence across the country, a disc jockey in Fargo, North Dakota, turned the record over and played "To Know Him Is to Love Him." The haunting, ethereal ballad, with Kleinbard's soft voice drenched in the famous Gold Star echo, struck home. Out of nowhere, the record blew up the charts all the way to number one. In Hollywood, things were still possible.

WITH "JENNIE LEE" streaking into the nationwide Top Ten, suddenly Jan and Arnie were rock and roll stars. Their first public performance happened the Friday night in June that school let out, at the Pasadena Civic Auditorium on a bill with jazz saxophonist Bud Shank and singer Bobby Freeman, whose hit, "Do You Want to Dance," was shooting up the charts only slightly ahead of Jan and Arnie. He was a Black kid from a vocal group at San Francisco's Mission High School whose demo caught the ear of a visiting record executive. Freeman was a cocky yet likable character. Jan invited him to a midnight party at his garage following the show to celebrate Freeman's eighteenth birthday.

Jan knew Ralph Mathis, brother of Johnny Mathis, who sang with a Los Angeles vocal group called the Ambers, and Ralph knew Freeman from San Francisco. They all came together. As usual, the place was packed with Barons, their girlfriends, their girlfriends' girlfriends, a mass of happy teenagers, dancing and singing along to records, sneaking beers in the driveway, banging on the piano, and more singing. School was out for summer. Their cars crowded the steep driveway and the roadside above where there was no sidewalk.

Mary Sperling was a sophomore who had been to parties at Jan's garage before. Jan had recorded her and three girlfriends singing one of the first songs he and Don Altfeld wrote. She had also interviewed Jan and Arnie for a column she wrote for the *Santa Monica Outlook.*

"Arnie beats bongos and I play piano," Jan said. "We were just fooling around in my garage a couple of weeks ago, and within a couple of hours we'd written the music and lyrics to this song. Just for kicks, we went into Hollywood to make a record of the song for our own use. The funny part is we had no intention of doing anything professional with the song. Mr. Lubin heard our song, took us over to Arwin Records, got together a group of musicians directed by Don Ralke, and we made the record."

Parties like these had been a regular feature at the Berry house on Linda Flora since Jan returned from San Francisco the year before. The Berrys had five children younger than Jan living in the house too, and there was an older stepsister who didn't. They gladly accommodated their son's friends and had long grown accustomed to the clamor of voices and music coming from that end of the house.

Besides sampling Jan's radio station record collection, they spun the Jan and Arnie record—both sides—repeatedly. Bobby Freeman brought an acetate of his next single, "Betty Lou Got a New Pair of Shoes," and everybody agreed it sounded like another hit. They gave "Do You Want to Dance" plenty of plays, too. With both his record and the Jan and Arnie single riding high in the Top Ten that week, the night's giddy platter party took on the air of a minor summit meeting.

During that summer, the two teens got to be Jan and Arnie. They reunited with their high school buddies from the Sleepwalkers when they played the El Monte Legion Stadium with Kip Tyler and the Flips. They did a two-week sweep of the East Coast with Frankie Avalon, Link Wray, and the Kalin Twins; they made another appearance on *The Dick Clark Saturday Night Beechnut Show* to receive a gold record for "Jennie Lee" and perform their follow-up, "Gas Money"; and they did a weekend of dates in San Francisco with Sam Cooke, where Jan and Arnie first saw Lou Adler, the sole white guy in the Cooke party, although they were too intimidated to hang out. They finished the summer appearing on another sold-out Dick Clark concert at the Hollywood Bowl that included many of their friends, singing their hit wearing Bermuda shorts in the warm California evening—an altogether triumphant moment.

To Arnie Ginsburg, this was all a frolic. The eighteen-year-old had already enlisted with the Navy Reserves and was due for military service the next year. This rock and roll deal was Jan's big idea and he thought he might as well take it for a ride, but there was no need to take it seriously, too. Arnie told Mary Sperling about his plans to join the Navy for her article in the *Santa Monica Outlook* (Jan told her he hoped to go to UCLA). When Jan and Arnie posed shirtless for teen magazines, acting out the group's beginnings in the gymnasium shower room, and engaged in all the typical teen idol antics, it left Arnie cold. He took no pleasure in the pointless adulation and grew slyly contemptuous of the whole affair. He had a rubber stamp made of his signature so he didn't have to sign autographs. He truly hated show business. He was never comfortable performing, and he was also beginning to chafe under Jan's controlling instincts. Jan was driven and focused, while Arnie was looser and more casual. Arnie knew it would all come to an end anyway in January, when his Navy

Reserves hitch started. They appeared on the December cover of *Dig* magazine, where they promised to perform at a New Year's Eve party for one lucky contest winner. Madelon Sullivan won the event and threw her party at the Henderson Youth Center in Nevada, but for Jan and Arnie, the party was over.

5

BLONDE-HAIRED
EVERLY BROTHERS

DEAN TORRENCE HAD not been back long from boot camp. He had managed to stow away his gear at his parents' house and register for school in time for the fall 1958 semester at Santa Monica City College. On this sunny, not-quite-summer-any-longer Sunday morning, he was winding his way down Sunset Boulevard in his freshly waxed pickup to see about getting into the weekly football game with his old high school buddies. He looked forward to being a regular guy again, playing ball and seeing old friends, but he had no idea where he stood with Jan. He had not been in touch with him since getting back from Fort Ord.

Six months earlier, Pvt. Torrence had been shining his shoes at five in the morning at Fort Ord when one of his high school pals who had signed up with him came over excitedly, carrying a transistor radio tuned to a San Jose radio station. To Dean's surprise, out of the tinfoil speaker sputtered "Jennie Lee." Dean couldn't believe his ears. He could tell instruments had been added, a saxophone solo and more, but otherwise it sounded just like the recording they'd made in the garage. He waited expectantly for the disc jockey to announce the record. "That was 'Jennie Lee' by Jan and Arnie," he said.

Jan and Arnie? What happened to the Barons? Dean was confused, alarmed even. That night, he called Jan from the pay phone on base. Jan explained what happened and told Dean they had re-recorded the song without him. It wasn't a satisfying phone call, and when Dean retired to the barracks, his mind was crowded with dark thoughts. He wasn't angry at Jan so much as frustrated with himself for blowing his big chance. When he could finally wrangle a weekend pass and get back to Los Angeles, he went by the house on Linda Flora for an awkward meeting with Jan, Arnie, and Joe Lubin, who eventually told Dean he was a distraction and asked him to leave. That was the last time he had seen Jan.

At the Palisades High football field, the old gang welcomed Dean back into the fold. All his friends from the Barons were there, including Jan. They exchanged greetings, and Dean was secretly impressed that Jan was playing football like the old days and not hanging out with Annette Funicello or Dick Clark. After the game, which the Barons won handily, everybody piled into their cars and drove down the hill to State Beach. Sitting on the wall, Dean asked Jan about Arnie. "He and Jennie Lee are working on a new act together...or he joined the Navy," Jan said. "I can't remember which."

At the end of the afternoon, Jan suggested Dean come up to his house on Linda Flora and work on some music with him. Dean followed Jan's turquoise Chevy up the hill. They quickly got lost in the garage, pounding piano, singing songs, listening to Jan's ever-expanding record collection. Dean finally remembered he had a date with his girlfriend that night. He called her and told her he was making music with Jan and he would call her tomorrow. He went back to the garage and sat down on the piano bench. He wasn't going to blow it a second time.

♪

BRUCE JOHNSTON MAY have been only sixteen years old, more than ten years younger than his bandleader, but he could tell Kip Tyler was a creep. He was full of himself, and about half as talented as he thought he was. In September 1958, Kip Tyler and the Flips cut a firecracker of a record, "She's My Witch," with Johnston's tinkling piano spiking into Dave Shostac's ferocious sax solo. It went nowhere. Just like all the Kip Tyler records. Even though he was still in high school, Johnston was beginning to see beyond Kip Tyler and the Flips.

Johnston had nourished ambitions in the record business since day one. Before Kim Fowley had been unceremoniously shuffled off into military service, the two had plotted undertaking many musical projects under a firm they called Modern Age Enterprises. They had the nucleus of a musical operation with Shostac, Nelson, and guitarist Deasy from the Flips. Johnston had also developed contacts in the rhythm and blues scene like guitarist Arthur Wright from John Dolphin's office. He had watched from the sidelines as Jan and Arnie and Phil Spector and Marshall Leib bluffed their way onto the hit parade; they made it look possible. With Fowley off in the Army for the time being, Johnston forged ahead on his own. He glimpsed the process on occasional freelance jobs playing piano or singing background vocals, and he picked up cues wherever he could. Johnston also wrote his own songs and had pushed to have them recorded since that fateful day at Dolphin's.

Johnston found a new partner in Jerry Cooper, another pal from Uni High, and together they cooked up a couple of songs. He was taking his bandmates and leaving Kip Tyler, who was not happy to lose his band again. There was going to be a dispute if Johnston tried to call his band the Flips. He booked studio time, found a bass player from the R&B scene, and went into the studio to make his Bruce and Jerry record. He typed out a letter to Fowley, away in basic training, to report the details of the session, along with some social notes and comments about the Pagans not interrupting homecoming this year.

```
MODERN AGE ENTERPRISES, INC.
15, 461 MILLDALE AVENUE
BEL-AIR, CALIFORNIA


BRUCE JOHNSTON, PRESIDENT
KIM FOWLEY, VICE PRESIDENT

KIM,
EVERYTHING IS GOING VERY WELL HERE IN LOS
ANGELES. WE RECORDED THE REST OF 'TAKE THIS
PEARL' AND 'I SAW HER FIRST'. LAST NIGHT WE
RECORDED THE VOICES. LAST WEEK WE RECORDED
THE MUSIC PART OF IT. WE USED DAVE SHOSTAC
ON SAX, SAM NELSON ON DRUMS, JOHNNY OTIS'
BASS PLAYER HARPER COSBY ON BASS, MIKE DEASY
ON GUITAR, AND MYSELF ON PIANO. I WILL KNOW
TODAY AT TWELVE NOON WHAT LABEL THE RECORD
WILL BE ON. I THINK IT IS GOING TO BE CAPITOL
RECORDS. THAT WILL BE COOL. MOST LIKELY OUR
NEXT RECORD WILL BE THE ONE YOU AND I WROTE,
'SAY WHAT'S IN YOUR HEART'. KIP TYLER DOES
NOT LIKE US BREAKING AWAY. THE BAND IS STILL
TOGETHER UNDER THE NAME THE JAMBOREES. IT WAS
GOING TO BE THE SLEEPWALKERS BUT THOSE GUYS
DOUBLE CROSSED ME. I WILL NOW DOUBLE CROSS
```

THEM. INSTEAD OF PUTTING BRUCE AND JERRY AND
THE JAMBOREES, I WIL PUT BRUCE AND JERRY AND
THE SLEEPWALKERS. IF THEY TRY TO USE THE NAME
SLEEPWALKERS AT ANY APPEARANCES WITH OUT MY
PERMISSION, I CAN SUE THEM. SOMEDAY I WILL
EXPLAIN THIS IN GREATER DETAL.
     FRIDAY NIGHT I WENT TO THE U.C.L.A.
HOMECOMING. IT SURE WAS NOTHING. NO RIOTS OR
ANYTHING. THE SOCIAL SCENE HERE IN L.A. AS
FAR AS I CAN SEE IS DEAD. OF COURSE I HAVE
BEEN WORKING WITH THE RECORD AND THE BAND AND
HAVE NOT BEEN ABLE TO SEE PEOPLE. I AM GOING
TO VANISE HIGH SCHOOL. (I DON'T THINK THAT IS
THE WAY YOU SPELL IT. THE SCHOOL IS OUT IN THE
VALLEY) I AM GOING WITH A GIRL BY THE NAME OF
GINA MASCHIO. SHE GOES TO UNI. HER MOTHER IS
A SINGER, CONSTANCE MOORE AND HER FATHER IS A
MOVIE PRODUCER. SHE SPENT MOST OF HER LIFE IN
PRIVATE SCHOOL. SHE KNOWS ALL THE SOCIAL KIDS
WE DO (JOYCE, DART ETC.) SHE THINKS OF THEM AS
WE DO. THAT IS ALL. OH—WHEN WILL YOU BE BACK?

     BRUCE JOHNSTON, PRESIDENT
     MODERN AGE ENTERPRISES, INC.

The Bruce and Jerry record ended up on Arwin Records, the Doris
Day label, home of the Jan and Arnie records. The company plugged
"Take This Pearl" as the A-side, when the other track, "I Saw Her
First," was arguably stronger. The record was released in March 1959
and disappeared without a trace. Also, Johnston in his letter to Fowley
meant Van Nuys High School. Although he still planned to attend
UCLA in the fall, Johnston couldn't think of much but music and

girls. He couldn't even correctly spell the name of the high school where he was currently enrolled.

♪

WHEN KIM FOWLEY returned from basic training, his father had taken him back, provided he went to school. Figuring his son would make a good accountant or maybe do well in publicity, he enrolled Kim in the Willis School of Business. Shortly after, Douglas Fowley left for several months in Brazil to direct a B-movie called *Macumba Love* starring June Wilkinson, an actress best known for her bust. He told his son, "No parties, don't wear my clothes, and don't use my car," and off he went.

On a bright Wednesday morning in February 1959, Kim was walking to school when he encountered a bespectacled teenage girl watering her front yard and sobbing. Kim stopped to inquire what had happened, and she burst out, "They've died—Buddy Holly, Ritchie Valens, and the Big Bopper." The tragic news from snowy Iowa hit Fowley like a sledgehammer. His rock and roll heroes had died; he felt the need to enlist, to commit his life to rock and roll, to step into the void they left behind. A dramatic gesture was needed. He threw his schoolbooks into a nearby trash can, went back to his father's house to grab a bunch of his father's clothes and his TV set, loaded everything into the backseat, and stole the car. He drove straight to Gold Star Studios in Hollywood, where Eddie Cochran had cut "Summertime Blues" and the Champs made "Tequila," like he was heading for church.

Gold Star was indeed a temple of rock and roll. Behind the Santa Monica Boulevard storefront windows with venetian blinds and the studio name written in gold script, they made rock and roll records.

Opened in 1950 by engineers Dave Gold and Stan Ross, the studio boasted extraordinary echo chambers built by Gold himself. Studio A was large enough for orchestral sessions, and Studio B down the stairs by the parking lot was often favored for rock and roll. Fowley gained entrance by handing over one of his business cards for his monthly column in *Dig* magazine: KIM FOWLEY — RECORDSVILLE — RHYTHM & NEWS.

He told members of the Champs he met standing around the parking lot outside the studio that he wanted to do an article about how to make a record, and they agreed to show him. Booked into Studio B, the Champs — or at least those members of the Champs who were currently disputing rights to the name with bandleader Dave Burgess — were waiting for Johnny and Dorsey Burnette, who showed up shortly thereafter to play guitars on the session. Fowley knew who the Burnette brothers were — authentic Memphis hillbilly rock and rollers who wrote hit songs for Ricky Nelson.

In Studio A, Fowley found arranger Danny Gould passing out music for a full-scale Gogi Grant pop session. Fowley used the same interview gambit, and Gould walked him through the process of making a pop record. Fowley soaked all this up like a sponge. That night, he spent his last twenty-two cents on french fries at the Hollywood Ranch Market and parked his father's Studebaker Golden Hawk on Selma Avenue. He curled up in the backseat to sleep, perchance to dream, in the heart of Hollywood.

The next morning, a vision came to him. Not exactly a vision, but a dark-haired, handsome man walking down the street carrying a guitar, who looked for all the world like a real rock and roll cat. Fowley jumped out of the car and stopped the guy. "What do you do?" Fowley wanted to know.

"Who the fuck are you?" came the perhaps not unreasonable reply.

Fowley laid out his *Dig* magazine spiel again, dropping a few names he'd collected the day before at Gold Star. The man introduced himself as Nick Venet. He came from the East Coast, where his first job in the record business had been picking hits for the jukebox in his father's diner in Baltimore. He moved to Los Angeles to become an actor and landed a small part in the Paul Newman movie *Rally 'Round the Flag, Boys!*, but got sidetracked into music, singing demos for a few bucks until one was sold to RCA Victor in 1957. Although his single, "Flippin'," was not a hit, it fostered a brief foray into a singing career. Once that cooled off, Venet found himself writing songs for other artists. Venet was at that moment on his way to meet with a music publisher. Fowley convinced Venet to let him act as his agent and to promise they would split anything above $250 that Fowley got for his song.

Fowley dazzled the music publisher with bullshit. He told the publisher that he was nineteen years old and he knew what kids liked. He demanded $500 for the song and the publisher gave it to him. Venet was so impressed he took Fowley back to the house where he was living with his girlfriend and her mother, Virginia Dodd, a rundown old rummy whose father had been married to silent-screen siren Barbara LaMarr. With hers broken, they put Kim's father's TV in the living room and let Fowley sleep on the floor with her chihuahua dogs.

Fowley tried hustling songs as Venet's agent, but mostly he was getting by through petty theft at parties, rifling purses and such. He and Venet made the rounds. Venet took Fowley to meet actress Tuesday Weld, who he knew from his movie role. They caught the Phil Harvey Band at the Rainbow Roller Rink in Van Nuys, Phil Spector and some cronies doing deep, twangy guitar instrumentals à la Duane Eddy, wearing long, black raincoats. The Teddy Bears had come and gone, and Spector, who Fowley had known from the Sleepwalkers, was giving this concept a shot. Venet decided he would take Fowley to meet Lou Adler.

Adler and his partner Herb Alpert had recently left their artist and repertoire posts at Keen Records and were now operating out of an office above an auto parts store run by a man named Lenny Poncher, who booked and managed Latin bands. Adler and Alpert had written a lot of songs and made plenty of records, but they were looking for their next move, still trying to land their first big score. Adler was a cool, haughty hipster managing kingpin KFWB disc jockey B. Mitchel Reed, and was very much an up-and-comer on the scene with an eye out for the big time. He listened impatiently as Fowley ran down some of the talent he thought he could deliver, starting with Bruce Johnston. Adler knew Johnston and said he sounded too much like Sonny Knight, the smooth R&B crooner behind "Confidential." Next.

Fowley kept in touch with the old neighborhood. He knew that Dean Torrence was back from Fort Ord—he had run into the unpleasant jock when they were both serving basic training in Monterey—and he knew that he and Jan Berry were making music together again. Adler was interested. He remembered Jan and Arnie. He asked Fowley what their music was like. Kim told Adler they were blonde-haired Everly Brothers who sang like they were Black. He explained that the most likely obstacle would be Bill Berry, underage Jan's rigid father, but he left Adler with the phone number and the vague suggestion that he would check back when he returned from his Air Force Reserve encampment in Idaho.

6

HERB B. LOU

AT TWENTY-FOUR, Lou Adler was a grown man with adult desires. He had been raised with deprivation and he wasn't going to live like that anymore. He was handsome, genial, wicked smart, and aggressively ambitious. He favored continental suits and smoked Lucky Strikes. Adler intended to succeed in the music business. Having finished serving his apprenticeship at Keen Records, he was ready to step out on his own.

There was nothing in Adler's background that would have prepared him for life in the arts. His father, Manny, who barely spoke to his son (although he would sometimes yell at him), was a mechanic and truck driver. His mother, Josephine, was the supportive, nurturing aspect of his life. Books and music were not part of their household. They lived barely above the poverty line, Jews in the Mexican neighborhood of Boyle Heights in Los Angeles, and Adler escaped to the Navy as soon as he could. In 1953, he returned from duty in San Diego and Okinawa with a tattoo of Popeye on his arm, which needed to be removed, and signed up for classes at Los Angeles City College, especially classes with girls. At night, he sparred in the various Hollywood dance contests held at clubs like the Tail Spin on Cahuenga Boulevard, good enough to win sometimes. Dancing in these Hollywood hot spots until closing, Adler frequently fell asleep on the ride home at four in the morning.

Adler held down a bunch of aimless jobs. He sold insurance. He worked in a clothing store. He hustled dance lessons at the Joe Lanza Dance Studio on Western Avenue. He was intrigued with the idea of songwriting, and with a piano-playing friend cut primitive demos in penny arcade record booths. In 1958, their girlfriends introduced Adler and Herb Alpert.

Alpert was the first real musician Adler knew. He was a jazz trumpet player, especially fond of Clifford Brown. His older brother was a drummer who used to rehearse his group in the family living room in the Fairfax district; young Herb Alpert was leading his own trio by age fifteen. Alpert graduated from Fairfax High School in 1953 and studied music for a year at USC but spent too much time chasing girls and playing gigs. Before long he dropped out and joined the Army. Alpert served in the Sixth Army Band and gigged his way through military service. After getting out of the service in 1956, Alpert married his high school sweetheart, Sharon Lubin, and they had a son, Dore. He was making a living in square society dance bands at Beverly Hills hotels when he met Adler.

Adler and Alpert wrote four songs together and shared the cost for a demo recording, with Alpert supplying the vocals. Although there was no way for amateur songwriters to get their material considered by major labels like Columbia, RCA Victor, or Capitol, the feisty independents along Vine Street would listen to anyone who walked in the door. Adler and Alpert sold their first song on their first stop. With the exception of Specialty Records, where an artist and repertoire guy named Sonny Bono advised them to find another line of work, they found a buyer for their songs everywhere they went. They placed every single one of their songs — even "River Rock" by "Froggy" Landers and the Cough Drops — and the man who bought the last remaining song, the estimable Robert "Bumps" Blackwell, also hired them for forty-five dollars a week to work with him as assistant junior artist and repertoire men at Keen Records.

Bumps Blackwell was already a major figure in the world of rock and roll, having supervised all the earth-shattering hits by Little Richard at Specialty Records ("Tutti Frutti," "Long Tall Sally," "Rip It Up," "Good Golly, Miss Molly," etc.) and conducted experimental pop recordings with the lead vocalist of the popular Soul Stirrers gospel group, Sam Cooke. When Specialty recoiled at their sanctified singer going secular, Blackwell took Cooke and his tape of "You Send Me" to Keen Records, where it shot to number one on the hit parade and established Cooke overnight as a teen heartthrob. Blackwell looked at Adler and Alpert and saw a couple of hip, young white guys who could help him keep in touch with that market.

In June 1958, Adler signed his first session log for a Sam Cooke recording of the Adler-Alpert song "All of My Life," which would be his first single since "You Send Me" not to make the charts. Cooke was a charismatic personality, suave and engaging, and a brilliant talent — the sort of man who lit up the room wherever he went. He was in the thick of the Los Angeles rhythm and blues world, and while Alpert, with a wife and young son at home, may have resisted some of the more lurid and tawdry aspects of life among the R&B crowd, Adler dove right in.

Adler had brought home an acetate of his Sam Cooke song, hoping to play it for his father, but was only able to put it on the phonograph in his room and have his father yell through his closed bedroom door to turn it down. Adler left home shortly after and

began dating a dancer from Boston who lived in an apartment building on St. Andrews Place in Midtown. Cooke kept an apartment in
the building where his old circle of gospel groups like the Pilgrim
Travelers lived with him in a kind of extended family. Adler became
Cooke's constant companion, rising daily in the late afternoon,
eating breakfast at dinnertime, staying out at the California Club,
the 5/4 Ballroom, or wherever until the clubs closed, adjourning
to the after-hours joints, getting home at dawn, sometimes alone,
sometimes with company.

When Cooke left Keen Records for the greener major-label pastures
of RCA Victor, Adler and Alpert packed their bags and settled into
new offices over the auto parts store, where they started Herb B. Lou
Productions to make records and manage acts. Keen had provided
Adler and Alpert with considerable experience in the studio. They had
made a lot of records for Bumps Blackwell, though nothing remotely
approaching a hit. They worked with a procession of little-known
vocalists at Keen: Milton Grayson, Marti Barris, Johnny "Guitar"
Watson, the Salamas Brothers, and the Valiants and their lead singer,
Billy Storm. They tried a jazzy instrumental with the Herbie Alpert
Sextet. When Keen didn't want a record, they would often throw it out
on a label of their own, like the "break-in" record called "The Trial"
by Herb B. Lou and the Legal Eagles, which used snippets of existing
hits as comedic commentary (a specialty of the duo Buchanan and
Goodman) on their Arch Records. They released the first pop record by
gospel singer Lou Rawls of the Pilgrim Travelers, "Love, Love, Love,"
on their Shar-Dee Records, a label they named after their girlfriends,
Sharon and Deanna. Before they left Keen, Adler sorted through the
Sam Cooke tapes still on the shelves and found a song they wrote
called "Wonderful World," which almost made the Top Ten when
Keen released the single after Cooke went to RCA.

Adler was poised to make a move. He and Alpert had spent hundreds of hours in the recording studio with Cooke and other musicians. He was watching Lenny Poncher manage the Latin acts. The tip from Kim Fowley about the high school kids that looked like the Everlys but sounded Black appealed to him. He had watched Sam Cooke slide effortlessly into the *American Bandstand* world of Philadelphia white kids like Fabian, Bobby Rydell, Frankie Avalon, and all the other clean, well-scrubbed rock and roll teen stars. Adler and Alpert drove up to Bel Air to meet these blonde Everlys. As they pulled down the steep incline of the Berry driveway, they saw the two boys standing outside the garage. Adler got out of the car and surveyed the two beach boys, both over six feet tall, barefoot, and squinting as they smiled at him in the sunlight.

"If you guys sing as good as you look," he said, "we're going to have a hit record."

Adler and Alpert were dressed sharp in suits and ties. Jan played them his and Dean's latest work, "Jeanette, Get Your Hair Done"—a piece highly influenced by Bobby Freeman's "Betty Lou Got a New Pair of Shoes"—written about Jan's Uni High girlfriend Jeanette Anderson. Her pregnancy during their last semester at school had been the scandal of the campus. She was about to have Jan's baby and give it up for adoption, even though she and Jan had already broken up.

While they were impressed with "Jeanette," Alpert had another song in mind for Jan and Dean: "Baby Talk," by a group called the Laurels. Adler and Alpert had the good sense to keep the boys in the garage, and together they spent the next two months working on the two-minute song while Adler convinced Bill Berry to sign off on his management contract. Jan had become expert at tape splicing. He would find a "bomp" he liked from one take and cut it into another where he thought it would sound better. He made so many edits that the back of the master tape was covered with white splicing tape. They used Jan's two Ampex recorders, slightly out of sync, which gave the recording its signature echo—not a true echo, but a delay, a sound that was unique to the garage. Alpert wrote an arrangement for the piece and went into the studio with keyboardist Ernie Freeman and his top-flight R&B session players (Alpert and Adler had not worked with many white acts before Jan and Dean). The musicians had problems matching the wavering tempo, but they eventually created a solid rhythm track for the vocals, which was the exact opposite of the usual process.

Jan and Dean no longer had a record deal. When Jan had taken Dean into the Arwin Records office and introduced him as Arnie's replacement, the label informed him their services would no longer be needed. After Adler and Alpert first took "Baby Talk" to Keen, who passed, they made a deal with Lew Bedell and Herb Newman, flush from their number one success with the Teddy Bears' "To Know Him Is to Love Him" on their Doré Records. The label wanted to keep the name "Jan and Arnie," and an attempt was made to cut a deal with Arnie to use his name, but Arnie refused. Dean was ready to go along and be the new Arnie but was thankfully spared that indignity.

Adler married his girlfriend, Deanna, a stunning beauty who came from money. With new furniture and a new white Thunderbird, they moved into the Sycamore Riviera, an apartment building in Hollywood with a few other show business tenants. Adler took Jan and Dean clothes shopping and outfitted them with stacks of matching sweaters. He wanted them to look like California. He knew their blonde hair, tanned skin, and Westside casual style would offer stark contrast to the dark-haired Italian boys from Philadelphia in their coats and ties on *American Bandstand*. He posed them for photos in white polo shirts or striped sweaters, jeans, and tennis shoes. Adler even made Jan dye his hair blonder, the better to look like Dean's brother. Adler really pushed the sun-and-beach California angle.

Released in May 1959, "Baby Talk" won the nightly "Voice Your Choice" contest on KFWB — perhaps not coincidentally hosted by B. Mitchel Reed, another Adler-Alpert client — not just once, but eight nights in a row. Even Jan with his organized phone brigades couldn't put in that kind of fix. He took Dean on his Wallichs Music City raids to switch singles around in the store, but the record was selling already. Across Vine Street from Wallichs, a huge poster of the two teens, impossible to miss, hung outside the Doré Records office. The record took off on Los Angeles radio and shot to number one, though the rest of the country wouldn't come around until a September performance on the ABC-TV Saturday night primetime Dick Clark show. By October, an appearance at an autograph party at a shoe store in Lakewood, almost suburban South Los Angeles, went deliriously haywire when more than five hundred teens, mostly girls, swamped the place. Five police units needed to be called. Jan and Dean were officially on the scene.

KIM FOWLEY SAW the 45 RPM of "Baby Talk" for the first time in the remote disc jockey booth of KGEM ("The Voice of the Treasure Valley") in the Howdy Pardner Drive-In in Boise, Idaho. Seeing as he was stuck in this God-forsaken armpit of creation, stationed at the Garvin Air Force Base, he had connived his way into sharing a disc jockey shift with a young lady he was trying to date. Fowley called Adler on the phone, and if he expected to be recognized, Adler gave no sign he did. When Fowley told Adler that he was a disc jockey, Adler asked him to play the Jan and Dean record. Fowley assured him he was already playing it and ran down some strange scheme about having Jan and Dean sign to Chancellor Records of Philadelphia with Fabian and Frankie Avalon. Fowley offered to manage the arrangement from a West Coast office. He had already posed this idea to Chancellor—after telling Chancellor he could deliver Jan and Dean—and felt encouraged. Adler certainly didn't want to be impolite to a disc jockey who said he was playing the Jan and Dean record, but he gave the call no further thought after hanging up.

When Fowley returned to Los Angeles a couple of weeks later, he went straight to the Rainbow Roller Rink in Van Nuys, where Jan and Dean were making their public debut on a bill with actor James Darren from the new movie *Gidget*. "Baby Talk" was all over Los Angeles radio, and the place was a zoo. He spied Jan and Dean walking into the show. Still wearing his full Air Force uniform and dragging a duffel bag, Fowley climbed over the velvet rope to greet his old University High classmates, who pushed past him without so much as a nod of recognition. Following behind them was Adler. "I'm Lou Adler, manager of Jan and Dean," he said. "Is there a problem here?"

While Fowley stared at Adler dumbfounded, Adler turned and walked away. He had expected some recognition or reward for introducing Adler to his new charges. He desperately wanted, at least, some small acknowledgment that he, Kim Fowley, had played a role in this glorious rock and roll triumph. Instead, all he got was the cold shoulder. He had wanted Lou Adler to teach him the music business; Fowley thought bitterly, I guess he has. Fowley picked up his duffel bag, hitch-hiked back to the Hollywood bowling alley where he was staying, and went to sleep in tears of rage.

Hollywood still called Fowley, and he soon found his sea legs. He had known Jimmie Maddin for a while; Maddin was the sort of character a lot of people knew. He was a sometime disc jockey and television host, a red-hot saxophonist from the swing era who dug rock and roll, and owner of the Summit nightclub in Hollywood. Maddin was also running the music department at American International Pictures and hired Fowley as his assistant. Fowley's job was to show up in the morning and answer the phones until Maddin shook off his hangover and made it into the office, usually around two in the afternoon. Maddin let Fowley sleep in his nightclub and eat a free dinner, and paid him ten dollars a week—big money.

For the soundtrack to *Ghost of Dragstrip Hollow*, another fine American International Pictures production, due for release in July 1959, Fowley supervised his first recording session. He rounded up Bruce Johnston and Sammy Nelson. Nelson knew guitarist Richie Podolor, who had been leading a traveling version of the Pets after "Cha-Hua-Hua" turned into a decent mid-chart hit. Podolor's parents had been so encouraged by his success in the music business at such a young age, they sold their used car dealership and opened a recording studio, operated by Richie's older brother, Don: American Recording Studio, next door to the Hollywood Palladium at Hollywood Boulevard and Argyle Street. To help him produce his first session, Fowley brought someone he knew with at least some experience making records, Nick Venet.

The assembled group cut two guitar-based instrumentals at American Recorders, and Podolor overdubbed bass. They named the band the Renegades since the songs were called "Geronimo" and "Charge." The band even drove to Santa Barbara to promote the record on an after-school TV dance party. Podolor, who thought he wrote the songs, was astonished to discover, when the single was released, both songs credited to Nick Venet. Twenty-two-year-old Venet was the one with the most experience in the record business, and he knew the value of a copyright. Venet also landed a third song on the soundtrack, and Fowley found a spot for a song Bruce Johnston co-wrote with singer-actress Judy Harriet, another scrappy newcomer who had been one of the first batch of *Mickey Mouse Club* Mouseketeers and recorded the original version of "Tall Paul" before Annette Funicello made the song a hit. These teenagers were scrambling to grab the lower rungs of the ladder to success. There wasn't always room for everyone's hand.

♪

AFTER KIP TYLER AND THE FLIPS, Johnston had found a job for himself and Nelson at a club called Rocky's in the Valley with a saxophonist named Bobby Rey, who offered Nelson ten dollars to do a demo session for him at a studio. That ten-dollar session led to another. And another. Soon Nelson, sick of hauling his drum set all over town, settled down as the unofficial house drummer at American Recording. In their spare time, he and Podolor experimented with the sound of his drums. They spent months working on tuning Nelson's drums, trying different microphone techniques like miking the bass drum separately, looking to discover ways to make the drums more animated, more articulate.

Since his days at Uni High playing solo for dancers at lunch-time, Nelson had thought the drums were everything rock and roll really needed. He felt certain there was some tribal call in the drums that he could tap into to make a rock and roll hit. He and Podolor often discussed the idea. Several strains were running through Nelson's head — the swing beat to the 1953 hit "Caravan," by Ralph Marterie; the old trap drummer in the pit band at the New Follies Burlesk playing with Jennie Lee; and the driving, thrumming beat of "Peggy Sue" by Buddy Holly. Also "Topsy II" by Cozy Cole had brought the drum solo back to radio, reviving an old Benny Goodman swing number for the rock and roll crowd. Nelson and Podolor dreamed of making such a record. They already had a title: "Teen Beat."

Nelson was fooling around in the studio one afternoon when Kip Tyler came in. They no longer worked together, but Tyler stayed in touch. As Nelson pounded out a jungle drum tattoo, Tyler started dancing around. "Ooh, that's good," he told Nelson. "Do that again." That was how Nelson accidentally happened across the beat that would rock the nation.

When it all came together for Nelson, American Recording was booked solid, so he went down the street to Western Recorders and cut a nineteen-dollar demo of "Teen Beat" on an acetate. He played the track for some publishers at American Recording, but they didn't think anybody would be interested in a drum record. But Nelson was undeterred. He took the acetate to disc jockey Art Laboe because he had recently released a hit bongo drum specialty by Preston Epps called "Bongo Rock" on his Original Sound label. Laboe loved "Teen Beat" as soon as he heard the first few bars.

In July 1959, a couple of weeks later, Laboe brought Guybo Smith, Eddie Cochran's bass player, and jazz guitarist Barney Kessel into the studio to beef up the basic band of Nelson, Podolor, and Bruce Johnston. He had Smith tune his bass strings down to match Nelson's drums and brought the Johnny Horton record "The Battle of New Orleans" to demonstrate the martial beat he wanted. Laboe and the engineer spent hours later doing laborious work using a primitive graphic equalizer.

The boys dreamed up names to use on the record — Sam and Rich; Sammy, Richie, and Bruce — but when Nelson called Laboe to talk about the record's release, Laboe told him he would release the single under the name "Sandy Nelson," and Laboe and Nelson would be sharing the songwriting credit. Nelson complained that wouldn't be fair to Bruce and Richie, but Laboe told him the record had always been his idea. Nelson also objected to the name Sandy—his real name was Sandor, but he always thought Sandy sounded like a girl's name. He argued that he was known around town as the drummer Sammy Nelson. Laboe said that wouldn't matter when the record was a national hit, and hung up.

Nelson told his discouraged bandmates, once again cut out of the credit, that he would make it good to them if the record made money, but that didn't really make anyone happy. The next day, Podolor reported for boot camp, having previously received his draft notice, and didn't think about the record again until he was in the Army and heard it on the radio.

"Teen Beat" was a phenomenon that spent four months on the charts, rising to number four and selling more than seven hundred thousand copies. Art Laboe didn't have a contract with Sandy Nelson, who was suddenly the most famous drummer in rock and roll. Kip Tyler, his old bandleader, acting as his manager, took Nelson to Imperial Records; his end of the deal was another Kip Tyler record nobody heard. At Imperial, Nelson came under the supervision of executive Eddie Ray, a veteran of the R&B record business. He rushed Nelson into an album called *Sandy Nelson Plays Teen Beat*, a bald attempt to cash in on the hit single, including a re-recording of the original. Twenty-year-old Nelson was more than slightly cowed to be in the studio with his hero Ernie Freeman, whose record "Jivin' Around" Nelson used to play at parties. He had done the number with Bruce Johnston in the Sleepwalkers, and now he found himself covering the song with its composer sitting at the keys. Nelson had only recently left high school, and he wasn't entirely certain he was ready for what came next.

7

NANCY AND TOMMY

JILL GIBSON HAD no idea what Jan Berry was doing in the halls of University High in the fall of 1959. Hadn't he graduated with her sister's class the year before? Jill knew Jan from some parties she'd attended during the eleventh grade with her Barons boyfriend Joe Amsler. Since Amsler joined the Army after graduation the summer before, they had been seeing much less of each other and had basically drifted apart. Jill, who was introverted but not shy, had always nursed a secret crush on Jan. He was a good-looking bad boy who didn't care what you thought, a quality she found highly appealing. Jill hadn't exchanged more than a few words with him, and here he was walking up to her in the near-empty school hallway, a toothy grin spreading across his face.

One look at Jill Gibson and you knew she was from California. It wasn't only the silky blonde hair, lustrous tanned skin, piercing blue eyes, and sharply etched cheekbones, but the nonchalance with which she carried her beauty, as if it was such an accepted part of her life that it barely mattered to her at all. If she felt exceptional, it wasn't because of her looks. She wasn't a social girl with dozens of friends and a busy calendar. Although she never lacked for male attention, Jill preferred to spend her time alone, painting, drawing, or playing her guitar, maybe writing a song. Her home life was dreary; her travel agent father lived under the thumb of his cold, controlling British wife. Jill had little to do with her parents and stayed behind a closed bedroom door as much as she could, but she was close to her more outgoing, compliant older sister, Jane, the good daughter. Jill was the sullen rebel.

In actual fact, Jan Berry had not graduated with Jill's sister, but at midterm a semester later. In February 1959, he entered pre-med at UCLA and pledged to the Phi Gamma Delta fraternity, although he chose to live at home rather than move into the Fiji house on campus. Jan took attending college only slightly more seriously than he did high school and continued to concentrate much of his energies on making music in the garage with Dean. He still had time to play. He knew Jane Gibson from school and Barons parties, and he knew her younger sister Jill through her connection to Joe Amsler. But this meeting in the hallway at University High was the first time they had spoken to each other one to one. Without standing on ceremony, Jan asked Jill out, and she said yes.

From the beginning of their relationship, Jan and Jill made music together, spending hours in Jan's garage, Jill strumming guitar, coming up with melodies, Jan fitting lyrics to her music. Jill learned violin in elementary school, but by high school she played guitar and sang folk songs, often originals that she wrote herself or with her high school friend Tracy Newman. She was something of a beatnik and once pledged with another high school friend that they would wear only black for the rest of the year. Much that passed between Jill and Jan went without words. The romance bloomed quickly, and soon they were going steady.

Dean met Judy Lovejoy at State Beach. Daughter of actor Frank Lovejoy and actress Joan Banks, the attractive, personable blonde teenager attended Marymount School for Girls, the elite Catholic school on Sunset Boulevard near UCLA. Her parents belonged to the exclusive Sand and Sea Beach Club, part of the Oceanhouse hotel on the site of the fabulous hundred-room beach house built by newspaper baron William Randolph Hearst for his mistress, the silent film star Marion Davies. Judy had spent enough time with the smart set, so one weekend she walked off on the sand, up toward State Beach, where the Uni High kids hung out.

Dean was a fresh-faced cutie with a goofy grin who looked more like thirteen than his actual nineteen years old. He lived at home with a younger sister; his parents called him Dean-O to distinguish him from his father, also named Dean. Judy had her own T-bird, her own phone, and lived in a Beverly Hills mansion with her movie star parents. Dean couldn't help but be impressed. Before long, they were double-dating with Jan and Jill. The two blonde beauties posed in swimsuits with their backs to the camera next to their blonde boyfriends for a publicity photo at Castle Rock near State Beach, waves crashing in the background, the boys dressed in matching madras shirts and shorts, already pushing the whole California dream.

While Jan and Dean had spent that summer flogging "Baby Talk" at live appearances — often lip-synched — around the Los Angeles area with a couple of out-of-town trips to work with Dick Clark, Jan was now carrying a full academic load at UCLA, and Dean was equally involved in classes at Santa Monica City College. Both sets of parents were adamant that they stay in school because the rock and roll thing would never last. It was already slowing down after the Top Ten success of "Baby Talk." The follow-up single came and went, as did a subsequent third single.

Dean provided the perfect comic foil for Jan's hijinks. They were both big Laurel and Hardy fans, and they brought some of the old-fashioned comedy team spirit into their rock and roll act, which was not necessarily confined to their live appearances. They frequently staged fake fistfights in public, falling over each other in restaurants, Jan pretending to have seizures, causing public scenes for their own amusement, while their girlfriends looked the other way and rolled their eyes. Dean brought the touch of humor that balanced Jan's often malicious bad-boy act and may have even softened it some. But the antics weren't always upbeat and light-hearted.

Over Thanksgiving weekend, they flew to Hawaii to take part in a concert celebrating statehood, along with the Four Preps, Jimmy Clanton, and their University High pal Sandy Nelson, who had become a major attraction since "Teen Beat" hit the charts (Sandy brought his mom on the trip). Lou Adler found himself pounding on Jan's door, where he was sequestered with a teenage girl who turned out to be the daughter of the admiral in charge of the naval base. Her father was looking for her, and Adler told Jan he needed to get her out of his room. Jan did not react well. He took a fire extinguisher and broke all the lights above the room numbers on the entire floor. It cost them more to check out than they made on the trip.

TOMMY SANDS SAW the engagement at the Cocoanut Grove as the culmination of three years of hard work. This would be his crowning moment since he had burst on the scene as an overnight sensation starring in the television play *The Singing Idol*. He'd been working as a professional musician since the age of eight, when he began making weekly appearances on the radio in his hometown of Shreveport,

Louisiana. He was only fifteen years old in 1952, when he first came
to the attention of "Colonel" Tom Parker, who was then managing
country star Eddy Arnold.

Colonel Parker groomed young Sands, first as a cowboy movie
star, and later as a rock and roll singer he briefly offered to RCA
Victor as an alternative to Elvis Presley when Parker was experiencing difficulties separating Presley from his recording contract with
Sun Records. Sands was cut from the same Southern rocker cloth
as Elvis; they even knew each other early in their careers. When
the producers of *Kraft Television Theatre* called Parker about casting
his boy Elvis in *The Singing Idol*, Parker recommended Sands and
referred them to his manager. *The Singing Idol* vaulted Sands into
the forefront of rock and roll when it aired nationwide in January
1957, and landed him a record deal within the week at Capitol
Records. His debut disc, "Teen-Age Crush," went to number three
on the charts, sold eight hundred thousand copies, and established
Sands as a star.

For Sands, appearing at the Cocoanut Grove was a symbol of
having arrived in show business in Hollywood. Located off the lobby
of the thousand-room Ambassador Hotel on Wilshire Boulevard's
"Miracle Mile," the elegant supper club still had the Arabian Nights
décor and artificial palm trees that had come straight from the set
of Rudolph Valentino's *The Sheik* when it first opened in 1921. The
nightclub was built into Hollywood fables; it was the place where
Bing Crosby and Frank Sinatra entertained foreign leaders, early
Academy Awards ceremonies were held, and Joan Crawford and
Carole Lombard danced the Charleston. It was the town's big room,
and teen idol Sands had been moving away from rock and roll into
mainstream show business almost from the moment he hit the charts.
His new manager was a former Hollywood studio publicist named

Ted Wick. His latest single featured Sands swinging to the big band sound of Sinatra arranger Nelson Riddle.

Sands and his quartet had worked to get this far. They had played all the big TV shows—Ed Sullivan, Perry Como, Garry Moore—and did all the major nightclubs in the country, in between flying in and out of Hollywood for sessions at Capitol Records. His new album, *Sands at the Sands,* was a big band affair recorded live at the Sands Hotel in Las Vegas. But the Cocoanut Grove was the big one. Hollywood was his hometown now, and the opening-night audience was filled with celebrities, gossip columnists, and his friends and fans. Sitting ringside at a table where she couldn't be missed was Nancy Sinatra.

Tommy Sands was a crooner for a new generation. Standing on that stage in a fresh tuxedo, singing those songs with the orchestra blasting behind him, he couldn't have reminded Nancy of anyone more than her father. She never took her eyes off him the entire night.

Backstage after the show, Sands and his band entertained a breathtaking array of well-wishers, acquaintances, and friends, each announced by the maître d', and every name would bring a shock of recognition and a glance between the delirious musicians. When Nancy Sinatra was announced, the band members looked at each other with big smiles of disbelief. She made a beeline for Sands.

Since graduating University High and dropping out of USC after one semester, Nancy had been contemplating a career in show business. She was nineteen years old, still living at Carolwood with her mother and siblings. She had drifted away from her high school friends and brushed up her stenography skills at the Willis secretarial school. In March 1960, the month after meeting Tommy Sands, she was in New York taking crash courses in voice, dance, and drama when she was asked to represent the Sinatra family at the ceremonial greeting of Elvis Presley on his return from the Army. Nancy sat demurely in her smart tweed suit on a folding chair in an Air Force base hangar awaiting the scheduled press conference. On her lap, she held a box of ruffled tuxedo shirts—a gift from her father suggested by Colonel Parker. Parker had negotiated an unprecedented $125,000 fee for the first television appearance by his lad Elvis after leaving the Army, on a special, *The Frank Sinatra Timex Show: Welcome Home Elvis.* Nancy was waiting for the plane to touch down, as appointed, when Presley landed in a near-blizzard at Fort Dix, New Jersey. As exciting as this duty was, her mind was elsewhere.

Although they had known each a little more than a month since that night at the Cocoanut Grove, things were cooking on high heat between Nancy and Tommy Sands. Only that morning, he had called from Los Angeles and asked her to marry him. She was planning to fly straight home after Elvis's press conference to have Tommy meet her at the airport with an engagement ring and her mother in tow, but the same blizzard that was blowing when Elvis landed delayed her flight for more than twenty-four long, lovelorn hours. She wound up spending the night with her grandparents in Weehawken, New Jersey. Nancy called her father to tell him the news. He issued no warnings or criticism. "Okay, Chicken," he said, "if that's what you want."

The television special with Elvis was filmed a couple of weeks later at the Fontainebleau Hotel in Miami, and Nancy's appearance on the show when it was broadcast the following May would be her professional show business debut. Her presence also served as a bridge between generations, her father's audience and the Elvis fans, who were more her age. She certainly looked the ingenue in the Vegas-style opening number with the rest of the cast: her father, Sammy Davis Jr., and Joey Bishop. She performed a stilted, inconsequential dance routine with two male dancers during her father's hosting duties. She and her father sang an awkward duet—Sammy Cahn rewriting the lyrics to "You Make Me Feel So Young" as "You Make Me Feel So Old." She wore a cunning little décolleté frock and sang in a surprisingly bland little-girl voice, somewhat overshadowed by her father's smothering presence. A star was not born.

Once they were engaged, Nancy insisted on joining Tommy and the band on the road, although her parents only agreed if her mother, Nancy, or his mother, Grace, went along to chaperone. Nancy was no virgin. Her mother had helped arrange an abortion for her the year before, and did so without judgment. Big Nancy understood; she herself had undergone the procedure in 1947 while she and Frank were estranged. But under the watchful eyes of their mothers, the lustful couple had difficulty keeping their hands off each other, even saying goodnight at their hotel room doors. If only for the sex, Nancy could hardly wait to be married.

Sands dedicated his swinging new song, "That's Love," to his fiancée on the Tennessee Ernie Ford TV show. She sported a four-carat, emerald-cut diamond engagement ring. They planned to hold the wedding that winter after he completed basic training for the Air Force Reserves at Lackawanna Air Force Base in Texas, but her father was scheduled to film a movie in Hawaii, so they moved up the date.

On Monday, September 12, 1960, Nancy Sinatra and Tommy Sands were wed in front of three dozen friends and family at the Sands Hotel in Las Vegas. The twenty-three-year-old groom looked dashing in his airman third class Air Force uniform, and his twenty-year-old bride wore a street-length dress from her father's designer, Don Loper. Her mother watched in silent horror, seeing her own life flash before her eyes. Her father cried when he saw her in her wedding dress with the bouquet and pear-shaped diamond earrings that he gave her. Frank waved off any photographs ("It's Nancy's day," he said), while the newlywed couple happily posed for a phalanx of photographers, cutting the wedding cake, kissing, and smiling. It was a match made in movie-magazine heaven.

8

ALLEY OOP

IN EARLY 1960, Kim Fowley was working for Arwin Records in Beverly Hills as a kind of go-fer and office manager. He had been whining to his boss at American International about the Jan and Dean deal, and they cooked up the idea of trying to license the six Jan and Arnie sides from Arwin for re-release. Fowley got Marty Melcher on the phone and made his pitch. Melcher told him to come over to the office and was surprised to see the tall, gawky nineteen-year-old show up. Taken by the kid's *chutzpah* and gift of gab, Melcher offered him a job, and Fowley moved in—literally. He began sleeping in the office, storing his dirty socks and clothes under the sofa. His bosses simply thought he was first in the office every morning.

Less than two years out of University High, Fowley remained close to his old musical associates. To Fowley, Hollywood was a small town. He was hustling every day, rubbing sticks together trying to make a spark, waiting for his first big deal. When he had nothing better to do, he would hang around the lobby of American Recorders, the studio owned by Richie Podolor's parents, where his Sleepwalkers pal Sandy Nelson was part of the scenery. One afternoon at the studio, Fowley ran into Nelson, who had recently returned from a grueling three-month bus tour with Freddy Cannon, Dion and the Belmonts, and Skip and Flip. Nelson told Fowley that Flip was also back in town and had come by the studio but had just stepped out. A few minutes later, when he returned, Nelson introduced Fowley to Flip—Gary S. Paxton—the tormented hillbilly genius who was going to change his life.

Paxton had driven from the Pacific Northwest in his '58 Oldsmobile to make his fortune in Hollywood. Skip and Flip had scored three hit records the year before, but Paxton hated performing live and was having personal problems at home. He wasn't the most stable personality. A child of unwed teenage parents, Paxton had been adopted and renamed shortly after his first birthday. He was sexually molested by a neighbor at age seven and misdiagnosed with polio at eleven. When he was a teen, his strict Christian adoptive parents moved from a farm in Kansas to Arizona, and Paxton, who had long found refuge in music, started playing rock and roll. He started a band called the Pledges with a college student six years older named Clyde Battin. The Pledges made a couple of local singles, including "Betty Jean," a rocking love letter to seventeen-year-old Paxton's fourteen-year-old bride.

The band broke up after a woman approached Paxton at a restaurant and identified herself as his mother. He immediately left Betty Jean and their young son in Tucson and went to live with his mother in Seattle. Betty Jean filed for divorce. Paxton found work in nearby Tacoma with a country band led by a then-unknown singer named Buck Owens, picking up ten dollars a night. To make ends meet, Paxton picked fruit by day. As he was working in an orchard with the radio blasting out of the rolled-down windows of his truck, he heard a familiar song.

The local label where the Pledges had made their records had sold the year-old masters to an East Coast company that released a single, "It Was I," renaming the group Skip and Flip after the poodle dogs that belonged to the label owner's wife. The record was headed into the Top Ten in July 1959 when Paxton (now Flip) returned to the fold and joined Clyde (now Skip) Battin on the road. Skip and Flip appeared on *American Bandstand,* made more records, the whole program.

When Betty Jean and their son turned up in Seattle, having dropped the divorce, Paxton was already engaged to another girl. Then Betty Jean got pregnant again. Paxton was tired of the road and driving back and forth between the two women when he was home. He suspected Battin of having an affair with his wife. In February 1960, Paxton quit the group, piled into his Oldsmobile, and headed for Hollywood, promising both women he would send for them when he made it. He never saw either of them again.

Paxton rented a seedy room for $7.50 a week at El Centro and Selma in the middle of Hollywood. He wandered into American Recorders two blocks away because that was where he had recorded the last Skip and Flip single—a cover of the old Marvin and Johnny R&B hit "Cherry Pie." There he met Kim Fowley, who immediately started to schmooze him. Fowley took Paxton to Arwin Records and introduced him to Marty Melcher. Meeting Doris Day's husband made Paxton think Fowley was somebody who knew people, important people. In Paxton, Fowley found someone with genuine musical talent—he could sing, write, and play guitar. Fowley could supply the hustle and strategy; he told Paxton he had learned to think Jewish. Fowley knew how Hollywood worked.

Fowley could take Paxton around and introduce him as Flip of Skip and Flip and, because he had hits, he was treated as a celebrity.

Everybody assumed he had money. Fowley and Paxton took a lot of meetings. Fowley kept up the front, even though they were both broke and starving. He quit his job at Arwin and then started running errands for disc jockey Alan Freed. The father of rock and roll radio had moved to Los Angeles in May 1960 and opened shop on KDAY. Fowley was sleeping on a cot in Happy's Chevron, next to American Recorders, working as the night watchman of the filling station at Hollywood and Argyle. He and Paxton formed a music publishing company called Maverick Music and printed business cards with the number for the pay phone on the corner.

Paxton always claimed he met songwriter Dallas Frazier in a gas station outside Bakersfield on his way from Seattle to Los Angeles. Frazier was the son of dust bowl immigrants straight out of *The Grapes of Wrath*, and he had been plugging away in the country music racket since he was twelve years old. Fowley and Paxton officially launched Maverick Music when they sold a Dallas Frazier song, "Sugar Babe," recorded by the shopworn R&B act Gene and Eunice, to a small-time label in Gardena. But they knew they had found something special when they heard Frazier's next song, "Alley Oop," obviously inspired by records by the Coasters. Frazier dreamed up the lyrics as he was musing on a newspaper comic strip about prehistoric cavemen (*There's a cat in the funny papers we all know...*) years before, while working heavy machinery at a cotton mill his father managed in the San Joaquin Valley.

From his phone booth office, Fowley called Lute Records. He had already been talking with label owner Al Kavelin, a bandleader from New York popular in the Thirties who had recently started the independent label after Marty Melcher fired him from Arwin Records. Kavelin had only been in business a couple of months and managed a few releases, but nothing that didn't sink without a trace.

Although Fowley had to hitch-hike to the Lute offices, he talked Kavelin into giving him $200 and put together an epic session days later at American Recorders. He hired veterans of the R&B scene for the session. Keyboardist Gaynel Hodge had been part of the Hollywood Flames, sang with the Platters, and co-wrote the Penguins hit "Earth Angel." Bassist Harper Cosby worked for Johnny Otis, who had recently crashed the charts with "Willie and the Hand Jive." And drummer Ronnie Selico played on all the Olympics' hits, including "(Baby) Hully Gully."

Sandy Nelson came along for the session but didn't take the drum chair. He found an empty bottle to clink and a garbage can to scream into after every time Paxton sang *Look at that caveman go*. Paxton brought along a red-haired girlfriend named Diane Mutz from Long Beach. Dallas Frazier showed up with a pal from Bakersfield, a song-writer named Buddy Mize. They all sang along. Somebody brought a generous supply of hard cider, and the session soon devolved into a drunken morass. Paxton had to take a chair to sing and had to read the lyrics off a brown paper bag. As he finished the vocal, he fell off the chair, his voice fading from the tape as he slipped away from the microphone.

Because Paxton thought he was still under contract to the label that had signed Skip and Flip and didn't want to risk using his name on the record, they needed to find a new one. This was outlaw rock and roll, and they needed an alias. Fowley pointed to the intersection outside the studio, Hollywood and Argyle, and the group had a name, the Hollywood Argyles

When "Alley Oop" burned up the charts in June 1960, Fowley and Paxton were caught by surprise. They weren't used to success. After first sending out a bunch of imposters to play as the group at the El Monte Legion Stadium for ten dollars apiece, Paxton decided he could use some ready cash while waiting for "Alley Oop" royalties to come rolling in. He and Fowley put together a road version of the Hollywood Argyles—all white, unlike the studio version—and Paxton only had to do three or four shows before he remembered how much he hated it.

♪

SANDY NELSON MOVED out of his parents' place and rented a small house in the woodsy end of the North Hollywood hills. The same day, he bought a new Chevrolet Impala station wagon, with a payload big enough to haul around a set of drums. After a booking agent got him a spot on the Dick Clark primetime Saturday night show but neglected to tell Nelson, Clark sued him, and the American Federation of Musicians had to step in to settle the affair. When Nelson did finally appear on Clark's New York City show, host Clark went backstage to greet Nelson personally. "I just wanted to make sure you were here," he smiled.

If Clark had showed up three minutes earlier, he might have wondered, because Nelson had spotted a spiral staircase leading to the storm drain system and had been exploring subterranean New York until a couple of minutes before Clark peeked into his dressing room. Outside of the miserable bus tour with Freddy Cannon and Skip and Flip, Nelson played only a few select gigs. He did a couple of shows in Northern California with Jan and Dean. Dave Shostac watched in amazement as Nelson, late for his stage call, leaped the railing and landed on his drum chair at San Francisco's Cow Palace; Nelson was often given to crazy physical feats of derring-do like scaling the outsides of buildings.

Nelson also picked up a few session jobs. He played on the hit

"A Thousand Stars" by Kathy Young and the Innocents. Young was a fifteen-year-old high school girl who approached Innocents manager Jim Lee at a show at Pacific Ocean Park and ended up with the Innocents backing her in the studio on what would become a Top Ten hit. Nelson also did sessions with rock and roll firestarter Gene Vincent, already on the other side of the bell curve of his career. It was only after Nelson's best collaborator, Richie Podolor, got out of the Army, where his skills as a classical guitarist had landed him soft duty in special services, that things began to happen again.

Theirs had always been a contentious relationship. Although Podolor was still sore over the "Teen Beat" songwriting credits, he put his feelings aside and started working with Nelson again. Nelson brought him to Imperial, where, recording under his first two names as Richie Allen, Podolor scored a modest hit with the twangy instrumental "Stranger from Durango" in October 1960. He and Nelson teamed up for a few shows, double-billed but playing in the same band; half the show would be Richie Allen, the other half Sandy Nelson. They toured the Northwest in a car, but after more kids asked for Nelson's autograph, Podolor stopped speaking to him for the entire ride back to Los Angeles.

"ALLEY OOP" BY the Hollywood Argyles took off on the charts and didn't stop until it reached number one in *Billboard*. Paxton and his girlfriend moved into more spacious quarters at the El Jardin apartments on Hayworth Avenue in West Hollywood. Fowley's status suddenly changed with the clutch of chiselers and kibitzers that hung around the front of Nickodell's on Selma and Argyle, feet up on car fenders, cracking wise and talking tall, while shunning lower forms of life like Fowley. They were the real Hollywood Argyles. Fowley and Paxton found the same group of hustlers on the sidewalk in front of the Brill Building in New York, where they traveled after the record hit the charts, and were not greeted like penny-ante pikers; they were embraced. Ersel Hickey, who had a hit two years before with "Bluebirds Over the Mountain" and kept an office upstairs, treated them to drinks at Jack Dempsey's. They met with Mike Stoller of the songwriting team Leiber and Stoller, who recognized that "Alley Oop" was an homage to their work with the Coasters. In their office on the ninth floor of the Brill Building, Stoller offered to produce the next Hollywood Argyles record, but Fowley and Paxton had better ideas.

Lou Adler didn't like Kim Fowley, but that hardly made him unique. Almost nobody liked Fowley. Adler, however, could do something about it. He knew "Alley Oop" was going to be a smash as soon as he heard it, and he also knew that Kavelin's little Lute label did not have the distribution pipeline for a nationwide hit. He pulled together a plan to cover the record as quickly as he could. This kind of hijacking was common in the record industry; a hit song could have a half dozen different versions hit the streets within weeks or even days of each other. Pop songs could be retooled for rhythm and blues or country and western markets, and vice versa.

Dean Torrence had known Don Drowty from University High and on campus at Santa Monica City. Drowty was raised in foster homes around Santa Monica and was an unsparingly polite yet insistent young man with a stylish flat-top haircut and a strong, clear singing voice. He and two friends sang together as the Pastels, not that they were getting anywhere. At Adler and Alpert's Sunset Boulevard offices, the Pastels were introduced to guitarist Tony Moon, a fully trained musician adept at arranging vocal harmonies. Adler and Alpert had been looking at Drowty and his friends, another set of Westside beach bums who sang like they were on a street corner in the Bronx, but they hadn't yet landed on what to do with the group.

When Adler and Alpert took them into Western Recorders to cut their version of "Alley Oop," Jan and Dean came along. Jan clinked on a Coke bottle and Dean sang in the background chorus with everybody. Engineer Dayton "Bones" Howe suggested naming the group the Evergreens, then Adler added Dante (Don), and they became Dante and the Evergreens. Adler put the tape on a plane to New York for Madison Records, where he had arranged a deal, and the single was on the streets by the end of the week. Both versions of "Alley Oop" hit the national charts in the first week of June 1960.

"Alley Oop" threatened to become a minor obsession in Los Angeles music circles. Rhythm and blues bandleader and session musician H. B. Barnum pulled together a group of his own studio musicians and cut yet another version of the song, calling their group the Dyna-Sores. Even Fowley and Paxton got in on the act, covering their own hit in pidgin English as "Cholley Oop" by the Hong Kong White Sox. The Hollywood Argyles and Dante and the Evergreens battled for supremacy pretty much market by market. Although the Argyles won the number one slot on the *Billboard* charts, Dante and the Evergreens were number one at the jukebox industry trade magazine *Cash Box.* The Argyles were tops in Los Angeles, but the Evergreens ruled in New York City, where the group performed at the Apollo Theater—only the third white rock and roll act to play the Harlem theater, after Buddy Holly and Duane Eddy.

Fowley took the Evergreens' cover of "Alley Oop" as a hostile act. He considered Drowty an enemy from high school. He suspected Jan of stealing his Del-Vikings album he brought to a party at the Berry house, and he could have been right—Fowley was the kind of pathetic wretch that Jan would have looked down on and treated accordingly. And Adler was the sort of smart Jew that Fowley resented because he thought they ran Hollywood; he had been brought up around that kind of thinking, and he could be profanely anti-Semitic (he could be profane about anything). He took the cover of his song personally. And he could have been right.

Fowley fostered ambitious plans with Paxton to crash the coalescing rock and roll record business growing in Hollywood. He had no grand design or vision but was driven by an almost innate need to succeed — at any cost — and not simply to succeed, but to see his enemies fail. If Fowley was single-minded about moving their pieces down the board, Paxton was more careless, often heedlessly irresponsible.

Paxton's apartment at El Jardin was always overrun with musicians sleeping on the living room floor. Paxton, customarily dressed all in black, made himself scarce, his growing collection of hot rods parked out front. He polished off a fifth of Jack Daniel's a day. Paxton found a hot band at the Hollywood Legion Lanes called the Cordials and sent them out on the road as the Hollywood Argyles. Meanwhile, he played around town on weekends for cash at sorority and fraternity parties at USC and UCLA with another version of the Hollywood Argyles that sometimes included Fowley's pal Bruce Johnston on keyboards.

Fowley was the front man for their operation. He and Paxton made records cheap and fast by the dozen. Fowley found talent everywhere. Doug Salma of the East Los Angeles R&B act Doug and Freddy was walking down Sunset Boulevard carrying a portable Wollensak tape recorder, trying to get someone to listen to his tape, when he saw Fowley standing on the sidewalk outside the Hollywood Palladium. Fowley took Salma into the filling station bathroom to use the electricity and loved Salma's version of the Bobby Freeman song "Need Your Love." Fowley remembered Bruce Johnston singing the hell out of the song with Kip Tyler and the Flips at the Rainbow Roller Rink. He washed his hands and took Salma to El Jardin for Paxton to hear it.

When the three guys from the Innocents walked into American Recorders, Fowley was holding office hours, haranguing someone on the phone, feet on the desk. They had come from Adler and Alpert's office, where they had gone to see Herb Alpert, but he was too busy, and they split. The year before—as the Echoes—Jim West, Darron Stankey, and Al Candelaria had cut a single with Adler and Alpert, when they were still working for Keen Records. When these fellows said they had just come from Herb B. Lou Productions, Fowley perked up. If it meant beating Adler out of something, he wanted to hear what they had.

For Fowley, Adler became a minor obsession. Fowley needed to have enemies to justify his poisonous worldview, and Adler fit the bill. Feeling persecuted left Fowley free to do what he wanted. He still nursed resentments towards Adler over the Jan and Dean affair, and, of course, he hated Jan and Dean and had hated them since high school. The opportunity to swipe a song from Adler was irresistible. He leaned forward to listen with special interest.

While Stankey strummed his guitar, the three launched into "Honest I Do," a slight, simple ballad lit up by the high tenor vocal—falsetto almost—of Jim West. Fowley pulled Paxton out of a session and made him listen, then told the Innocents to come back that afternoon for a recording session. They had to finish the lyrics in the car on their way home to the San Fernando Valley before returning to make the record. Fowley quickly sold the master to Jim Lee at Indigo Records, who signed the group to a record deal and personal management.

But Fowley wasn't done. When "Honest I Do" hit the Top Ten in September 1960 (number one in Los Angeles), Fowley sold an extra song left over from the session to Al Kavelin of Lute Records, who pumped out "Tick Tock" in an effort to hijack the Innocents' follow-up hit from Indigo Records for his own label. It was the sort of sleazy move common to bottom feeders of the record industry like Fowley and Kavelin. Although the record failed to catch much of the breeze left by "Honest I Do," the song would not go unnoticed by Fowley's nemeses Lou Adler and Jan Berry. The rock and roll record scene in Hollywood was still a tiny cabal.

PART 2

DAYLIGHT

Southern California,
where the American dream came
  too true.
                    — Lawrence Ferlinghetti

9

SURF MUSIC

Spring 1961

DON ALTFELD WAS sitting at the piano with his girlfriend, Donna
Saunders, in his parents' living room, playing the old Frank Loesser–
Hoagy Carmichael song "Heart and Soul." It was a simple song for
people who didn't know how to play the piano. As they were playing,
Altfeld thought of the new hit by the Marcels—a remake of another
old standard, "Blue Moon." While he and Donna continued their
four-hand exercise, he shouted to Jan Berry, who was hanging out on
the couch, "Hey, Jan, come over here and put some 'bomps' on this."

Jan leaned over their shoulders and did just that.

Jan and Dean definitely needed a new idea. It had been almost
two years since "Baby Talk," and in the here-today-gone-later-today
world of rock and roll, they teetered on the edge of extinction. Adler
had kept them on television, and they made local appearances on
weekends and toured briefly during school vacation, but they badly
needed a hit. Jan breezed through his first semester of UCLA then
took off the fall semester, while Dean struggled with a full load of

courses at Santa Monica City College plus additional advanced art classes elsewhere.

Jan had even floated a trial balloon with a solo single in February 1961 under the name Jan Barry, changing the spelling at the suggestion of Dick Clark. Adler threw the single out on a label he named Ripple Records, after the cheap wine, and nothing much happened. Jan and Dean never stopped making appearances together, despite fan magazine headlines that screamed "Why Did Jan and Dean Break Up?"

After the Dante and the Evergreens record, Adler and Alpert had signed a deal with Madison Records as independent producers, a new idea gaining currency in the record industry. They had built a stable of acts that included not only Jan and Dean and Dante and the Evergreens, but also pop singer Deane Hawley and R&B vocal group the Untouchables. There wasn't a lot of money — the Dante and the Evergreens single may have gone Top Twenty, but Madison Records never paid Adler and Alpert one dime — and now the plan was to record Jan and Dean on "Heart and Soul." Adler was traveling with the guys over the weekend and, with what little money they had left, booked studio time while they were out of town, for Alpert to record the basic track and his arrangement.

Calm and clear-eyed, Herb Alpert was a bright, engaged, ideal collaborator. But he was also a bebop jazz musician who dug Clifford Brown, Miles Davis, Dizzy Gillespie — a cat from the land of Oo-Bla-Dee. He was no snob; he loved rhythm and blues music, and he had even made some questionable records, but he had never consciously made a record he didn't like. Until now. It wasn't that he didn't like "Heart and Soul"; he hated it. Alpert thought it was a piece of junk, or worse. It was so bad that it made him question what he was doing with his life. Left alone in the studio with the firm's dwindling resources, his artistic instincts rebelled. Rather than lay down the instrumental track for "Heart and Soul," he spent the session cutting one of his jazz numbers instead. It would mean the end of his partnership with Adler.

The partners had few assets to divide. Alpert wanted the Ampex tape recorder and Adler wanted Jan and Dean. They came to an agreement quickly, and Herb Alpert walked out the door with the Ampex under his arm, twenty-five years old, a wife and young son at home, into an uncertain but preferable future. They parted on less than amiable terms.

Back in school that spring semester, Jan Berry was walking out of class down Westholme Avenue on a sunny day, with "Heart and Soul" playing in his head. He was taking over from Alpert as musical director and arranger. He had sketched out all the vocal parts that morning, and did the instrumental arrangement in his head while he was driving to the studio. He and Adler had put together their last few hundred bucks for the session.

Adler called Don Kirshner, co-owner of Aldon Music, who had told Adler on his first trip to New York to let him know if he ever wanted to be in the publishing business. Kirshner ran the hottest company in the business, with songwriters like Carole King and Gerry Goffin, Neil Sedaka and Howard Greenfield, and Barry Mann and Cynthia Weil. Kirshner was a brash young newcomer who started out in Washington Heights selling songs with Bobby Darin. His partner, Al Nevins, was an older, more experienced music man. These guys were the center of the New York music business from their office at 1650 Broadway. Hollywood was far away from Times Square, and outside of Capitol Records, the music business in Los Angeles was strictly nickel and dime. Adler signed on as the West Coast office of Nevins-Kirshner.

Adler wanted to place Jan and Dean with Liberty Records, the

Hollywood company that was quickly becoming the largest independent in town. The label was now far beyond the Chipmunks
and novelty records, with hits by Bobby Vee, Gene McDaniels, Timi
Yuro (of Fairfax High), the Ventures, and even cowboy actor Walter
Brennan. Jan loved the idea and quickly became obsessed with signing
to Liberty. He had sold Liberty a master he and Altfeld produced by
a group of Latino friends from Uni High who called themselves the
Gents, and he liked dealing with the label. Another endorsement
came from Uni High friend Dick St. John, who had formed a duo
with another old Uni High friend, Mary Sperling, called Dick and
Dee Dee, and they were signed to Liberty. The problem was Liberty
Records didn't like "Heart and Soul." They were willing to sign Jan
and Dean, but they wouldn't release "Heart and Soul."

Adler took the master to Challenge Records, a modestly successful
independent owned by cowboy star Gene Autry that had some success
with rock and roll records by the Champs and others. They made a
quick deal for the single and a follow-up, then Adler continued his
negotiations with Liberty. Oddly enough, another version of the
Frank Loesser–Hoagy Carmichael chestnut was released a month
before by an authentic New York vocal group, the Cleftones, who'd
been around since Jan and Dean were singing in the locker room
showers. But Jan and Dean managed to catch their own Westside
street corner sound on their rendition and followed the Cleftones
up the charts. "Heart and Soul" brought practically washed-up Jan
and Dean back to life just in time to watch the Los Angeles record
scene explode.

When the record originally came out in May 1961, the B-side was
a song titled "Those Words," a typical Jan and Dean ballad written
by Lou Adler and Jan Berry. The "tick-tock" that opened the record
gave it away at the top, but "Those Words" was clearly a ham-handed,

copyright-infringing rewrite of "Tick Tock," the Innocents record that Fowley released (and co-published) after "Honest I Do" hit the charts. The Jan and Dean B-side was quickly swapped out for a remake of one of the songs on Jan's solo single, but apparently those guys could not resist picking on Fowley.

♪

BY SUMMER 1961, the traffic jam stretched three miles every week-end night along the Balboa Peninsula below Newport Beach, where thousands of teens jammed the grand Rendezvous Ballroom to hear Dick Dale and the Del-Tones. A decadent Jazz Age palace built on the seashore with a twelve-thousand-square-foot dance floor, a former swing emporium where big band king Stan Kenton once held forth in all his glory beside the sea, the Rendezvous had been more or less down and out when Dick Dale started throwing his dances there the year before.

Dick Dale was a former Elvis impersonator who had developed a singular style on the electric guitar. Attacking his bottom strings with a machine-gun flurry of staccato strokes, Dale drove a thunderous, roaring sound out of his guitar, drenched in reverb, that washed over his audience in a visceral wave. He worked with Leo Fender at his nearby guitar plant in Fullerton to hot-rod his Fender Stratocaster guitar, fine-tune the reverb unit, and build an amplifier powerful enough to withstand Dale's brutal treatment. Fender developed the Fender Showman amplifier for Dale and named it for him because that was what Fender thought Dale was—a showman.

The South Bay, of course, had long been an epicenter of surfing on the California coast. Hawaiian transplant George Freeth introduced surfing to California shores in 1907 at Huntington Beach, and the great Duke Kahanamoku surfed those breaks in the Twenties. The throngs at Dick Dale's shows at the Rendezvous tracked in sand from the beach. They started calling what he did "surf music."

Surfing had exploded around the Southern California beaches. The movie version of *Gidget* had been released in spring 1959 and offered the outside world its first look at California beach culture. The real Gidget, Kathy Kohner from University High, visited the movie set the summer after graduating and met the star who portrayed her, Sandra Dee, who was almost the same age. Kohner saw the movie the next year in an auditorium in Eugene, Oregon, where she was attending college. Her life had veered off the beach and never went back, but Gidget left her mark. The movie marked the beginning of romanticizing California beach culture.

Surfer magazine made its debut in 1959. Up and down the coast, a filmmaker named Bruce Brown had been packing school auditoriums showing his 16 mm silent surf films and providing wry live narration. There was a swell coming in from offshore. These people were building their own culture. Surfers prided themselves on their freedom from convention, their rejection of established values, their alienation from mainstream society. In a sense, they ran a parallel course to the more cerebral, indoor pursuits of the beatniks. Surfers had their own social attitudes, clothing, and slang—all the makings of a successful subculture. What they needed was their own music.

A few miles away, the Belairs were filling to capacity and beyond the Knights of Columbus and Elks lodge halls they were renting to throw teen dances in the South Bay. Fans of instrumental rock and roll acts like Duane Eddy, Johnny and the Hurricanes, and the Ventures, the five-piece Belairs featured the articulate lead guitar of Paul Johnson. In summer 1961, the Belairs released a single, "Mr. Moto," which was followed the next month by the first record from Dick Dale and the Del-Tones, "Let's Go Trippin'," on his own Deltone Records. Surf music was spreading inland.

Bruce Johnston caught the wave early. He had been working for more than a year at Del-Fi Records, the label started by former bandleader Bob Keane in 1958, where Ritchie Valens made all his records. Johnston entered UCLA at age eighteen in September 1960, but he had his hands full already as a staff producer at Del-Fi and songwriter for Keane's Maravilla Music. He produced and wrote the rest of an album to go with the hit single by Ron Holden, "Love You So," that his boss bought from a Seattle label. He arranged sessions for Little Caesar and the Romans. He wrote songs for the Bob Keane Orchestra. He produced the Pharoahs, the singing group who made the original "Louie Louie" with Richard Berry. He pieced together the remaining tapes to make the third album by Ritchie Valens, who had died in the February 1959 plane crash that also killed Buddy Holly and the Big Bopper. Johnston was a teenage rock and roller serving a serious apprenticeship in the record industry, stockpiling valuable experience, finding his way, and living in comfort on Chenault Street in Brentwood.

"Do the Surfer Stomp" (parts one and two) by Bruce Johnston, released in January 1962, could have come straight from the bandstand at the Rendezvous Ballroom. The dance step was already a well-established part of the routine: kids stomping their feet in unison, raising a room-shaking wallop on the beat. Johnston, who actually surfed when he could find the time, picked up on the raucous dance beat and tailored the breaks in the song to encourage the dance the surfer kids had perfected in the South Bay. While the record made nary a ripple outside the Southern California counties, it made a small splash around town, where people were beginning to pick up on the whole surf thing.

♪

AFTER FOUR OR five failed singles for Imperial Records, Sandy
Nelson knew the future of his recording career looked dubious. He
could tell he was not quite the attraction he had been in the wake of
"Teen Beat" only the year before. He played a few gigs, accompanied
solely by a guitar player, at exciting places like Bakersfield, Oxnard,
and Fresno. He went ahead and took a tour in January 1961 as substitute drummer for the Ventures after the band's regular drummer,
Howie Johnson, was injured in a car crash. (The Ventures were one
of the leading rock and roll instrumental groups after their summer
1960 Top Ten hit "Walk—Don't Run.") The taxing tour took Nelson
and the band through the Pacific Northwest and, weirdly, Nebraska.
Nelson made note of the chains, tire changes, and salt rotting the
trailer. Not only were conditions arduous, the band also lost their
shirt on the tour, although sales rose slightly when, halfway through
the tour, they decided to add Nelson's name as a special guest.

All the time he was on the road with the Ventures, Nelson continued to experiment with new patterns and beats. On his return to
Los Angeles, he started working on his ideas with Richie Podolor.
Before Podolor would agree to collaborate, they drew up an agreement that guaranteed Podolor's royalties, retroactive back to "Teen
Beat." Podolor still felt cheated of his due. Without Podolor, Nelson
had made many uninspired records with session musicians. His longtime pal Bruce Johnston had been involved in Sandy Nelson's sessions
since "Teen Beat," when he used his shoes to muffle the piano. After
one album session, Johnston and Nelson repaired to Tijuana to get
drunk, watch strippers who took off everything, and sit in with the
local rock and roll band in the bar. The label kept handing Nelson
material to record he didn't like but recorded anyway. Nelson longed

for the chemistry he had enjoyed with Podolor, no matter how hard it was for the two of them to get along.

They set up in the new studios on Santa Monica Boulevard that Podolor's parents had moved into after leaving the Hollywood Palladium. Nelson, alone with an engineer, messed around with miking his drum kit up close, putting mics under the floor tom, in front of the bass drum. He cut a lot of drum tracks and edited the pieces into one flowing number. A couple of days later, he brought in Podolor to overdub some guitar. Podolor wrote a melody for the drum track and played guitar all over it. Nelson had to pull him back, make him play simple octaves. They had a contentious relationship, but they were like an old married couple that agreed to fight. The magnificently titled "Let There Be Drums" was another miracle hit for Nelson, scorching its way into the Top Ten in August 1961. The *Let There Be Drums* album with the adventuresome ten-minute "The Birth of the Beat" also sold a ton of records. Nelson's recording career was back on track, safe and secure, galvanizing his status as the first star drummer of rock and roll.

T.J. SKARNING MET Dick and Dee Dee at the Chicago airport in November 1961. The forty-four-year-old promoter with a pencil-thin mustache booked tours of the Midwest from his Artists Management Bureau office in Minneapolis. He had dropped a bundle presenting Elvis Presley in 1956, but Skarning had the far reaches of the rural Midwest covered as a concert producer. The surprise Dick and Dee Dee hit "The Mountain's High" made number two on the charts in September, and they were booked on a three-week tour with Jan and Dean and Jerry Fuller, hitting such hot spots as Des Moines,

Iowa; Fargo, North Dakota; La Crosse, Wisconsin; and other exciting points in between. Skarning escorted Dick and Dee Dee to his car, where Jan and Dean were standing around waiting.

Mary "Dee Dee" Sperling had attended University High for a year and knew Jan from his garage, where he had recorded her and some girlfriends on a couple of experimental tracks. Dick Gosting also knew Jan from University High, although he was a couple years behind him. He changed his name to Dick St. John when he became a recording artist and the record label changed Mary Sperling's name to Dee Dee without telling her, which did not make her especially happy. Neither did her singing and songwriting partner — she already had a boyfriend — taking full credit for their collaboration "The Mountain's High," which they had written together for the B-side of their first single. When some disc jockey in San Francisco flipped the record over, "The Mountain's High" detonated and flew up the charts. Dick and Dee Dee were the headline act on this tour.

Skarning packed the two nineteen-year-olds into the backseat of his late-model four-door Ford sedan with Jan. He put Dean in the front seat, and off they drove down the highway to Iowa. The band and Jerry Fuller followed in a second car. After the first weekend of shows, they stopped in Sioux City, Iowa, on their way to Madison, Wisconsin, nearly four hundred miles away. Dean called Lou Adler from a pay phone but got disconnected as a big rig diesel blew by, drowning out whatever Adler said after "I have some terrible news…" When Jan got Adler back on the line, Adler told him the Berry family home at 1111 Linda Flora had burned down that morning in a devastating wildfire that swept through the Bel Air hills, taking with it nearly five hundred homes.

Clara Berry had evacuated with two-year-old Stevie — Jan's son with Jeanette Anderson, who the Berrys had secretly adopted and were raising as their own—and the baby, Billy. Jan's brother Kenny and father, Bill, managed to drive up the hill on back roads to make their way around the blocked access; they arrived in time to see the final wall on their home collapse. Jan's 1958 Corvette—his "Charming Chariot"—burned to a crisp in the driveway, right alongside Jill Gibson's treasured T-bird and Bill's sailboat. The garage was gone, along with the massive KJAN record library, Jan's tape archive, and thousands of dollars of recording gear. All cinders.

There wasn't much time to absorb the news. Skarning hustled everybody back into the car and headed down the highway. Inside, the car was silent, only the sound of the tires humming on the road. Finally, Jan spoke up. "I invite you all to a rubble party," he said.

With long miles between concerts and shows every night of the week, sometimes two per day, Skarning was perennially stressed about the schedule. Everybody felt cramped in the four-door sedan. Jan and Dean held M&M fights over the backseat and Jan once kicked the back of the driver's seat in frustration so hard that Skarning lost control of the car and nearly crashed. Jan and Dean delighted in torturing the poor fellow, ditching him in a drugstore at one brief stop, hiding while he looked for them, and then, when he came back from searching, complaining about him making everybody late.

But it was the appearance of Randy that most unnerved Mary Sperling. "Randy" was a character Jan played in restaurants, slurring his speech, contorting his face, and acting like he was having a seizure. "We just picked him up at the mental institution, ma'am," Dean would tell the waitress. "Don't bring him a fork or knife, just a big spoon."

"How do I cut my burger with a spoon?" Jan slurred to Dean.

"Relax, Randy," Dean said.

Jan addressed the waitress in his put-on voice. "Bring me a knife and fork," he pleaded, while Dean firmly shook his head no. The waitress hurried off. When his food came, "Randy" covered his plate in ketchup and Dean led him out of the restaurant, tripping and falling as they went. Back in the car, Jan and Dean thought the brain damage act was downright hilarious. Randy made frequent appearances on the trip. They even talked Dick St. John into trying his hand at the seizure act and walked out of the restaurant like they didn't know him, leaving St. John squirming helplessly on the floor. The tour ended in wintry St. Paul, Minnesota, and Skarning sent Jan and Dean home to sunny California with the second half of their fee, a whopping check for $1,314.28.

10

HE'S A REBEL

AFTER UNIVERSITY HIGH, Jill Gibson had entered USC in fall 1960 and lived in a dorm for a semester but couldn't work up interest in much beyond her music and astronomy classes. She spent most of her time working on her car. She was supposed to meet Jan one afternoon at Adler's office on Sunset Strip and, in order to reach his office upstairs, she walked through the downstairs office of the John Robert Powers Agency, one of Hollywood's top model agencies, where Nina Blanchard first laid eyes on her. Blanchard saw Jill's California-girl look and knew that was a fresh idea for the modeling scene. She told Jill she was about to start her own agency and asked if she would come to work for her, modeling.

In high school, Jill had tumbled into a spot in a television commercial for Ban Roll-On deodorant. It involved little more than walking up to someone's door and paid several thousand dollars. While she was not averse to making such easy money, Jill was leery about trading on her looks. She didn't feel especially beautiful, and she resented how much value people put on her looks while ignoring the more meaningful parts of her character. She didn't have any great interest in clothing and didn't like to wear makeup, but she accepted Blanchard's offer nevertheless.

Jill picked up plenty of modeling work. She did catalogs, newspaper ads, and sometimes runway shows downtown with other models. She was encouraged to move to New York—Los Angeles was a remote secondary market in the fashion industry—but she had no interest in relocating and very little interest in modeling. She modeled for designer Peggy Hunt, *le dernier cri* in Hollywood high fashion, and worked runways with Peggy Moffitt, the model famously associated with designer Rudi Gernreich. Eighteen-year-old Jill lived in an apartment in Westwood with her sister, Jane, and modeling paid the rent.

Jill was a dazzling young woman who could quietly command the attention of a room with nothing more than her natural radiance and unspoiled, unpretentious manner. She and Judy Lovejoy went to a party in December 1961 at the home of Russ Titelman, an Aldon songwriter whose older sister had been Phil Spector's girlfriend at Fairfax High. Neither of their boyfriends—Jan and Dean—accompanied them, and they were messing around at the piano, Jill playing and singing, Judy harmonizing, goofing around with some Jan and Dean songs. The irony wasn't lost on the other partygoers who crowded nearby, but the girls sounded good together, and Jill could really sing, although it was not something that she was especially interested in doing. Then Phil Spector slid on the end of the piano bench with Jill and started to take an interest in what they were doing.

The next week, Jill and Judy met with Spector at the Beverly Hills office of Terry Melcher, the son of Doris Day, who was being produced by Spector for Columbia Records. Judy Lovejoy knew Melcher; their parents were in movies together. She introduced Jill, who sat around the office, talking, playing piano, and singing with

Spector, who wanted to take Jill and Judy into the studio. Spector knew who the boyfriends were, but he liked the idea of these two gorgeous blonde West Coast girls harmonizing on his songs. Oddly enough, it was Adler — not the boyfriends — who insisted that Spector couldn't produce their girlfriends and told Jan that *he* should take them into the studio. Jan found a couple of songs and worked on the records in earnest during January and February 1962, but nothing ever came of it.

Jill Gibson was much more than someone's girlfriend. At a time when women were largely defined by their relationships, she was independent, free-spirited, wholly herself — qualities that made her all the more attractive to Jan. He could tell that — like himself — Jill would never do anything simply because somebody told her to.

♪

IN APRIL 1962, a bunch of music business buddies headed down to Tijuana, Mexico, to catch the bullfights — record company guys Joe Smith and Tommy LiPuma, disc jockeys B. Mitchel Reed and Bobby Dale, promo man Jerry Moss and his new partner, Herb Alpert. They went to see *torero* Carlos Arruza — who was, along with the famed Manolete, one of the greatest Spanish bullfighters of the Forties — in his triumphant return from retirement as a *rejoneador*, or bullfighter on horseback. The grimy seaside border town, only a couple of hours from Los Angeles, was a steaming cauldron of sex and sin, a banquet of prostitutes, strip bars, and clip joints catering to day-tripping *gringos*. El Toreo de Tijuana was a rundown bullring in the center of town that had been there in various incarnations for more than sixty years. Tijuana — always a fun trip.

Herb Alpert had split up with Lou Adler one year before and

was only now getting back into the record business. At first after leaving Adler, disenchanted and disgusted, he took a job as a gym instructor—he had always been a good-looking guy who liked to stay in shape; he had even flirted with the idea of becoming a movie actor briefly—but found himself before long writing songs with his next-door neighbor. Alpert thought one song in particular would be perfect for pop singer Gogi Grant and made an appointment to demo the material for her producer, Dick Pierce of RCA Victor. Sitting at the piano in Pierce's office, Alpert showed him a couple of originals and his arrangement of a standard from the Thirties, "Gonna Get a Girl." Pierce offered him a record deal. Alpert, who had never before thought of himself as a vocalist, made a couple of singles for RCA under the name Dore Alpert, although union rules kept him from playing trumpet on any of the sides. At the time of the Tijuana trip, he was making tapes on the old Ampex he took from Adler in his own garage at 419 Westbourne Drive in West Hollywood and had a new partner, Jerry Moss, a promotion man he first met in New York when Moss worked the Dante and the Evergreens record.

Moss, a savvy, affable gentleman with a warm, ingratiating smile, who fell into plugging records in New York City after leaving the Army in 1958, had moved to Los Angeles two years earlier. He bumped into Alpert at Martoni's, the Cahuenga Boulevard music industry hangout, and they rekindled their association, hanging out at La Cienaga piano bars, Alpert often sitting in with his trumpet. His deal done at RCA, Alpert had a new song he wanted to release. Moss was also interested in putting out a record by an actor friend. They decided to join forces, each contributing one hundred dollars, and they started Carnival Records.

Alpert had been toying with a melody he picked up from songwriter Sol Lake, who led a society trio with Alpert's brother, Dave, on drums. Alpert, too, played occasional dates with Lake, who showed him the tune. Lake had dozens of songs recorded—"Roly Poly" by Doris Day in *Pillow Talk* was one recent example—without any real success. Alpert listened to Lake's song and was unimpressed. At first. Then he couldn't get the tune out of his head. Lake played the song on piano and had some crazy idea about recording the piece he called "Twinkle Star" on a celeste.

In his garage, Alpert transferred the melody to the trumpet, then added a second horn part. He toyed with the tempo and fussed endlessly with the song in his workshop. Finally, he phoned Sol Lake and played it for him over the phone. "What's that?" asked Lake, who didn't even recognize his own song.

Attending his first bullfight, Herb Alpert was overwhelmed by the pageantry. The small open-air bullring was tucked among the downtown traffic and crowded streets and filled with spectators. There were flags waving in the sunshine and bright and brassy mariachi music from the band led by Miguel Bravo in the stands. Maestro Bravo had led the house band at the Agua Caliente Casino, an elegant Tijuana emporium that closed in the Thirties, and was a close friend to Rafael Méndez, said to be the greatest trumpeter of his lifetime.

Alpert and his pals were drinking, carrying on, and getting swept away in the atmosphere. Alpert had never before heard the heroic lead trumpets of a high-gloss mariachi band, which blended so seamlessly into this Mexican pastoral playing out before his eyes. Between the sober ceremonies of the ring, the costumed horses and riders, the festooned lances, and the festive mix of blood lust and this robust, ornate brass band music, unlike anything he had heard before, Alpert was transfixed. Inspiration lodged in his brain like a bullet. He knew what to do with "Twinkle Star."

Back home, he and Moss released their Dore Alpert single, "Tell It to the Birds," in July on their Carnival Records label in Los Angeles, where they pumped it up to number sixteen on KFWB (it didn't hurt that Alpert's old pal B. Mitchel Reed was banging the song nightly on his top-rated show). Moss sold the master to Dot Records for $750. Moss's other record, with the actor, came and went without notice, but they used the money from Dot to finance the recording of the retooled "Twinkle Star." Alpert had re-voiced the horn parts on his arrangement, taking everything slightly south of the border. He wanted to evoke the pageantry and exotic flavor of the bullring without making overtly Mexican music. It was Southern California music... with a Spanish accent. Alpert borrowed bullfight crowds yelling "*Olé*" from the sound effects library of Liberty Records and hired studio musicians for an off-the-books session at Conway Recorders in Hollywood. Moss got the picture. He named the song "The Lonely Bull" and, honoring the source of the inspiration, called the group the Tijuana Brass featuring Herb Alpert.

They needed a new name for their label because it turned out Carnival had already been taken, so they put their initials together and released "The Lonely Bull" in August 1962 on a label they called A&M Records.

♪

STEVE DOUGLAS HAD returned to Los Angeles a couple of years before, after spending almost two years touring and recording with Duane Eddy, his blazing sax solos on Eddy's records cutting new trails for rock and roll saxophone, culminating with his 1960 tour de force "Peter Gunn," in which Douglas navigated the charts with his sole tenor where composer Henry Mancini required six saxophones. He had been squeaking by playing sessions, mostly rhythm and blues section work with arranger Maxwell Davis, staff producer at Kent and RPM Records, and contracting the occasional date, when Phil Spector called and asked him to put together a band for a session later the same week.

Douglas knew Spector from Fairfax High, even though he was a couple of years ahead of Spector. Their mothers were friends, and Douglas's mother made him let the pushy little kid play in his band when they were in high school. The acne-riddled punk could play guitar, though, and they developed an uneasy truce of a friendship. About the time Douglas left Duane Eddy and returned to Los Angeles, Spector had moved to New York to work with Leiber and Stoller.

In New York, twenty-year-old Phil Spector had proved to be quite the *wunderkind* in the studio, producing hits by Ray Peterson ("Corinna, Corinna") and Gene Pitney ("Every Breath I Take") and attracting the attention of the high and mighty in the New York record business, like Ahmet Ertegun of Atlantic Records and Freddy Bienstock of Hill and Range Songs—Elvis's publishers in the penthouse of the Brill Building. And he had written the Ben E. King hit "Spanish Harlem" with Jerry Leiber. Now, with Los Angeles–based Lester Sill, Spector had started his own label called Philles Records, and they had considerable success on their first outings with a girl group called the Crystals.

The Crystals were poised for the crucial make-or-break third release when Aaron Schroeder, Gene Pitney's music publisher, played Spector a new Pitney composition called "He's a Rebel," and Spector instantly recognized the song for what it was. A smash. Spector grabbed the song and rushed off to Los Angeles to record it.

He had not worked in Los Angeles since recording "I Love How You Love Me" with the Paris Sisters, a self-conscious 1961 masterpiece for Lester Sill's Gregmark label that Spector obsessed over in the studio for countless hours. He was sick of New York studios with their restrictive union rules that forbade overdubbing, not to mention the snooty older studio musicians in their coats and ties who looked down on rock and roll as beneath their jazz-world credentials, no matter what was actually paying their rent and putting food on the table.

Spector knew he wanted to make this record in Studio A at Gold Star with its sumptuous echo, and phoned Stan Ross about booking the dates. Ross, who was planning a Hawaiian vacation, hedged about being able to engineer the session. Spector expressed some urgency; he had information that producer Snuff Garrett was also fixing to cut "He's a Rebel" with a singer named Vikki Carr at Liberty. The Crystals were not able to make the session, and Spector didn't care. His record label owned the group name; it was entirely up to him who the Crystals were. Lester Sill recommended a vocal group called the Blossoms, who had been studio regulars in Los Angeles for years, singing background vocals for everybody from Sam Cooke to Bobby Darin. Spector called the lead vocalist to come to Gold Star for an audition.

Darlene Wright was a twenty-three-year-old preacher's kid from Texas who grew up singing in Baptist churches and had a husband, a baby, and a mortgage. Lester Sill picked her up and drove her to the studio. She was surprised to be called in by herself and even more surprised by the short, sullen producer wearing sunglasses in the already dark studio and reeking of English Leather. He sat at the piano and sang her the song in a reedy, monochromatic voice. Unlike most other producers, he wanted her to learn the song from sheet music, not the demo. As she worked her way through the song, Spector encouraged her to use the rough bottom edges of her voice, to step on the gas and apply some gospel fervor. The entire enterprise seemed strange, but Wright thought the song was little more than a trifle and the flat fee of $3,000 Spector offered was a king's ransom, so she didn't think there would be much more to this than a good payday.

On Friday, July 13, 1962, the band gathered at Studio A in Gold Star Studios on Santa Monica Boulevard to cut "He's a Rebel." Spector had called an especially large group, far beyond the standard rock and roll session. He wanted two bass players, which seemed unusual to Douglas and the other Los Angeles session players, but using two bass players on big R&B sessions was standard in New York; one on standup bass and one on Fender. The only musicians on the session Spector knew were bassist Ray Pohlman and guitarist Howard Roberts. Douglas collected Jimmy Bond as the second bassist, Nino Tempo on second saxophone, guitarist Tommy Tedesco, pianist Al De Lory, and a drummer he knew from a club in the Valley named Hal Blaine.

Darlene Wright was there with the other Blossoms, who were joined by a male vocalist comfortable singing in the female range named Bobby Sheen. The arranger had been recommended by Lester Sill because of his work with Sill's partner and Duane Eddy's producer, Lee Hazlewood. His name was Jack Nitzsche. Spector was distressed to discover that Stan Ross was not behind the board; in his place was Gold Star staff engineer Larry Levine, who had helmed many sessions at Gold Star—he cut Eddie Cochran's "Summertime Blues," among others.

From his chair in the control room, Spector drove the session like a maniac. He was searching for a sound, and he wouldn't stop until he heard it. He would start with the guitar players and have them play the first four bars over and over. He would have them play fifth notes, then change it to sixteenths. He would let them play and bring in the other instruments, then stop and start with the guitars all over again. The other musicians would sit and wait for their turn to come in, but never the guitar players. He kept them playing for hours. Howard Roberts's fingers were bleeding. All the time in the booth, Spector, operating at full-roar volume, was riding engineer Levine to bring up this instrument, bring up that instrument, until this unholy gushing mulch pulsed out of the speakers.

As the tapes finally rolled, Al De Lory, skittering little stabs of bebop scales up and down the keyboard, locked into a four-finger gospel phrase that anchored the entire arrangement, and drummer Hal Blaine drove the band into each chorus with propulsive fills. Steve Douglas delivered a fire-breathing solo in the middle eight, and the band themselves were shocked and amazed at the huge sound they were making. By the time Darlene Wright and the other singers laid their parts into the blend and Wright scorched the lead vocal, the session shifted into some transcendent level where nobody in the room had been before. They were making a number one hit—but it went beyond that.

This was the big bang of Los Angeles music—the moment a new generation of studio gladiators stepped into the arena. These were rock and roll musicians, not slumming jazz players or wizened rhythm and blues veterans. Saxophonist Steve Douglas had never heard jazz; he picked up the instrument after hearing sax breaks on New York rhythm and blues records by players like Sam "The Man" Taylor, Jimmy Wright, and King Curtis. He didn't know a flatted fifth from a fifth of Scotch. Hal Blaine, who hurried back from an out-of-town date with Peggy Lee to make the session, had spent three years backing Tommy Sands. These musicians spoke a different language. They were the young rebels in T-shirts and jeans, rough and ready to rock and roll. With guidance and direction from a handful of ecstatic visionaries, they were going to reshape American popular music.

11

THE BEACH BOYS

ON OCTOBER 22, 1962, President John F. Kennedy went on nation-wide television to announce that the United States had discovered the presence of Soviet nuclear missiles in Cuba and was sending the U.S. Navy to quarantine the island and turn away Soviet cruisers attempting to deliver more missiles. The world appeared to be on the brink of nuclear war. Frank Sinatra was convinced the end was at hand.

His pal, White House press secretary Pierre Salinger, had called over the weekend to warn Sinatra there might be trouble. Sinatra put his pilot on twenty-four-hour alert and stocked his private plane with four weeks' worth of water and rations. He phoned his latest flame, South African dancer and actress Juliet Prowse, in New York City and urged her to fly somewhere safe, certain New York would be the first place the Russians would sizzle. Prowse told him she would ride it out.

He called his daughter Nancy, also in New York, and told her to watch the president's speech on television that night, and for her and husband Tommy to pack their bags and be prepared to leave New York immediately after the speech. One of his aides was waiting for fourteen-year-old Tina Sinatra outside Marymount School, where fear and panic were racing through the hallways, and whisked her back to Carolwood Drive, where Big Nancy drove her and Frank Jr. to the Sinatra compound in Palm Springs in her Buick Riviera. Tommy and Nancy flew in from New York, and the Sinatra family huddled together in the desert around television news broadcasts, waiting for the end of the world.

Tommy Sands had taken his bride and moved to New York exactly because of the stifling, smothering clannishness of the Sinatra family. He quickly tired of the daily phone calls, the weekly family dinners, the boundless loyalty to Nancy's father. Nancy experienced considerable difficulty adjusting to married life herself; she started seeing a psychiatrist. In New York, they rented a one-room apartment on East Fifty-Fifth Street. Nancy took drama classes and singing lessons, but she was conflicted about her career and had old-fashioned ideas about how to be a wife that weren't necessarily working.

Tommy's career was faltering. He was no longer recording for Capitol Records, and his film career had stalled after he played opposite Annette Funicello in a 1960 Walt Disney remake of the Victor Herbert operetta *Babes in Toyland*, and a subsequent piece of fluff called *Love in a Goldfish Bowl*—pure studio hokum in which he starred with Fabian, another fading teen idol haplessly trying to transition into the movie business. Nancy had been pestering her father to help her husband's film career, and Sinatra did arrange for Sands to play a role in his upcoming film *Come Blow Your Horn*, but Sands knew the director and producer didn't really want him. He did not want to owe his success to his wife's father and begged off, claiming he wasn't right for the part.

In New York, Tommy enrolled in classes with Lee Strasberg at the Actors Studio. He worked at writing a screenplay and took a part in a regional theater production in New Jersey, before going out of town for a run in the musical *Remains to Be Seen* at the Tenthouse Theater in Chicago. The entire Sinatra clan came out every night and would repair to their hotel suite after and call Nancy's father, wherever he was—Las Vegas, Beverly Hills—while Big Nancy sat on the couch, eating hard candy from a bag and waxing nostalgic about being married to Frank.

Young Nancy started a recording career at Reprise Records, a label owned by her father, and signed to be handled by her husband's manager, Ted Wick. The record label teamed her with producer Tutti Camarata, the Disneyland Records musical director who made Annette's records and a former swing-era trumpet player who wrote arrangements for Jimmy Dorsey before graduating to television and motion picture work. Camarata cut a timid, squeaky-voiced Nancy on a piece of bubblegum, "Cuff Links and a Tie Clip," released in August 1961, an entirely inauspicious debut that nobody noticed. The next record, "Like I Do," was a Top Five hit in Italy, and Nancy dutifully followed up with an appearance on Italian television's popular variety show *High Fidelity*. She did the grand opening of Korvettes Records in New York City and made a round of pointless promotional visits to radio stations to boost her next release, "June, July and August," which wasn't even a hit overseas.

Nancy had no idea who she was. She was unsculpted clay, a puppet to record producers who made her sound like a thousand other anybodies. Nancy needed to find out who she was. What did it mean for her to be married? She thought she'd got married because that was what good girls did when they wanted to have sex, and she certainly thought of herself as a good girl (she also definitely wanted to have sex). She knew her father thought she was a good girl too. Was she her father's daughter or her husband's wife? Did she want to have a marriage or a career? Having both seemed impossible to balance or reconcile. Her relations with men were skewed. She had grown up with her father *in absentia* but still looming over every kernel of her life. She wasn't just anyone's daughter, but what did it mean to be *his* daughter? Her mother never sorted out what in her life was distinct and separate from the powerful vortex that was Frank Sinatra. Why should it be any easier for his daughter?

♪

AS FAR AS Jan and Dean knew, it was going to be another routine high school hop, the Valentine's Day dance on Thursday, February 14, 1963, at Hermosa Beach High School. They drove down to the date never expecting to find destiny waiting. Jan and Dean did not keep a band but simply taught their songs to backup bands backstage before shows. There were only about five Jan and Dean songs, and the remainder of the program was drawn from commonly recognized rock and roll standards, usually including a Chuck Berry number or two. As was not unusual, Jan and Dean were shown to a vacant classroom that would serve as their dressing room, where they would meet the evening's backup band and run through their set. Tonight's band was already on the scene waiting for them, a group called the Beach Boys, who Jan and Dean had been wondering about for the better part of a year.

One sunny day the previous spring, they had been cruising down the Pacific Coast Highway in Dean's bitchin' custom-painted, fuel-injected Corvette with the radio blasting. Dean had spent months hand-sanding the fiberglass and removing all the chrome. He had the Japanese body shop he frequented paint the car with about twenty coats of Chinese red lacquer, until it gleamed like a candied apple. The little slashes on the sides that were usually painted white, Dean painted black. For Christmas, his girlfriend, Judy, gave him a hand-crafted Nardi wooden steering wheel made in Italy with his name engraved on one of the spokes. He was one cool twenty-two-year-old.

The boys loved their fast cars. Jan bought a new Corvette Stingray, and the two of them would roar up the highway, going to dates in San Francisco at heroic speeds in excess of one hundred miles an hour. They were wild, fearless drivers. Jan would race from Tiny Naylor's drive-in at Sunset and La Brea in Hollywood all the way down Sunset to the beach. Dean was in three or four crashes with Jan driving. "You haven't been killed yet," Jan would remind him.

It had been a chilly year and a half since "Heart and Soul." Their record career, of course, had slumped as soon as they finally came on board at Liberty in October 1961. The label took Adler off production and tried staff producer Snuff Garrett. They even brought in the Liberty chief's teenage son, Lenny Waronker, who was a smart young kid, but his mother had to drive him to the sessions. Whenever they cruised, Jan and Dean tuned in KFWB to hear the hits of the day. Down the highway they were rolling when an eerily familiar sound burst out of the car radio speaker.

Bomp...bomp...dit di dip

They looked at each instantly. Somebody had cribbed the background vocals from "Baby Talk," and they both recognized it immediately. Then the song started.

Surfing is the only life, the only way for me...

This was beyond their comprehension; a song about surfing? Outside of the few hardy souls along the coastline who actually attempted the sport, who could possibly care? As few people at Uni High who surfed, what did this matter to kids living inland, say in San Bernardino; did they even know what surfing was? When the radio announcer said the name of the group, the Beach Boys, they had to agree it was kind of cool and they liked the record. But why wouldn't they—it was practically a Jan and Dean knockoff.

Now here they were, almost a year later, in this South Bay school bungalow with the "Surfin'" group—the Beach Boys. Good-looking, slightly awkward Brian Wilson with his lopsided grin was clearly their leader; he played bass and sang. His little brother Carl was the guitarist and their middle brother, Dennis, played drums, although he was home nursing injuries from a recent car crash while a substitute filled in. Their cousin Mike Love sang lead, and a thirteen-year-old kid from across the street named David Marks played rhythm guitar. They wore creamy blue plaid Pendleton shirts as band uniforms and were clearly excited to be working with stars the magnitude of Jan and Dean. The Beach Boys, however, were on their way up. They had recently signed with the mighty Capitol Records and released a second surfing-inspired single, "Surfin' Safari," that slowly made its way into the Top Twenty nationwide, but they were still playing high school hops in the neighborhood.

The Beach Boys hailed from nearby Hawthorne, a flat, landlocked neighborhood of one-story houses bought on the GI Bill after the war, the streets lined with jacaranda trees that bloomed bright purple every spring. A couple of dozen blocks from the Wilson family home, Mattel produced the Barbie dolls. Their angry, controlling father, Murry Wilson, was a failed amateur songwriter who worked in the sheet metal business and had taken a serious interest in his sons' rock and roll enterprise. His oldest son, Brian, emerged from family after-dinner sing-alongs with a love of harmony and a gift for melody, although his surf songs sprang wholly from his imagination. Surf? He didn't even know how to swim. But Dennis was an adventurer who would take the twenty-minute bus ride down Manhattan Beach Boulevard to watch the surfers from a perch on the seawall, return home and tell his brother about it. Innocent teenage hodad Brian, California kid that he was, intuitively grasped the metaphor inside surfing.

Sitting around their makeshift dressing room, Jan and Dean ran down their ten-song program with the band, who were prepared and alert. Jan and Dean were intrigued enough to watch the Beach Boys' opening set. Teenager Carl Wilson made a serious impression as a guitarist on Dick Dale's "Let's Go Trippin'" and the Belairs' "Mr. Moto." They threw in a couple of standard rock and roll dance songs like "Louie Louie" and "Johnny B. Goode," but it was the two surfing songs which closed their set that made Jan and Dean go crazy. They watched as the Beach Boys ripped up the high school dance with their two originals.

Jan and Dean whipped through their polished act with the Beach Boys backing them up in about half an hour and exited the stage after closing with "Baby Talk." They were already back in the class-room when the promoter told them that they had run short of the contracted time and he wanted them to play longer. They huddled with the band, who offered to go back and repeat a couple of the songs from early in the Jan and Dean show. Jan and Dean were adamant, however; they wanted to sing the surfing songs with the Beach Boys. They all went out and sang "Surfin'" and "Surfin' Safari" to their hearts' content.

On the ride home, Jan and Dean could not contain their enthu-siasm. Surf music was all they could talk about. Their latest single, a cover of the Forties big band hit "Linda," was showing signs of life, a welcome warming trend after the long, cool winter since "Heart and Soul" more than a year before, but that was suddenly yesterday's papers. As Adler moved more firmly into his music publishing and management role at Nevins-Kirshner, Jan had finally assumed control of their record production and, even though he had already produced sessions uncredited for Jan and Dean and others, "Linda" was his first official Jan and Dean production. But Jan had seen the future at the Valentine's Day dance. He had no specific idea what he was going to do, but whatever this Brian Wilson was up to, Jan wanted in. He made sure to get Brian's phone number.

Brian went to Lou Adler's office at 6515 Sunset Boulevard, next to Dino's Lodge, the next week to meet with Jan and Dean. He was tall, clear-eyed, eager, and a huge Jan and Dean fan. He and Jan sat at the piano in the office and Brian played him a new song, "Surfin' USA." Immediately Jan wanted the song for Jan and Dean, but Brian explained that wasn't possible because the song was going to be the next Beach Boys single on Capitol. Dean objected that the song copied Chuck Berry's "Sweet Little Sixteen" and that Brian could get in trouble doing that. Brian told Dean that he had discussed this with his father, Murry, who assured Brian that it was allowed. Jan wanted to record their own versions of "Surfin'" and "Surfin' Safari" for the album they were currently making, and Brian, excited to have somebody else record his songs, agreed to have the Beach Boys back up Jan and Dean in the studio.

Adler already knew Brian; Nick Venet, who had taken an A&R job at Capitol Records and was producing the Beach Boys for the label, had introduced them the previous fall. Hoping to sign him to Aldon as a songwriter, Adler had taken Brian to New York City in August 1962 to meet Don Kirshner, the man with the golden ears who ran the music publishing company. Kirshner presided over the most hip, cool, and successful group of songwriters in the business from a corner office with a red piano where his songwriting staff assembled every Friday to play their latest works. They hung a sign on the door that read GAME IN SESSION — DO NOT DISTURB, which meant nothing to Toni Wine, the fifteen-year-old songwriter and demo singer with chestnut hair down to her waist who Kirshner had recently signed. She barged in. They were throwing wadded up pieces of paper at a hoop on the back of the office door. "Do you want to play or root?" Brian asked.

"Root," she said.

She was taken by the bushy blonde California kid in the cute pinstripe button-down shirt. Kirshner was not so impressed. He offered a paltry $50 a week as an Aldon songwriter to Brian, whose second record, "Surfin' Safari," had just hit the charts. When Brian dared to express some objection, Kirshner lashed out. "Don't come on like Tarzan with me," he told Brian.

Nevertheless, despite Kirshner's insulting behavior, Brian brought home the songwriter's contract Adler hoped he would sign. His father, Murry, flew into a rage. He wanted the Beach Boys to be a family business, which he intended to run, and he wanted nothing to do with music business professionals like Adler, who he saw as highway robbers trying to come between him and his boys. Brian brought the contract back unsigned, but he liked to hang around Adler's office and bang out tunes on the piano.

Adler wanted to encourage collaboration between Brian and Jan, even though both the Beach Boys and Jan and Dean had exclusive contracts with record companies who would strenuously object to such associations. Jan and Brian decided to put together a clandestine session on Monday night, March 4, at Conway Studios on Highland Avenue in Hollywood—a slightly out of the way studio where the session could be kept quiet.

At Adler's office, Brian played them another song, "(When Summer Comes) Gonna Hustle You," that they both loved and wanted to record. Jan excitedly pressed Brian for more. He had another song, but it was only partly finished. He played them the melody and sang the line *Two girls for every boy*. Jan was sold. He told Brian he knew how to finish the song, and Brian told him to do whatever he wanted with it. Jan made Brian play it over and over.

Brian started hanging out. He sparked new energy in Jan, who immediately began to absorb Brian's approach to arranging harmony vocals. Jan impressed Brian as deep and knowledgeable. Jan explained his system of double-tracking vocals and instrumental parts to Brian, who was only beginning his career in recording studios. Jan, at age twenty-two, was a cagey veteran with hundreds of hours in the studio and nearly two dozen records to his name, including two gold records. They started writing together. Don Altfeld began work with them on "She's My Summer Girl," but Brian and Jan finished it by themselves.

Two weeks after the Conway sessions, where the Beach Boys and Jan and Dean quickly recorded "Surfin'" and "Surfin' Safari" to complete the new Jan and Dean album, cleverly titled by Adler *Jan and Dean Take Linda Surfin'*, Jan convened the session to record the unfinished song Brian had handed over during that first meeting at Adler's office, now titled "Surf City." Jan had passed Brian's song to lyricist Roger Christian, a top-rated Los Angeles disc jockey and hot rod nut who Murry Wilson had solicited to work with Brian on car songs. Brian introduced Christian to Jan, and Christian came back with a set of lyrics. He was a car person, not a beach guy, and he got a few details wrong, which Dean corrected.

When Jan cut the instrumental tracks in March at United Studios in Hollywood, drummer Hal Blaine pulled together a crew that included guitarists Glen Campbell and Billy Strange, bassist Ray Pohlman, keyboardist Don Randi, and on a second set of drums, Earl Palmer. Blaine and Palmer played synchronized drum parts to beef up the bottom end, a pairing that became a hallmark of Jan and Dean sessions. When it came time a month later to record the vocals, Jan brought in his three Latino pals from the Gents, Tony Minichiello, Vic Diaz, and Manuel Sanchez, to fill out the background vocals. Jan was producing the trio on another project of their own. He also invited Brian Wilson, who gladly joined the mix. The one person who didn't sing on the record was Dean.

Brian watched in quiet awe as Jan conducted the session. Jan explained to Brian the advantages of hiring session players to cut instrumental tracks; Brian was still making his records with the Beach Boys playing on the tracks. Jan led all of them through twelve over-dubs of the background vocal parts. Brian and Tony Minichiello supplied the siren-wail falsettos in the background chorus. Jan and Brian sang the lead vocal in unison, which he also double-tracked. Jan's arrangement opened the record with Brian's cornerstone lyric — *two girls for every boy* — blasted like a clarion call all on its own before the thunderous band piled in behind the vocalists.

When "Surf City" by Jan and Dean hit number one on the charts, Murry Wilson went haywire. His son's first number one hit was not only shared fifty-fifty with someone outside the family, but the song's entire copyright had gone to Jan's publisher, Screen Gems, for which Murry Wilson blamed Adler. He was furious and unleashed his anger toward Jan and Dean at every opportunity. He called Jan a "song pirate" and told Brian he could no longer see Jan or associate with him in any way — a demand Brian gave all the attention it deserved.

At the same time, Roger Christian and Dean said nothing about being left off the songwriting credits, because they both knew complaining would do no good with Jan Berry. He did what he wanted to do, and if he wanted the song credited to Brian Wilson and Jan Berry, that was how it was going to be. Dean was happy to go along for the ride, and Christian wasn't in any position to object either.

With the promise of sex trumpeted in the record's opening moments, "Surf City" captured a California of the mind that was instantly understood by teenagers across the land. Cars, sun, sex, and surf; *Gidget* set to a rock and roll beat. It was the last innocent American summer before November 22, 1963, and Jan and Brian had provided a timely twist on any enduring Norman Rockwell ideals. Something about the appealing scenario was distinctly all-American, but it was a new, improved America—a California kind of America—and it was embraced whole-heartedly by teens across the country whether they lived near an ocean or not. Somehow the tuneful mind-movie of girls in swimsuits, cars without rear windows, and ocean waves struck an unexpected resonant chord in the youth of the final days of the New Frontier.

THE FIRST
ALL-GIRL SURF BAND

TERRY MELCHER WENT to high school in Beverly Hills and looked down on Westside kids like Bruce Johnston when they first met in 1960. Melcher was working at the service station near his parents' office building in Beverly Hills. His mother was movie star Doris Day, and his father was her manager and third husband, Marty Melcher, who adopted Terry when he was eight years old. They owned an office building on Canon Drive, where Marty Melcher presided over the Day show business empire, which included a profitable music publishing company, Daywin Music, and a less successful record label, Arwin Records, that may have existed, at least in part, as a means to divert taxable income into a money-losing enterprise. Marty Melcher was that kind of businessman. He was also a strict, controlling father who wouldn't let his son closer to the record company he owned than the service station on the corner, no matter how much the kid wanted to be in the music business.

Bruce Johnston was half of Bruce and Jerry and had his first record released on Arwin. He stopped by the record company to be taken to an afternoon TV dance program, *The Lloyd Thaxton Show*, when Terry happened to be at the office, and they were introduced. They did not hit it off immediately.

Terry was a tall, handsome, blonde California boy who looked like his mother, freckles and all. His relationship with his adopted father was fraught. When Marty Melcher was dating his mother, he enlisted young Terry (and his grandmother) in the courtship, helping convince a dubious Day to marry him, but once they married, he grew angry and tyrannical. Marty dispatched his young son to military school and East Coast boarding schools before allowing him to finish his last two years of high school in Beverly Hills while living at home on North Crescent Drive. Melcher kept his wife largely sequestered, and Terry's most frequent daily contact with his mother was through the house intercom. After dropping out his first year at Principia College, a Christian Science college Marty found for him in Elsah, Illinois, Terry was put to work by Marty in the mail room of the William Morris Agency.

Terry borrowed money from a friend to finance a demo recording of him as a vocalist. While his parents had no objections to Terry going into show business, neither wanted him to be a performer. He timidly brought the recording home, and a predictable scene ensued... until his father listened to the record. The next day, Marty played it for Doris, and they were both surprised at how good it was. A record deal was easily arranged at Columbia Records, where Doris Day was one of the reigning stars. The label naturally insisted he use the name Terry Day, but they not only went for the first flop single, they ordered a follow-up. Terry was smart enough to insist on bringing in an outside producer, an up-and-coming New York hotshot named Phil Spector, although "Be a Soldier" fared no better when it was released in November 1962. Terry soon decided he was more interested in behind-the-scenes work.

Terry entered a program in New York for trainees to learn how to produce records, where he came under the wing of David Kapralik, head of A&R at Columbia Records. While Columbia was the distinguished major label with leading programs in classical, Broadway, and jazz, the company had no current hits. Columbia was home to old-fashioned pop artists like Johnny Mathis, Ray Conniff, Tony Bennett, and Andy Williams, whose shelf lives were growing shorter by the day. Kapralik saw in twenty-one-year-old Melcher a bright and capable young man who could bring Columbia into the twentieth century, or at the very least, maybe produce a couple of hit records.

Kapralik returned Melcher after his training to the Los Angeles office of Columbia Records in December 1962 under the avuncular Irving Townsend, who oversaw a frontier outpost of the Columbia operation run out of a three-story building at 6121 Sunset Boulevard, with the studios on the ground floor and the offices on the third. Under Townsend's tutelage, Melcher went to work as a producer, beginning with an album of ice-skating music by an organist.

By spring 1963, surf music was sweeping the Southern California teenscape, although it had not yet broken out beyond the region. Still mostly relegated to the five counties around Los Angeles, this raging phenomenon appeared poised to spread across the country. While the popularity of the sport was certainly on the rise—Top Forty radio stations in Los Angeles started broadcasting surf reports daily—local teens were going further than that, adopting the fashion, the lingo, the bleached-blonde hairdos; the whole surfer ethos was spreading beyond the beaches.

While surf music had been the exclusive province of

Hollywood-based independent companies, major label operations in Los Angeles moved to cash in on the trend. Capitol Records not only signed the Beach Boys, but also coughed up an astronomical $50,000 to acquire Dick Dale and the Del-tones, the highest advance paid since RCA signed Elvis Presley. East Coast labels ignored the fad, but Dick Dale's album *Surfers' Choice* on his own Deltone Records had been the top-selling album for more than a year at Wallichs Music at Sunset and Vine, practically in the shadow of the Capitol Tower. The West Coast A&R department of RCA Victor inked a Boulder, Colorado–based band called the Astronauts and fired up Henry Mancini on a surf single.

At Columbia, A&R producer Terry Melcher signed Bruce Johnston, whose "Do the Surfer Stomp" record had quietly sold more than one hundred thousand copies over the past eighteen months. Johnston's band had become a favorite at USC and UCLA frat parties.

In March, Melcher and Johnston pulled together the usual suspects — saxophonist Steve Douglas, drummer Hal Blaine, bassist Ray Pohlman, guitarists Tommy Tedesco and Glen Campbell, along with other session players — and quickly cut a dozen numbers from the surf songbook, including the Beach Boys, Dick Dale, the Ventures, even a new version of "The Original Surfer's Stomp." Johnston played piano and sang, although most of the selections were instrumentals, and Columbia quickly dumped out an album from the sessions called *Surfin' USA* by the Hot Doggers. For Melcher and Johnston, these were early experiments in the studio.

In April, Melcher and Johnston took a weekend getaway that would cement their partnership in the spring awakening of Lake Arrowhead, a year-round scenic beauty and natural wonder ninety miles east of Los Angeles, where Melcher's parents had recently bought a charming $75,000 home with a gabled roof and decks on every level, overlooking the lake. Melcher often partied at his parents' retreat with buddies and gals. He was a young Hollywood aristocrat who had dated ventriloquist Edgar Bergen's gorgeous daughter, Candice Bergen, when she was a high school senior and he was five years older. They broke up when he started seeing songwriter Jackie DeShannon, a twenty-two-year-old knockout who didn't have homework. Melcher's parents lived down the street from Danny Thomas, and he was close with Danny's daughter, Terre Thomas. Arrowhead quickly became a playground for Melcher.

He and Johnston spent the weekend laying the groundwork for their creative relationship, talking about his other big signing, a male vocal duo called the Opposites, who had a deal as songwriters with his father's publishing company. Melcher cut them singing a little-noticed rhythm and blues chart entry called "Here I Stand," renamed the group the Rip Chords, and that record was making a modest appearance on the charts.

For Columbia Records, even a mid-chart hit like "Here I Stand" qualified as a major success. The Opposites' Phil Stewart was a private investigator, and Ernie Bringas was a theology student and assistant pastor; both leaned more towards country and western in their musical tastes. To that end, for the Rip Chords' follow-up, Melcher was planning on cutting them singing the 1957 Ferlin Husky song "Gone," but he and Johnston got carried away rewriting the number that weekend. They also wrecked a speedboat and the pier. There may have been alcohol involved, but when they returned to Hollywood, they had transformed the country weeper into something unexpected — a rock and roll car song.

Cars, of course, loomed large in the thoughts, dreams, and lives of American teens. Melcher and Johnston didn't invent the car song; car songs were a wrinkle already tied to surf music. On the flipside of the Beach Boys' breakthrough surf record, "Surfin' Safari," was the keystone car song, "409" written by Brian Wilson with his first collaborator outside the group, Gary Usher, who met Brian because his uncle lived near the Wilsons in Hawthorne. On the other side of "Surfin' USA," the March 1963 smash that launched the Beach Boys juggernaut nationwide, was another car song, "Shut Down," written by Brian with Roger Christian, effectively establishing the genre in a single stroke. Usher collaborated with Brian's brother Dennis Wilson on a Benzedrine-fueled road trip to Tijuana during which they composed a pair of car songs, which they recorded and sold to Warner Brothers Records across town in Burbank as the Four Speeds, a single that saw some local action. The Beach Boys launched a booming cottage industry in the Los Angeles recording industry in surf and car songs.

Car songs combined with surfing on these records to elaborate this burgeoning California myth. The songs may have voiced simple sentiments, but they were laced with seductive images hinting at unimagined freedom and new vistas. Automobiles held a special place in the California mystique. Los Angeles was built for cars; alone among major American cities, Los Angeles had been laid out almost entirely after the development of the automobile. Long, broad avenues that roll on for miles crisscross the almost entirely flat landscape. With year-round sunshine and no salt on the roads to screw up the paint jobs, Los Angeles and cars were made for each other. In the prosperity that followed the war, almost anybody could afford a car. Every new building came with a parking lot.

Southern Californians invented hot rods. George Barris started making custom machines out of dreams at his North Hollywood garage in 1945. Airbrush artists like Ed "Big Daddy" Roth covered hot rods in flames and stripes. With the fluid culture of Southern California, all this popular art leaked into fine art circles with the "finish fetish" artists of the early Sixties in Los Angeles, whose work with poured resins and airbrushing was clearly influenced by hot rods and surfboards. Many of the artists were hot rod and surf enthusiasts themselves; Southern California was full of them.

In late April, Terry Melcher called a split session with the Rip Chords and Bruce Johnston, backed by the same band, more or less, that they had used on the Hot Doggers record. Singing with Johnston, Melcher had discovered his voice. They learned they could make a special sound together, and Melcher had opened up as a vocalist, found his confidence, and he and Johnston became beautiful partners in harmony. At the split session, the band disposed of the Johnston track "Surfin' Round the World," which featured prominent vocals from Darlene Wright—who had begun making solo records with Phil Spector as Darlene Love—and the other Blossoms, the veteran Los Angeles studio vocalists who were also the studio version of the Crystals, before turning to the Rip Chords track.

On the Rip Chords record, Melcher and Johnston assumed full control. They had turned the Ferlin Husky song "Gone" into a rousing rock flag-waver along the lines of the Isley Brothers' "Shout." Gracia Nitzsche, wife of arranger Jack Nitzsche and background vocalist, delivered a tongue-in-cheek recitation over the introduction as revving engines announced the body of the song—a rolling, gospel-flavored number with Johnston's street corner vocal group arrangements coming right out of his days at the El Monte Legion Stadium. Johnston and Melcher sang all over the track, madly overdubbing their Beach Boys–inspired harmonies. Leaving nothing to chance, they took over the record. Stewart and Bringas were background vocalists on their own record. They did better on the B-side, a Steve Douglas arrangement of another old country standard, "She Thinks I Still Care," although Johnston still decorated the close with falsetto flourishes.

Between the Arrowhead weekend and the "Gone" session, Melcher and Johnston had forged a powerful brotherhood. They were beautiful boys who sang together like blood relations and shared the same slightly absurd, sometimes snide sense of humor. Bel Air and Beverly Hills were not exactly far apart. In June, Johnston accepted a position on the A&R staff of Columbia Records to officially join Melcher as the label's West Coast rock and roll mavericks, even if they still wore coats and ties to the office. Melcher hired his old Beverly Hills friend Judy Lovejoy, who had broken up with Dean Torrence, to work as their secretary. When her father died of a sudden heart attack that October, he tenderly took her to a World Series game at Dodger Stadium, where his mother had season tickets, and held her hand through the game.

With the two Rip Chords singles both bubbling under, Melcher focused intently on the next release. These two modest successes were the only thing Columbia had happening in rock and roll for years. He wanted to blow on that ember. Melcher found the bare bones of a song from Carol Connors, an aspiring songwriter who sang lead vocal on the number one Phil Spector hit "To Know Him Is to Love Him" when she was still in junior high and known as Annette Kleinbard. She had been trying to wriggle her way back into the music business ever since. She was currently the anonymous female vocalist in the road edition of the Ray Anthony Orchestra. She played in a folk group, the Storytellers, whose lone single Lou Adler picked up for national distribution with the Aldon house label, but its modest Los Angeles success did not spread. Melcher buffed, polished, and rewrote the song, which, although credited to Connors and her younger brother, was co-published by Daywin Music, Melcher's family business. He apparently didn't need credit if he owned half the song.

"Hey Little Cobra" was custom-designed by Melcher to give

him and Johnston what they needed for a full-scale Beach Boys impersonation. Carol Connors knew about Cobras; she had crashed her boyfriend's AC Ace-Bristol, a British racecar that was a predecessor to Carroll Shelby's Cobra, the fastest production model car Detroit ever made. The membership of the Rip Chords had become confused by Bringas returning to seminary and Stewart hiring another pair of singers to join the touring group. No matter. At the October recording session, Melcher and Johnston didn't let any of the group near the mic; they overdubbed every part, Melcher singing lead and Johnston filling out the background chorus. Their Beach Boys impression was masterful, their dominance of the record complete. "Hey Little Cobra" shot to the top of Los Angeles radio on release in November, and the rest of the nation would catch on in the new year.

IT WAS A sunny April afternoon when Sandy Nelson headed out on his little Honda 50 motorbike from his home in the Hollywood hills along Mulholland Drive. He was going over the hill to the Burbank Airport, where he was planning to catch a plane to San Diego to see the woman he was engaged to marry. Winnifred and her sister had moved to Hollywood to see if they could make it in show business—their parents underwrote an apartment, but the closest they came was when one sister got engaged to marry a drummer. Along the ridge, the road bobs and weaves, running above the rim of the canyons high above Hollywood. Without much traffic, Nelson could zip along, enjoying the outdoors whizzing past him as he swooped around the curves.

Since the breakout *Let There Be Drums* solidified his standing,

Nelson had been pumping out albums that expanded the role of percussion in rock and roll, as well as catering to a more mundane market for instrumental versions of other people's hits. Imperial Records had put out six albums by Nelson the year before. He was a small factory, but he liked trying new ideas. His *Compelling Percussion* album featured an eleven-minute drum solo and an eight-minute experimental piece called "Civilization" that he recorded with Richie Podolor late at night, using found sounds they had collected at Nelson's place in the Hollywood hills. Los Angeles disc jockey Roger Christian played the track nightly on his post-midnight show. Nelson had a tidy band that worked steadily. These were all sunny days for Sandy Nelson.

He rounded the corner on Mulholland and turned onto Dixie Canyon Avenue, which would trail its lazy way over switchbacks and gullies down the hill to the San Fernando Valley. Nelson leaned into the first of the hairpin turns down the hill.

A giant yellow wave rose up in his face as a Los Angeles Unified School District bus swung halfway through the same turn, going up the hill. Before Nelson slid into the side of the bus, he lost control of the bike. His leg got caught in the wheel of the bus and he was pulled off the bike, while the bus screeched to a halt, stopping short of crushing his legs. The school kids burst out of the bus, screaming and crying. They thought he was dead.

An ambulance took Nelson to a North Hollywood hospital, where they tied off his arteries to keep him from bleeding to death. He had already passed out from shock. Specialists examined him. His knee was destroyed. They did not think he would walk again. His leg was alive, but there was no feeling in it. They put him in traction and awaited developments. He languished in the hospital for a couple of weeks without much change. The night nurse told him he had screamed all night when they brought him in. They didn't think he would make it at first, but here he was all these days later, surely on the mend.

Nelson was sitting up in bed, smoking a cigar, watching *The Red Skelton Show* on television with the night nurse. A piece of strawberry shortcake sat on a plate on the counter. Nelson asked the nurse to hand him the shortcake. The nurse reached over but then froze, a look of horror on his face, and hurried out of the room. An artery in Nelson's leg had burst and it was gushing blood like a garden hose. The nurse rushed back with the emergency room doctor, who clamped down the bleeding. He told Nelson they were going to have to amputate his leg tonight. They didn't even have time to bring in a surgeon; the emergency room doctor did the surgery.

KIM FOWLEY NEVER learned how to drive, an unpardonable sin in Los Angeles. He took buses to recording sessions or he hitch-hiked. In 1963, he was back where he started, renting a room at Virginia Dodd's house, where Nick Venet had let him sleep with the chihuahuas many moons before. He had been up and down many times since the Hollywood Argyles. He and Gary Paxton quickly blew through their "Alley Oop" score, what little they were paid. Their partnership ended shortly thereafter in a big blowup in July 1961. Fowley was tired of Paxton being the genius while he was the businessman. He wanted to be the genius too. Paxton was simply tired of obnoxious, pushy Fowley. He bought him off for $500 and sent him packing.

They had only managed one measly hit after "Alley Oop," with two guys from a band called the Downbeats. They sold the regional hit they recorded at KGEM in Boise, Idaho, to the Los Angeles independent label Gardena Records—a rock and roll version of "Chopsticks" called "Beatnik Sticks." When the label owner discovered that bandleader Paul Dick's middle name was Revere, he suggested they call the group Paul Revere and the Raiders. Paxton and Fowley put together another instrumental around a rocking Rachmaninoff riff, "Like, Long Hair," that landed the group in the Top Twenty, but that was their last hit together.

Paxton was all over the place, recording as a vocalist for Liberty, making surf instrumentals for fly-by-night labels, causing trouble wherever he went. He turned down an offer from Nick Venet to join him on the Capitol Records A&R staff for $50,000 a year. He was knocking around doing whatever he could when he ran into a couple of the guys from the Cordials, one of the bands he sent out posing as the Hollywood Argyles, who had a Boris Karloff routine they had worked into a dance record. When Paxton could not find a single label interested in picking up the master, he put the darn thing out himself on his own label and had one of the biggest-selling records of 1962 with Bobby "Boris" Pickett and "Monster Mash."

For a while, Kim Fowley was living the Hollywood high life with his "Alley Oop" bucks in the Park Sunset, where Eddie Cochran wrote "Summertime Blues" in his manager's apartment. Fowley, too, managed to score one good-size hit after the split with Paxton, although, typical of Fowley, it was a complicated, treacherous affair. Fowley had moved into a mansion with an older woman on St. Ives Drive above the Sunset Strip. She agreed to finance Fowley's production of an instrumental number he called "Nut Rocker," which was essentially a boogie-woogie version of the march from Tchaikovsky's *Nutcracker Suite*. Fowley hired some old-hand session players to cut the track (H.B. Barnum played the piano part), while his lady friend backed the pressing of some singles by the group, dubbed Jack B. Nimble and the Quicks. Before long she withdrew her support after Fowley did something to piss her off, so Fowley took his idea to Rendezvous Records, where the label chief agreed to cut another version of the record, provided Fowley did not attend the session. When "Nut Rocker" by B. Bumble and the Stingers started to climb the charts in spring 1962, Fowley's former partner came out of the woodwork and leased the Jack B. Nimble version to Dot Records. Although the B. Bumble record would eventually prevail, Fowley was nearly too clever for his own good.

Fowley hustled any work he could find. He was on the street daily. He knew everybody. When the Sharps, the R&B vocal group that used to play the El Monte Legion Stadium and shouted on Duane Eddy records, hit on a song they thought would put them back in business, they called Fowley from a pay phone booth early in the morning. Fowley had produced the quartet as the Crenshaws for Warner Brothers Records the year before. The group kept changing their name, and the members had recently joined the Black Muslims of Chicago. Fowley hired them to both cater and entertain a party, where the crowd went wild when the caterers broke into song and dance. They crowded around the receiver to sing him their new song, "Papa-Oom-Mow-Mow," and he instantly recognized it as a hit. But instead of producing it himself, he directed the group to Liberty Records, where they released the record as the Rivingtons in August 1962. Fowley settled for a small finder's fee.

Fowley stayed busy, even though the hits had thinned out for him. For a while, he was producing surf-style instrumentals with ski themes, like "Shush-Boomer" by the Alpines and "Ski Storm" by the Snow Men. Then he decided the world needed a rock and roll version of the Zodiac — "Astrology" — and chose that for his own

debut as a recording artist. Fowley needed to find some female background vocalists for the session and approached Mike Postil, another
young hustler, a year out of high school in the San Fernando Valley
and trying to make it in the music business under the name Mike
Post, who recommended a trio he was working with, sisters Terry
and Carol Fischer and their neighbor Sally Gordon. Through Postil,
Fowley hired the three women to sing background vocals on his
"Astrology," an idea whose time had not yet come. The girls sounded
surprisingly good, and Fowley inquired about their relationship with
Postil. "I own them," he told Fowley.

About the same time, in fall 1963, Fowley was picked up hitch-
hiking by a young man named David Gates with a guitar in the
backseat. When asked, he told Fowley that he was a guitarist and
songwriter. Fowley said that he was a record producer. Gates asked
what he was doing hitch-hiking. "I'm eccentric," Fowley said.

Gates was a young man beginning his career, starting to play a few
sessions, getting to know and be known. He lived in a house with his
wife and kids on Canyon Drive that he shared with a session pianist
named Russell Bridges, who did arrangements under the name Leon
Russell. They had belonged to a band together in high school in Tulsa,
Oklahoma. Fowley was renting a room down the street in Virginia
Dodd's house. They repaired to her living room, where Gates took
out his guitar and played Fowley a song he'd written called "Popsicles
and Icicles." Fowley heard a hit song in search of a girl group. He
called Terry Fischer and asked if she and the other girls had a contract
with Mike Postil or would they like to make a record with him? They
did not have a contract with Postil, she told Fowley, and the only
job he'd managed to find them was the lousy ten-dollar background
vocal date on Fowley's "Astrology" record. It was not lost on Fowley
that he was doing the same thing to Mike Postil that he thought

Lou Adler had done to him with Jan and Dean, as he calmly swiped Postil's girl group.

Fowley was working at Chattahoochee Records for Ruth Conte, a Hollywood gal who had made a lot of money in real estate and interior design. She started the label for her husband, John Conte, a second-rate radio actor and B-list TV announcer, whose records accounted for the first several releases. Fowley had taken an interest in the label, and Conte approved a one-hundred-dollar budget for the recording of "Popsicles and Icicles." Clyde (Skip) Battin of Skip and Flip did the vocal arrangements in the same living room where Gates had showed Fowley the song, wrapping the number in luscious Beach Boys–style harmonies. Fowley named the group the Murmaids to enhance that delicious connection, and he would later advertise the group as the First All-Girl Surf Band (as though the Murmaids played their own instruments).

"Popsicles and Icicles" blew up on Los Angeles radio on release in October 1963, climbing all the way to number one in the trade magazine *Record World* in February 1964. It was displaced the next week by "I Want to Hold Your Hand" by The Beatles. Fowley, sensing change in the wind, cashed in his interest at Chattahoochee, stuffed the dough into a suitcase with a stack of *Introducing The Beatles* albums on Vee Jay, and bought a one-way ticket to London.

13

BE TRUE TO YOUR SCHOOL

IN OCTOBER 1963, Dean Torrence agreed to meet with Barry Keenan at the Tommy Trojan statue in the center of the USC campus, where Dean had transferred from Santa Monica City College to study architecture. Dean knew Keenan from University High—Keenan belonged to the Barons Hi-Y club with Jan and Arnie. He had been the youngest stockbroker ever admitted to the Pacific Coast Stock Exchange and made a fortune by the time he was twenty-one. Keenan had invested money for Dean, who was still living at home with his parents and sister, and they did quite well.

Keenan was no longer doing so well. After a car crash left him addicted to painkillers, he lost all his money, his marriage disintegrated, and his mind was clouded and confused with drink, despair, and drugs. He arrived for the meeting with Dean carrying a three-ring binder containing a twenty-seven-page business plan. Dean brought a bag lunch.

Dean listened as Keenan spilled out a fantastical plan to kidnap Frank Sinatra Junior. Keenan had known Frank's sister Nancy at Uni High, and even once met the old man through her. He explained in great detail his crazy scheme to use the ransom money for short-term real estate and stock investments that would put him back on his feet. Once that was accomplished, he would then return the ransom. As a devout Catholic, Keenan knew he could not truly be forgiven without restitution. As Dean glanced at the "Plan of Operations" in the three-ring binder, Keenan laid out the intricate scenario and asked Dean for $5,000 seed money.

Dean didn't know what to think. Clearly, Keenan needed help. Dean gave him $500 and told him to get his life together. It was disturbing, but Dean didn't give it much more thought. There was already a lot going on in his life. He was on the verge of pop stardom, but he was still enmeshed in relationships from high school, still living in the same small town where he grew up. Keenan was a California kid gone rogue, and Dean couldn't tell the difference from high school pranks. In Dean's defense, he had a lot of other things on his mind.

Jan and Dean's second smash single of the year, "Honolulu Lulu," was headed toward the Top Ten. Adler came up with the title and Jan and Roger Christian hashed out the song at the Copper Penny coffee shop on Sunset the night Jan graduated from UCLA. Christian scribbled the lyrics on a paper napkin, which got left behind and thrown away. The songwriters had to return to the coffee shop at four in the morning to comb through the old coffee grounds and other garbage in the dumpster before coming up with the crumpled manuscript.

That fall, Jan had enrolled in med school at the California College of Medicine. He moved out of the rebuilt house on Linda Flora, into a spacious penthouse apartment in a modern four-story building on Occidental Avenue, with roommates Don Altfeld and Vic Amira, both also medical students. He had a great pad, a new Corvette Stingray, and a gorgeous, cool model girlfriend, Jill. Jan and Dean had recently finished shooting the pilot for a proposed TV series called *Surf Scene*, and there was talk of a movie role in the offing.

While Dean quickly forgot Keenan's plan to kidnap Frank Sinatra Jr., Keenan moved ahead with his half-baked idea. He used the money Dean gave him to hire an accomplice at one hundred dollars a week. Joe Amsler had also gone to University High and belonged to the Barons. Amsler had dated Jill Gibson for much of his senior year. Since leaving the Army, Amsler had been making a meager living abalone diving, fishing, and doing some amateur boxing. He had gotten married, and his wife was putting pressure on him to come up with some money. Keenan also brought in an older man, John Irwin, who had dated Keenan's divorced mother. He was a tough guy with a shady criminal past who Keenan thought might come in handy.

Initially, the trio followed Sinatra Jr. to Phoenix in November but failed to make the snatch. They made plans to grab him on November 22, the day Kennedy was assassinated, but scrubbed the mission after what happened in Dallas. Then Keenan hit up Dean for another $500. They stalked Sinatra Jr.'s engagement at the Cocoanut Grove, after which Irwin washed his hands of the affair and took a job painting houses. In December, Sinatra Jr. was playing Harrah's Club in Lake Tahoe with the Tommy Dorsey Orchestra, after which the whole act was set to leave for Europe. With Sinatra's travel plans pending and Keenan's funds exhausted, the time to move had come. Keenan took Amsler to Tahoe on the pretext of finding construction work and, once there, sprung the plan on him.

On Sunday, December 8, 1963, nineteen-year-old Frank Sinatra Jr. was relaxing in his boxer shorts and T-shirt with a trumpet player from the band when somebody knocked at the door of his hotel room. "Room service," the voice said. "We have a package for you."

Amsler and Keenan, carrying a box full of pinecones, burst

through the door. "Put it over there," said young Sinatra, suddenly looking down the barrel of the loaded .38 revolver in Keenan's hand.

The victims were told this was a holdup, and between the two of them they came up with twenty dollars and change. Amsler taped their hands. Keenan demanded one of them accompany him as a hostage to ensure the robbers' safety and started to take Sinatra, who complained he wasn't dressed. They let him pull on a pair of slacks and slip into loafers, then led him out into the snowy night. When Keenan realized he had left their second gun behind in the room and went back to get it, he found the trumpet player already untied and moving around the room. Keenan ordered him to sit in a chair and remain for at least five minutes so they could make their getaway.

They put a sleep shade over Sinatra Jr.'s eyes and threw him in the backseat of their Chevy Impala, only to pull over when they saw a roadblock on their way out of town. They took off his sleep shade and advised Sinatra not to say anything or somebody could get shot. They managed to slip through the roadblock, which they assumed was checking for chains on cars on the way out of town in the snow. They figured it would have been too soon for the police to have been alerted to the kidnapping. They put the blindfold back on Sinatra and fed him a couple of sleeping pills. They spent the twenty bucks from the holdup on gas because they didn't have any money of their own.

Sinatra Jr.'s manager phoned his mother, Big Nancy, at her Bel Air home (she had sold the Carolwood place in 1961 and moved to a smaller, three-bedroom home on Nimes Road). She called his father at the compound in Palm Springs, and Sinatra immediately rented a private plane and flew to Reno, which was as close to Tahoe as he could get during the blizzard. Sinatra received calls from attorney general Robert F. Kennedy, who assured him they had two hundred men working on the case already. He heard from Chicago crime boss Sam Giancana, who offered his own unique brand of assistance. And FBI boss J. Edgar Hoover called to advise Sinatra not to talk to anyone but FBI agents, who had set up a command post at the Mapes Hotel in Reno by the time Sinatra arrived. "We'll catch these clowns," Hoover told Sinatra.

Nancy Sinatra was in New Orleans upstairs in her room watching television, while her husband, Tommy Sands, was performing downstairs at the Blue Room of the Roosevelt Hotel, when Big Nancy called. She was torn between staying safe in New Orleans and jumping on the first plane home. When her husband came upstairs after his show, they decided to stay. FBI agents were already guarding their room.

On Monday, Dean received a call from Keenan, who wanted to know if he had heard the news on the radio. "Somebody kidnapped Frank Sinatra Jr. in Tahoe," he said. In an instant, Dean realized what had happened — Keenan had gone through with it. Keenan sounded calm, although he admitted he hadn't slept. The kidnappers had not yet made their ransom demands known; they were too scared to call Sinatra. Keenan needed more money. Dean couldn't believe what he was hearing, but he accompanied Keenan to the bank and withdrew another $500. Keenan drove back to Tahoe by himself to clean up his hotel room and pay the bill to cover his tracks. He put skis on the car roof and took one run down the bunny hill to make it look good before he drove back to Los Angeles.

The kidnappers went silent for thirty-six hours after grabbing Junior, while the Sinatra family waited in agony. Nobody slept. Big Nancy refused to take sedatives and walked the hallways, nearly hysterical. Around nine o'clock on the Tuesday morning, tough-talking John Irwin, now back in the fold, called and spoke with Sinatra. He put Junior on the phone for a second and told Sinatra he would call back with instructions. The kidnappers then went to the library for a Reno phone book and picked a service station in Carson City. Not knowing that was a half hour away from Reno, when they called back they gave Sinatra fifteen minutes to get to the phone booth at the gas station.

The service station attendant was there by himself when the phone rang and a voice asked for Frank Sinatra. He hung up. The phone rang again, and the voice asked for Frank Sinatra. He'd hung up again, thinking this was some kind of practical joke, when two cars roared to a stop in the station. A man jumped out of the lead car and ran up to him.

"I'm Frank Sinatra," he said. "Have I had any calls?"

The kidnappers asked for $240,000 in small bills, a weirdly low number, as Sinatra had already offered a million bucks for the return of his son. At this point, they had padlocked Junior in the back room of a secluded house on five acres in Canoga Park that Keenan had rented under a false name. Sinatra Sr. flew back to Los Angeles that night and joined the family and FBI at the Nimes Road house, where the phone finally rang about half-past nine. The kidnappers proceeded to bounce Sinatra and an accompanying FBI agent around West Los Angeles phone booths for several hours, until he was finally instructed to take the ransom to a service station on Sepulveda Boulevard and leave the money between two parked buses.

The kidnappers had been awake for days on various drugs, and their brains were fried, their nerves frayed. Keenan collected the ransom, but Amsler, who went with him, spotted someone he thought was an FBI agent and took off running. When Keenan reported back to Irwin that Amsler was missing, Irwin concluded Keenan had killed him. Around two in the morning, Irwin called Sinatra and told him he was bringing his son back and dropping him off, but Irwin got the location of where he had left Junior wrong, and when Sinatra drove out from Nimes Road to pick him up, he couldn't find him. On his way back to Nimes Road, he drove past Barry Keenan, who was also out looking for Junior and recognized Sinatra as he whizzed past him. Sinatra returned home furious, convinced he had been double-crossed.

Frank Jr., dropped at his request beside a freeway overpass next to the 405, had started to walk toward Beverly Hills, hiding in the bushes at every passing car, thinking it might be the kidnappers coming back. When he saw a Bel Air private police patrol car, he waved his arms to flag it down. As soon as he saw the sleep mask hanging around Junior's neck, the patrolman knew what the story was.

When the patrol car approached the Nimes Road neighborhood, he saw all the streets crowded with press and police and told Junior to climb in the trunk of the car. He drove through the crowds to the Sinatras' back door. The patrolman opened the trunk and Frank Jr. climbed out and embraced his hysterical mother. He turned to his father. "Dad, I'm sorry," he said.

The next day, Keenan dispensed chunks of the ransom to people he owed money. He called Dean. "I left you something nice in the shower," he said. Dean's mother had made breakfast for Keenan when he stopped by the Benecia Avenue home. In his shower, Dean found a paper bag stuffed with cash, clearly uncounted but amounting to more than $25,000. Dean panicked. Over a prearranged phone call from a pay phone, he made plans with Keenan to return the money, but not before seeing if he could hide the dough in the basement of Judy Lovejoy's parents' home in Beverly Hills. Two nights later, Dean handed over the money to Keenan at a Culver City gas station.

Jill Gibson learned about the whole affair when the FBI knocked on the door of the apartment she shared with Keenan's estranged wife, Donna, whose pregnant sister was also currently staying with them.

Jill was not aware that Keenan and his sister-in-law were writing a screenplay about a kidnapping. She was even more surprised to get a call from Joe Amsler, who she hadn't spoken with in years. He told her they played Monopoly with the ransom money.

The next day, the FBI arrested Amsler at his apartment with almost $170,000 in cash. They nailed Keenan at Imperial Beach, a few miles from Mexico, with almost $50,000 on him. Irwin, on his way to New Orleans with his share of the take, spent the night with his brother in San Diego and told him the story. While he slept, his brother turned him in to the FBI, who arrested Irwin the next morning at his brother's apartment.

Two days later, the FBI accompanied Dean to open a safe deposit box jointly rented by Dean and Barry Keenan at a Century City bank. They found $1,800 more of the ransom money and a confession letter from Keenan that would prove explosive at the trial. Justice moved swiftly. The trial began seven weeks later. The principals were sentenced to life plus seventy-five years, a half hour after the jury returned the verdict.

Both Jan and Dean testified. In his first visit to the stand, Dean swore that he knew nothing about the kidnapping, but he returned that afternoon to change his story. He confessed the safe deposit box had been used to pass secret messages between the two of them and that he innocently helped Keenan plan the kidnapping, never believing he would go through with it. He also admitted to receiving $25,000 in cash from Keenan. Dean told the court he came back a second time because he promised his parents that he would always tell the truth.

The defense tried to convince the jury that the kidnapping was a hoax intended to benefit Junior's career. Keenan went along with the story, although the letter found in the safe deposit box ultimately undermined his testimony (his lawyers were later charged with suborning perjury over this poisonous false testimony, although the charges were eventually dropped).

Jill Gibson, touched by his phone call, went to visit her ex-boyfriend Joe Amsler in Los Angeles County Jail, where he was being held. "Nobody will ever know the real story," he told her.

♪

JILL GIBSON EVENTUALLY quit modeling. For someone so unconcerned with her looks, that she made it as far as she did was remarkable. She never did manage to care about the work; it was simply an easy way to make money. The end came when she was up for a Max Factor TV commercial. She and another finalist were asked to close their eyes slowly. The agency picked the other model because they found a vein in Jill's eyelid to be too prominent. That was too much for Jill. She went to work at her father's travel agency — even that was better than modeling — and took an apartment in the same building as Jan on Occidental Avenue. That was mostly for appearance's sake; she spent most of her time with him upstairs in the penthouse.

Despite being closer to Jan, Jill was unhappy to be downtown so far from the beach. Always resourceful, Jan ordered four hundred pounds of sand delivered and spread over the patio outside the penthouse. They would lay their towels out on their makeshift beach and lie in the sun, although the sand gradually blew away.

Jan's three-bedroom apartment was built around an especially large living room, where he often spread out his large yellow score sheets on the floor while he did arrangements for recording sessions. He had minored in music at UCLA and taken courses in orchestration.

Jill often copied the scores for him. An upright piano was pushed up against the wall. Her sister, Jane, happened to live across the street with her husband and new baby daughter.

Jan and Dean weathered the Frank Sinatra Jr. episode, though not without sustaining some damage; they lost the TV series *Surf Scene* and their planned roles in the Columbia Pictures movie *Ride the Wild Surf*, although they still provided the title track. It didn't hurt them with the hit parade. After two big consecutive hits, Jan and Dean were a thriving enterprise. Jan was growing in his confidence and abilities in the studio. He wrote the arrangements and drew sharp, focused performances out of the players and vocalists; his command of record production allowed him to execute his exacting vision of his music. Nobody was making records any better in town.

In September, Jan had written "I Adore Him" with Screen Gems staff writer Artie Kornfeld on a rented piano in a Brooklyn hotel room while Jan and Dean were playing one of Murray the K's shows at the nearby Fox Theater. After "I Adore Him" gave the Angels their biggest hit since "My Boyfriend's Back," Screen Gems dispatched Kornfeld to the coast to mine more gold. He moved into the Occidental penthouse in November. With another Jan and Dean song, "Drag City," headed into the Top Twenty—written by Jan, Brian Wilson, and Roger Christian; Brian sang and played all over the record—Kornfeld worked on material for an album's worth of car songs.

Like surfing, the car song struck an emblematic note with young people across the nation. A symbol of freedom, possibility, self-sufficiency, the romance of the highway, all tied to life in Southern California as portrayed by these songs. It was a fresh sound blowing in from the West Coast, palpably white, firmly middle-class, free of irony, guile, or artifice. This music came direct from their young lives—late-night road races down Sunset Boulevard were as much a

UNIVERSITY HIGH SCHOOL

1
9
5
8

PTA Award Assembly with Frank Sinatra

Dean Torrance

CAMERA SHY
Arnold Ginsberg
Kim Fowley

Barry Keenan

Nancy Sinatra

Kathy Kohner

BEE FOOTBALL
Jan Barry (upper left) Dean Torrance (lower right)

From the pages of *Chieftain '58,* the yearbook for University High School. The students' futures were all ahead of them.

Jan and Arnie ("Jennie Lee"):
Jan Berry (*left*) and Arnie Ginsburg,
teenage rock and roll stars (1958).
*Michael Ochs Archives/
Stringer/Getty Images*

Blonde-Haired Everly Brothers:
Jan Berry and Dean Torrence
(1960). *Michael Ochs Archives/
Stringer/Getty Images*

Jan Berry and
Jill Gibson, at
Jan's UCLA
fraternity house
on their first date.

California Girls:
Jill Gibson and
Judy Lovejoy, on
the loose in a
photo booth
(1960).

Jan and Dean in California Teen Paradise: Bermuda shorts, bleeding madras shirts,
barefoot, with a couple of blonde beach bunnies who happened to be their
girlfriends, Jill Gibson and Judy Lovejoy, photographed at State Beach,
their high school hangout (1960).

"Baby Talk" producers Lou Adler (*center*) and Herb Alpert (*right*) in the studio with Jan and Dean (1959). *Ode Records*

Man About Town: Lou Adler with his *shiksa* princess and second wife, actress Shelley Fabares (1964). *Michael Ochs Archives/Stringer/ Getty Images*

Frank Sinatra with Frank Jr., age ten, and Nancy, age thirteen, at the Academy Awards in Hollywood, where their dad took home the Oscar for Best Supporting Actor (1954).
Bettmann/Contributor/Getty Images

ABC-TV publicity still for Nancy Sinatra's appearance on her father's television show when she was a senior at University High (1958).
ABC Photo Archives/Contributor/ Getty Images

Nancy Meets Elvis: With a box of ruffled shirts as a present, she greets the king of rock and roll at Fort Dix, New Jersey, on his return from military service in Germany, to publicize his upcoming appearance on her father's TV special (1960). *New York Daily News Archive/ Contributor/ Getty Images*

Tommy Sands and Nancy cut their wedding cake for the teen magazine photographers in Las Vegas (1960). *Bettmann/ Contributor/ Getty Images*

Kim Fowley, age nineteen, towers over Hollywood R&B music business veterans
arranger-guitarist René Hall, attorney Walter Hurst, and Hall's wife, Sugar (1960).
Collection of Alec Palao

"Let There Be Drums": Sandy Nelson was the first University High alumnus to make rock and roll history with his 1959 drum instrumental, "Teen Beat," but he solidified his position as the most famous drummer in rock and roll with this 1961 Top Ten. *Michael Ochs Archives/Stringer/Getty Images*

Terry Melcher as boy vocalist Terry Day (1962). *Michael Ochs Archives/ Stringer/Getty Images*

Bruce Johnston in madras sport coat on a teen dance TV show, promoting "Do the Surfer Stomp" (1962).

Summer Means Fun: Terry and Bruce recording in Columbia Studio A (1963). *Getty Images*

Jill Gibson photographs Jan and Bruce Johnston
in Honolulu (1964). *Jill Gibson*

Jan surfs Waikiki (1964). *Jill Gibson*

Jill Gibson's snapshots from Hawaii catch Jan and
Bruce Johnston fixing a flat tire. *Jill Gibson*

Terry Melcher emerges from a sugar cane field. *Jill Gibson*

Jan and Dean gone troppo. *Jill Gibson*

Bruce and Terry play statue. *Jill Gibson*

Jan and Dean, fall 1965 (photograph by Jill Gibson). *Jill Gibson*

Jan and Jill at their new Park Lane home, San Fernando Valley in the background (1965).

Jan and Dean's "Batman" sessions, photographed by Jill Gibson:
(*clockwise from top left*) bassist Ray Pohlman, guitarist Tommy Tedesco,
and drummers Earl Palmer and Hal Blaine (1966). *Jill Gibson*

Brian Wilson summons his people to meet him at Los Angeles International
Airport, on his way home from teaching the Beach Boys to play "Good Vibrations."
Among the family, friends, and other musicians assembled are his wife, Marilyn,
her sister Diane, lyricist Van Dyke Parks, Dean Torrence, Mark Volman of the
Turtles, and Danny Hutton (1966). *Guy Webster RPM Archives*

part of Jan's life as surfing—but across the rest of the country, they made California sound like the new world.

Brian Wilson spent a lot of time working with Jan in the studio, where Brian was taking mental notes and absorbing everything he could. Jan encouraged Brian to use session musicians rather than wait for the other Beach Boys to hold sessions. The core group of young session musicians Jan developed was also being used by Phil Spector, who now, after "He's a Rebel," did most of his recording in Los Angeles while maintaining his headquarters in Manhattan. With this platoon of rock and roll session musicians, Jan and the other producers pushed the music into new, more sophisticated shapes without sacrificing any of the fundamental drive of rock and roll. They were creating a new West Coast pop sound. Brian admired Jan for his strength of purpose and take-no-shit attitude, and looked up to him. At the same time, Jan was using Brian for his own purposes. With Jan, there were always wheels within wheels.

At the time, Brian was practically living at the Fairfax district home of his girlfriend's parents, Irv and May Rovell, where his girlfriend, Marilyn, lived with her two sisters, Diane and Barbara, who Brian also happened to find attractive. But even more, Brian was drawn to the warm, loving May Rovell, a calm and accepting presence in Brian's life entirely at odds with the household where he grew up. Only Carl was left living in the Wilson family home on West 119th Street in Hawthorne. Dennis, having been thrown out by Murry too many times to count, was living in an apartment in Hollywood. Murry also tangled with Beach Boys guitarist David Marks and his parents. He fired the teenager from the band in fall 1963, shortly after Brian's schoolmate from the original "Surfin'" sessions, Alan Jardine, rejoined after attending dental school.

Following two consecutive Top Ten hits that year pairing surf songs and car songs, Brian started to branch out into broader realms of expression. "Be True to Your School" was pure outgoing exuberance, cheerleading set to a rock and roll beat with glee club harmonies, while "In My Room," on the other side of the record, envisioned a world of introspective imagination behind a teenager's closed bedroom door, no doubt drawn from Brian's own life. Brian had left the beach and the drag strip behind and moved confidently into bold, bright vistas. He was painting pictures of teen life as he knew it from growing up in California.

The night of the Kennedy assassination, after a show in remote Marysville, California, Brian and vocalist Mike Love stayed up into the wee hours in their hotel room, trying to deal with the loss by writing a song. In "The Warmth of the Sun," a stunningly mature work, a level above anything they had written before, the beach was now a straightforward metaphor. Brian started writing the band's next single, "Fun, Fun, Fun," on a piano in Lou Adler's office and took a handful of session players — Steve Douglas, Hal Blaine, Ray Pohlman — into the studio with the Beach Boys when he recorded the song in January 1964. That record successfully translated a portrait of Southern California life, witnessed first-hand by Brian in the parking lot at Fosters Freeze on Hawthorne Boulevard in Hawthorne (*Well she got her daddy's car and she cruised to the hamburger stand now*), the local drive-in where Brian and the other Beach Boys ate many a cheeseburger. He saw a girl in her father's T-bird and went home to write the song. His artistic life was blooming even while he was straining under the constant interventions of his father, but with the Rovells, he had found a place he could be.

The Rovells' modest two-bedroom Sierra Bonita Drive house became Brian's sanctuary — his home, really — and a headquarters for a lot of his activities. He kept a two-bedroom apartment a couple of blocks away, but he rarely did more than change his shirt there. Jan spent much time at the Rovells' with Brian and, despite what Brian's father, Murry, thought or Capitol Records wanted, Brian loved writing, playing, and singing in the studio with Jan.

They wrote what they knew. They drew from their daily lives. Artie Kornfeld was visiting Brian at the Rovells' place when they decided to take a ride on Brian's moped. They crashed the bike when the wheels went out from under them on a sharp turn and scratched up their legs on gravel, bloody and raw since they were both wearing shorts. They pushed the bike back to Marilyn's home, laughing about how fast they had been going. As a New Yorker, Kornfeld knew the charmed lives these people led and realized there was a song in this. He and Brian started working on writing it almost as soon as they got back. They already had the title from Roger Christian.

Street racer Christian knew the part of Sunset Boulevard above UCLA where the road doubles back on itself. Voice actor Mel Blanc, the man behind Bugs Bunny, Porky Pig, Daffy Duck, Yosemite Sam, and all the others, had wiped out and almost died in a head-on crash at the spot in January 1961, a celebrated accident that gave this particular bend in the road a name all its own — "Dead Man's Curve."

14

SUNSET STRIP

LOU ADLER WAS waiting outside the Slate Brothers nightclub on La Cienega Boulevard's restaurant row to see comedian Don Rickles when he noticed a line outside the Italian restaurant next door. The last time Adler looked, Gazzarri's served spaghetti in clam sauce and had a little jazz trio in the corner. He elbowed his way into the club. The tiny dance floor was jammed. Adler could barely see the singer over the crowd. He was wearing a dark suit and tie, sported a glossy pompadour, and was playing an electric guitar. A drummer backed him while he sang old-fashioned Fifties rock and roll numbers—Little Richard, Chuck Berry, Fats Domino—and the joint was jumping.

The singer was named Johnny Rivers, and despite his relative youth he had been around a while. Rivers, born John Ramistella, played all over the South as a teenager. Originally from Baton Rouge, Louisiana, he bounced around Nashville, New York—where disc jockey Alan Freed shortened his name—and Los Angeles, where Ricky Nelson recorded one of his songs.

Rivers used to drink at the bar at Gazzarri's and came to know the owner, who asked him to take over the bandstand after his jazz trio gave him short notice. Rivers accepted and decided to model his guitar-and-drums act after Trini Lopez, who had recently hit with "If I Had a Hammer" from his album *Live at P.J.'s*, recorded down the street at the only place left on the Sunset Strip that had anything going on. The old-line Hollywood nightclubs like the Trocadero, the Mocambo, and Ciro's had faded like the Thirties stars who used to mob their rooms. The Strip was, for the most part, drying up and blowing away. Rivers hired drummer Eddie Rubin to back him at Gazzarri's, and within two weeks there was a line outside waiting to get in.

Adler noticed the crowd was not made up of teenagers like he would have expected, but well-dressed young people with money to spend. Dressed like he was going to appear before a judge, neat and clean Johnny Rivers was making this surly, swampy rock and roll palatable to a new crowd. Adler introduced himself to Rivers and they talked into the night. Rivers wanted to make a live record along the lines of Trini Lopez's, and Adler agreed to supervise the project. They rented the Wally Heider recording truck and spent two nights capturing Rivers's act at Gazzarri's. Adler edited and polished the recordings and took the tapes to New York to play for Don Kirshner.

As the lone sentry on the distant West Coast, Adler was out of the loop. Things had changed at Aldon ever since Kirshner sold the company in April 1963 to Screen Gems, the music wing of the Columbia Pictures studio. Screen Gems moved the New York office from the 1650 Broadway music building to more tony Manhattan quarters that the firm's big-name writers like Goffin and King, Sedaka and Greenfield, and Mann and Weil never visited. Adler was on the verge of being fired himself, although he didn't know it yet. When Adler played the tapes for Kirshner in New York, he passed on the Johnny Rivers deal. By the time Adler returned to Los Angeles, his replacements were at the office.

Adler didn't care. He had long been operating on his own out on the West Coast and had no special loyalty or ambitions with Screen Gems. Like Keen Records and Nevins-Kirshner, Screen Gems served its purpose in his education and career advancement, but he had outgrown the company. He had by no means made his fortune yet, but Adler could see a bright future for himself in the music business in Hollywood. California was young, fresh, and where the action was, and Adler knew the power was shifting. The Hollywood music business was still a small-time game, and he was perfectly positioned to steer the business in his direction. He could tell he was on the ground floor of something that was going to break big and soon. He was ready.

In a stroke of luck for Adler, his pal Elmer Valentine was planning to open a new club on the Sunset Strip, and he came to Adler for advice about music. A former crooked cop run out of Chicago on an extortion charge, Valentine had opened P.J.'s nightclub years before with some of his seamy Chicago cronies, but cashed in his end of the partnership to take over a former Bank of America building on Sunset and Clark. Valentine had recently returned from Paris, where he had visited the fashionable, swinging nightspot the Whisky à Go-Go, the type of club the French called a *discothèque*. Clubs featuring disc jockeys playing records were all the rage in Paris. Valentine wanted to open Hollywood's first discotheque. It was the right idea at the right time.

In January 1964, the Whisky a Go Go in Hollywood opened with Johnny Rivers on the bandstand. Valentine also built a platform above the raised stage for a disc jockey to play records over the club's massive sound system. On opening night, after the disc jockey failed to show, Valentine sent a waitress wearing a slit skirt up to the booth in his place. When she started dancing to the records she played, Valentine realized he had an entirely different attraction than he'd originally envisioned. He quickly recruited comely young dancers to accompany the disc jockey above the dance floor, where their go-go uniforms soon evolved to fringe dresses and white boots. They played records and danced during intermissions between Rivers's sets. The lines built up around the corner within weeks.

The Whisky lit up Sunset Strip. The place caught fire almost immediately, turning into the in-spot for the hip Hollywood crowd. The red leather banquette seating in the shadows under the balcony regularly attracted VIPs. Adler had his own booth. Jayne Mansfield and Steve McQueen became regulars. Rock and roll hit home in Hollywood, and the Whisky became the place to see and be seen, the now sound and the new scene. *Time* magazine ran a titillating photo spread. Television host Jack Paar did a remote broadcast from the club. The Beatles came to check out the action on their first visit to Los Angeles, and Valentine made sure to have Jayne Mansfield on hand to entertain them. John Lennon was able to convince her to let him glimpse her breasts. Hollywood nightlife held many wonders.

Rivers and Adler re-recorded the live album at the Whisky. Adler had not done that much production since splitting with Alpert, leaving the Jan and Dean records largely to Jan. He had supervised some Nashville sessions with the Everly Brothers for Aldon when they cut "Crying in the Rain," written by top Aldon songwriters Carole King and Howie Greenfield, but those Nashville guys operated on automatic pilot. He came out of the Whisky with new tapes, but he didn't hear the same live audience noise on the recording that he did in the room. He brought an audience of his own into a recording studio and overdubbed them clapping, yelling, and singing along, Jan and Jill among the throng. He had a hard time finding believers, but Adler eventually convinced Al Bennett at Liberty to put out the album on Imperial Records. In May 1964, four months after the club opened, the first single off the album *Johnny Rivers at the Whisky a Go Go*—a cover of a little-noticed Chuck Berry B-side, "Memphis"—exploded into the Top Ten. The album became a smash. Two months later, they released a second album of Rivers live at the Whisky.

At the same time, Adler had acquired a new set of partners. Freshly divorced, Adler was a man about town. He had been dating actress Ann-Margret and met her agent, Pierre Cossette. With another Hollywood show business professional named Bobby Roberts, a former tap dancer turned talent manager, Adler and Cosette formed Dunhill Productions, named after Roberts's dance act, the Dunhills. They put Adler on a salary and leased him a new Cadillac convertible. Dunhill opened an office on the second floor of 321 South Beverly in Beverly Hills. Now Adler was in a position to operate. In June, thirty-year-old Adler married his *shiksa* princess, twenty-year-old Shelley Fabares, the adorable, smart, funny actress from TV's *The Donna Reed Show* and hit recording artist of "Johnny Angel." She had recently signed a multiple-picture contract with Columbia. Movie magazines photographed their Bel-Air Hotel nuptials. Jan was Adler's best man.

AT DUNHILL, ADLER handed over day-to-day management of Jan and Dean to Bobby Roberts and concentrated on building the company. He also brought over songwriters Steve Barri and Phil Sloan, who Adler had only recently put together as a songwriting team. Sloan was another Fairfax High *enfant terrible* rock and roll singer and guitarist who had been making records since he was sixteen. Barri was a little older than Sloan, with a wife and baby. He still kept his day job behind the counter at Norty's Records on Fairfax Avenue. After an initial period of feeling each other out after their unceremonious introduction, the pair began to click. They were signed to the Dunhill music publishing company, Trousdale Music, for fifty dollars a week and went right to work writing surf and car songs, although neither knew how to surf or drag-race.

Sloan and Barri started singing on Jan and Dean sessions, bringing some precision to Dean's shaky falsetto and Jan's wobbly leads. They cut a set of their surfing songs for a deal Adler arranged with Eddie Ray at Imperial Records. They were going to be called the Baggys until Adler played the tape at his office for Rolling Stones manager Andrew Loog Oldham and vocalist Mick Jagger, who sneered, "Fantastic," and they became the Fantastic Baggys. Improbably, the single "Tell 'Em I'm Surfin'" slammed home on Los Angeles radio that spring. Surf was still up.

In March, Jan had lawyers renegotiate his contract with Screen Gems. Talks stalled. He was angered over restrictions in his agreement that kept him from writing with non–Screen Gems songwriters, assigning copyrights to other publishers, or even working as a producer on any outside projects. He wanted to expand his opportunities under the agreement. Screen Gems still had to approve any songs he wanted to record with Jan and Dean. He chafed against such constraints; Screen Gems could not tell him what to do. In fact, he told the president of Columbia Pictures to fuck himself. In those words.

He was also growing wary of Liberty Records' accounting procedures when it came to his royalties, and wanted Screen Gems to take responsibility for collecting the money he was owed. It wasn't enough to talk; Jan decided to act. He withheld his name from the copyrights of six songs he wrote with Roger Christian, Don Altfeld, and Jill Gibson, and assigned the publishing rights to Adler's Trousdale Music, an apparent subterfuge dreamed up by Adler and Jan to control the rights to those songs and not give them to Screen Gems. In June, when he did the same thing to the new Jan and Dean single,

"The Little Old Lady (From Pasadena)," Screen Gems filed suit.

Screen Gems accused Jan of stealing master tapes from United Recorders. In deposition, one Screen Gems executive testified that he believed Jan would destroy evidence in the face of allegations. They charged Pierre Cossette and Bobby Roberts with unlawfully inducing Adler to break his obligations to Screen Gems. The company also claimed to own Adler's Johnny Rivers tapes from the live Whisky album. With revenue to Dunhill and Jan and Dean frozen by litigation, the suit settled quickly, with Screen Gems winning the publishing rights on the contested songs and a portion of the royalties from the Johnny Rivers record. Jan would be allowed to produce other acts, but he agreed to record Screen Gems compositions on both sides of the next three Jan and Dean singles and at least one Screen Gems song on many more subsequent singles. Screen Gems would no longer have approval over every song he wanted to record, although his songwriting contract with them would remain intact.

Jan ran Jan and Dean. He and Dean were friendly, but not necessarily friends. They were like one of those old-time comedy teams they admired so much. They could enjoy working together, they appreciated the benefits of the partnership, but they lived vastly different interior lives. Dean lacked Jan's intense drive; he was a classic California kid who buried his feelings under jokes and smart-ass banter. He would go along with pretty much anything. But he did not spend much of his leisure time hanging out at Jan's Occidental Avenue apartment. Dean showed up to the studio when he was required to sing, but otherwise left recording to Jan. He knew that he had to do things Jan's way or not at all, and he accepted that. If he went along with Jan's program, he could afford a new car every year, pay his way through school, and even sock away some savings, since he was still living at home with his parents. Dean could stay cool, hang loose with that casual Southern California smart talk, back Jan's plays, and act the clown. That's what he was good at. Dean knew which one of them was the genius.

The strategy paid off. "Dead Man's Curve," released in May, was another Top Ten smash for the guys. Jan finished the song that Brian Wilson and Artie Kornfeld had started and added a thrilling arrangement. The song came from his life; that was his Corvette and Christian's XKE in the lyrics. Those two liked to drive fast. He obsessed over the drums in the introduction, constantly consulting with Brian on the piece. When the track first appeared on the *Drag City* album, Jan was still not done. He retooled sections, overdubbed new arrangements, more background vocals, brass flourishes. He put a harp behind his recitation, and he added the sound effects. He insisted engineer "Bones" Howe make the car crash at the climax last forever. The record was a towering achievement, the pinnacle of Jan's prodigious powers to this point.

For the other side of the single, Jan rewrote the leftover song from their original "Surf City" session with the Beach Boys, "Gonna Hustle You" — which the record company had reacted to with alarm over what they thought was the sexually suggestive word "hustle" — now transformed into "The New Girl in School." Jan recut the song with his hired gunslingers, packed the tracks with vocal parts, and produced a buoyant, sunny expression of male teenage lust, almost harmless, healthy, even wholesome. The production was so appealing, the label pushed "The New Girl in School" at first to radio stations, until somebody turned over the record and found "Dead Man's Curve." It was a brilliant record, masterfully produced, Jan's vision superbly executed, a complete mini-movie of the mind in three minutes and change. The song came to define not only the music of Jan and Dean but the life of Jan Berry.

15

SUMMER MEANS FUN

IN APRIL 1964, fresh from the ordeal of the kidnapping trial, Frank Sinatra arrived at the Hawaiian island of Kauai to film his directorial debut, *None But the Brave,* his first movie under a new deal with Warner Brothers. Sinatra had finally been able to deliver on his daughter's incessant lobbying and cast her husband, Tommy Sands, in a major role in the picture. The young marrieds joined the cast and crew on the island, although they were sightseeing in Honolulu when Sinatra almost drowned in the surf and had to be rescued by actor Brad Dexter; Sinatra's private plane whisked them back to the scene to find her father sitting up in bed eating eggs and peppers. The film was a joint Japanese-American production about a squad of American soldiers washed up on an island already occupied by the Japanese; it was a war movie with a message, an anti-war war movie. Sands ate every piece of scenery that came his way.

After their emergency retreat to the West Coast during the Cuban missile crisis, Tommy and Nancy had decided to return to California. They bought a brand-new bungalow-style home in the hills above Laurel Canyon, which they decorated with modern art and brightly colored upholstery. The tiny, ninety-pound brunette made her film debut in a lightweight teen movie called *For Those Who Think Young*, which starred James Darren of *Gidget* and featured Claudia Martin, Dean Martin's oldest daughter, in her own film debut. When they returned from Hawaii, Nancy was cast in a film starring her father, *Marriage on the Rocks*. At Reprise, she was still putting out insipid pop confections with producer Tutti Camarata; the pseudo-folk of "Cruel War" made a little noise...very little. Her career was barely more than a rumor.

Nancy's marriage had been troubled for some time. Sands had developed a sleek nightclub act, but he had been losing elevation for years and his frustration showed. Their Laurel Canyon home included room for a nursery, but the thought of starting a family terrified twenty-seven-year-old Sands, who was afraid to make the final commitment to adulthood and responsibility. He started seeing a psychiatrist. In those sessions, he decided to end the marriage, although he waited to tell his wife until after they had spent Easter weekend relaxing at the Sands Hotel in Las Vegas, after returning from the *None But the Brave* location.

When they came home for Easter Sunday, Sands unpacked his suitcase and then repacked it and hid it in the closet. He didn't want to spoil everybody's Easter. The next morning, he dressed for breakfast, wearing a coat and tie. Nancy assumed he had an early-morning meeting. Sands pulled his suitcase out of the closet and, standing in the bedroom, tried to explain what he was doing. He told his wife he wanted her to get a divorce as soon as possible, that she needed to get on with her life, that she would be better off without him. He was gone before his words sunk home. Nancy raced outside and beat on his car with her fists as he backed out of the garage and her life. She knew he would not come back.

Nancy went to the set of *Marriage on the Rocks*, and her hair-dresser and makeup artist did their best to patch up her puffy face and conceal her emotional distress, but she barely made it through the day. She moved into her mother's place on Nimes Road, and Nancy's teenage sister, Tina, came home from school that day to find her father cuddling and consoling her sobbing older sister.

♪

PERFORMING NO LONGER held any appeal for Terry Melcher; producing records suited his aristocratic style much better. In the past year, he had thrown himself into his partnership with skillful, willing Bruce Johnston, who signed on at Columbia as a staff producer for a modest $85 a week and took an office next to Melcher. As producers, they didn't participate in royalties, but they could order arrangements and then buy them from themselves for their sessions, which paid far better than their salaries. At a November 1963 session for the Rip Chords — again, without any actual members of the Rip Chords present — Johnston and Melcher knocked out three album tracks for the group and a fourth cut, "Custom Machine," which was released in January 1964 by an act they called Bruce and Terry. They tried out a live version at the Redondo Beach teen nightclub owned by KRLA disc jockey Reb Foster, the Revelaire Club, but quickly concluded their time was better spent in the studio.

Meanwhile, the growing Los Angeles recording industry was becoming an assembly line manufacturing surf and car songs. Johnston found himself recording with Steve Douglas, Hal Blaine, Tommy Tedesco, and the other musketeers all over town; they were the Kustom Kings for Mercury, the Vettes for MGM, the Catalinas for Bobby Darin's production company. It was a small town, with

Jan and Dean and the Beach Boys turning out hits from two studios on the same block of Sunset Boulevard, and Melcher and Johnston making imitations one block down the street. The same musicians played on every session.

When songwriter Steve Barri heard Melcher say they were planning a surf/summer/Southern California album, he and Phil Sloan whipped up "Summer Means Fun," which became the second Bruce and Terry single in April. While the record did not score consistently across the country, "Summer Means Fun" was a smash in Los Angeles and number one on KPOI in Honolulu. When KPOI disc jockey and concert promoter Tom Moffatt offered Bruce and Terry a slot on his big Fourth of July concert in Hawaii along with the Beach Boys and Jan and Dean, Melcher reconsidered his position on performing live.

Everybody had big hits. With "I Get Around" headed to number one, their fifth consecutive Top Ten hit in fourteen months, the Beach Boys were on fire. Jan and Dean were coming off the Top Ten smash "Dead Man's Curve," their fourth hit in less than a year. Another half dozen acts crowded the card for the two-night concert at the Honolulu International Center, but it was the sound of Southern California that was the center of attention. Melcher was concerned about how the Bruce and Terry performance would come off, so he hired session players Hal Blaine, Phil Sloan, and Glen Campbell to come along, even though they would cost more than Bruce and Terry were going to make. When Jan and Dean and the Beach Boys saw the session players were on the show, they were excited to use those guys as well, since they played on their records too. Of course, Melcher still paid. Neither Melcher nor Johnston had met the Beach Boys. This was shaping up to be one epic weekend.

Melcher was changing clothes in the dressing room, essentially a large men's room in the bowels of the Honolulu arena, when he felt a hard shove from behind. He turned around to see Dennis Wilson of the Beach Boys standing there with a grim expression on his face and his fists cocked in front of him, ready to fight. "Are you Terry Melcher—the guy who's been making all those records that sound like us?" he asked.

Melcher didn't know what to make of it. "Maybe they do," he said, "but that's not intentional. I guess it's just that we like what you and your brothers do a whole lot."

Dennis's face wreathed into an angelic smile and his fists fell by his sides as he brightened, and Terry Melcher suddenly became his new best friend. They met all the other Beach Boys, including Brian, who was keen to meet Johnston because of "Surfer Stomp."

It was a Hawaiian vacation disguised as a concert. Everybody brought their girlfriends (Phil Sloan brought his mother). The "Million Dollar Party" was set for three shows Friday night and Saturday afternoon and evening at the eight-thousand-seat Honolulu International Center Arena, the spanking-new complex in the heart of the city. Another concert was set for the Navy base at Pearl Harbor. They planned to extend their stay, take in some other islands, and make a real trip out of it. They bunked up at the Waikiki Grand Hotel with majestic Diamond Head outside the hotel room window and the perfumed ocean breeze carrying the scent of plumeria after dark in the warm tropical evenings.

At the show, Melcher, who had never spent much time on bandstands, stopped the band and started songs over, as if he were in the studio. They played "Hey Little Cobra," "Summer Means Fun," and a couple of others and got off, leaving Jan and Dean and the Beach Boys to their somewhat more elaborate performances. Phil Sloan, who had never played the instrument before, plucked at the bass until his fingers bled. Even though the Fantastic Baggys' "Tell 'Em

I'm Surfing" was all over KPOI, they wouldn't let him sing his song—even with his mother in the audience. There was a lot of horseplay backstage, culminating at the show at Pearl Harbor. Jan and Dean plotted to invade the Beach Boys' set wielding fire extinguishers and hid all the other fire extinguishers. The Beach Boys, of course, got wind of the planned attack and loaded up at the naval base PX with cream pies and shaving cream.

Ahead of the assault on the stage, however, Jan and Dean detoured through the Beach Boys' dressing room and pulled their clothes on over their own. Jan helped himself to Dennis Wilson's expensive silk shirt. Dean decided on a beautiful leather jacket belonging to Mike Love, and out on the stage they went, blasting foam from their fire extinguishers. The Boys were prepared. They dropped their instruments and started covering Jan and Dean with shaving cream and pies. With all the smoke and confusion, the battle raged in front of a greatly amused audience of sailors for nearly ten minutes. Only as the intruders retreated, their canisters sputtering on empty, did the Beach Boys notice whose clothes they were wearing.

While they were touring the Big Island and staying at the Volcano House, cruising down a mountainside with Terry Melcher at the wheel, Bruce Johnston in the front seat, Jan, Dean, and Jill in the back, Melcher veered off the road into a sugar cane field, plowing through the stalks and blowing out the rental car's tires. Jill took photos as they changed tires by the side of the road. These were bad boys from Beverly Hills.

BY THE TIME of the Hawaiian shows, the Beach Boys had become major stars, America's leading rock group. As their songwriter and producer, Brian had blossomed into a brilliant composer whose skills seemed to advance with every new release. His father's unending advice had soured into relentless criticism. He never let the Boys forget who knew best, no matter how far Brian's remarkable gifts developed.

The long-simmering confrontation burst into conflagration in April during the session for "I Get Around" at Western Recorders. Murry couldn't stop heaping abuse on Brian, complaining about the bass figure on the song, disparaging Dennis's drumming. Dennis put his fist through a wall and ran out of the studio. Murry kept hectoring Brian, telling him he was a loser and that he, Murry, was the real talent of the family. Finally, Brian raised some modest objection to his father's interference, and Murry turned indignant.

"Don't ever speak to me that way," said Murry. "I made you and the Beach Boys. Hear me. Without me, you are nothing."

Brian snapped. He tore off his headphones and slammed Murry against the wall. "Get out of here—you're fired," he yelled in his father's face. "You're fired as manager of the Beach Boys."

Murry slumped out of the studio, and Brian resumed his seat at the console and took a deep breath. "Let's get back to work," he said.

Murry spent a month in bed after Brian fired him, depressed and angry. Brian's parents bought a large new house in the suburb of Whittier (although they did not sell the Hawthorne place) but separated before they moved in after his mother discovered Murry's infidelities. The group was going through adjustments to success. Mike Love was getting a divorce. Al Jardine and Carl Wilson were buying houses. Dennis Wilson was spending money like a drunken sailor.

In addition to the first fully realized Beach Boys album, *All Summer Long*, Brian was producing a live album by the group, *Beach*

Boys Concert; a holiday album, *The Beach Boys' Christmas Album*; and a steady stream of hit singles. He was also working with Jan Berry on the writing and recording of the film soundtrack to *Ride the Wild Surf.* He sandwiched his songwriting and recording sessions between a hectic touring schedule. Brian never liked touring; deaf in one ear, he found it difficult to hear onstage. He greatly preferred the rectitude of the recording studio. Brian also discovered marijuana, and as with all of his enthusiasms, he threw himself whole-heartedly into smoking pot, while everybody around became a little horrified.

Brian Wilson needed to complete a new Beach Boys single before the group left for tour. He went into Western Recorders the first week of August to work on "When I Grow Up (To Be a Man)," a woefully innocent song from a twenty-one-year-old man. Life had been bearing down on Brian all year, as he balanced leading the Beach Boys with constantly mediating between the group and Murry. Firing him had only increased the pressure on Brian.

At Western Recorders, Brian invited Murry to attend the session. His chastened father came with their mother. A hundred yards down the street at United Recorders, Jan and Dean were working on the *Ride the Wild Surf* album. Adler was around. They heard Murry was on the block at the Beach Boys session and cooked up a scheme. Murry had never forgiven Jan and Dean for stealing "Surf City," and he reserved special anger for Lou Adler. But Jan and Dean knew that Brian had had enough of his despotic father and had given him his walking papers. When they heard that he was down the street at Western, they decided to put Murry on the spot. He had long vilified Jan and Adler as "song pirates," and Jan threw together a makeshift pirate's costume, kerchief over his head, patch over his eye, and walked into the Beach Boys session. As soon as he entered the room, Brian and the other Boys dissolved into laughter. They all got the joke. Watching his sons and the rest of them laughing at him, Murry boiled over with fury and stormed out of the studio. Brian felt the pressure rising.

In November, when the band flew to Europe, Brian suffered a panic attack on the flight. Before the plane touched down, Brian's sixteen-year-old girlfriend had received two telegrams imploring her to wait for his call. Over thousands of dollars of daily transatlantic calls, Wilson sought a lifeline with young Marilyn Rovell. When Brian landed back home, he wanted to get married that day and, since California required a three-day waiting period, he turned to Lou Adler, who made all the arrangements. Adler booked the wedding party at the Sands Hotel in Las Vegas, but Brian forgot his birth certificate, and everybody went home disappointed. They were married a week later in Los Angeles, and Marilyn moved into Brian's apartment.

Two weeks later, Brian was on his knees, sobbing, crying, screaming, shrieking, his face covered by a pillow, rolling in the aisle of a plane en route to Houston not long after takeoff. All the tentative control he had been able to maintain over this strenuous, challenging, pressure-cooker year fell apart in an instant, and the pent-up emotions came flooding out of him. His brothers wrestled him back into his seat and he went straight to a hospital once the flight landed, where they gave him tranquilizers. He still played the concert that night. The next morning, Brian locked himself in his hotel room, unable to stop crying, his stomach in crippling knots, until the Beach Boys' road manager came to take him to the airport to fly back to Los Angeles. He asked that his mother, and only his mother — not Marilyn and certainly not Murry — meet him. On landing, Brian asked her to take him to their vacant old home in Hawthorne. He wandered the empty rooms with his kind-hearted mother, trying to make sense of what had happened since he left this last safe place he knew.

♪

AFTER SEVERAL WEEKS in the dreary hospital in North Hollywood where they had cut off his leg, Sandy Nelson was transferred to an orthopedic hospital in Hollywood, where he would spend the next several months. Doctors contemplated further amputation because his leg had started growing gangrene, but one orthopedic surgeon came in and burned away the gangrene with sulfur in nightly twenty-minute sessions. Nelson didn't feel anything, and eventually the surgeon beat back the gangrene without further surgery.

Imperial Records owner Lew Chudd covered Nelson's hospital bills. Chudd was a decent man who paid his royalty accounts honestly and cared for his artists. Disappointed to have lost his two bestselling acts—Fats Domino and Ricky Nelson—to other labels, and with his other hit artist, Sandy Nelson, lying in a hospital bed, unlikely to ever walk again, let alone play drums, Chudd sold Imperial to Liberty Records and retired. Nobody ever accused Liberty president Al Bennett of paying royalties honestly.

It had been a difficult recovery. When the day came for Nelson to test his artificial leg in the hospital gym, he found the sensation strange, uncomfortable. He was sitting on the edge of the cot in despair, wallowing in grim thoughts, when he looked up and saw a twelve-year-old boy with two artificial legs, romping on the parallel bars and grinning at Nelson like he knew a secret. Nelson instantly understood how much heart this would take, but the boy gave him the confidence to move forward and literally take his first steps. Seven months after the accident, Nelson strapped on his new leg again and walked for the first time — the same day President Kennedy was assassinated.

Out of the hospital, money was not his problem. Nelson drew $1,000 a week from his deferred royalty account at Imperial Records. He sold his two-story Hollywood hills home with the massive upstairs master suite and bought a new home with fewer stairs, in upscale Brentwood. He immediately began building a recording studio in his garage off the kitchen. He had been planning to marry, but sadly his engagement did not survive his accident. His new next-door neighbor kept inviting him for drinks at the local cocktail lounge. Nelson resisted but finally went, and there he met a young lady who in short order became pregnant. They married, but there turned out to be some complications with the young lady's previous marriage not having been fully dissolved. Off they went to Vegas for their second wedding, and the eight-months-pregnant bride had to tear her groom away from the roulette tables for the ceremony.

Nelson masked his pain with codeine and alcohol, but he concentrated considerable effort on learning how to play bass drum with his left foot. He applied himself. He strapped a board to his artificial leg so he could play the hi-hat and went about relearning how to play drums. When his wife complained about him spending $5,000 on an Ampex recorder for his studio rather than furniture for their house, one of his friends told her, "I'd like to see you make money with a couch." When his mother came to visit and saw him with his baby daughter on his lap, surrounded by his wife, her parents, and her brother, she told Nelson he looked like a caged wolf.

But Nelson was happy being alone in the garage, building his studio, working on the drums. He began making music again. His Imperial Records supervisor, Eddie Ray, suggested he start over. Cutting a new version of "Teen Beat" — released in September 1964, it was called "Teen Beat '65"—was not the unsentimental Nelson's idea of starting over, reconnecting with his beginnings, or anything like that. It was strictly a record company strategy to recycle the catalog; the single put Sandy Nelson back on the charts and radio airwaves for the first time in two years, a mere seventeen months after he went under the bus.

♪

THAT FALL, TV producer Bill Sargent decided to host a special two-day live concert at the Santa Monica Civic Auditorium that would be filmed using his patented Electronovision, a closed-circuit video technology that would allow the video to be converted to film for display on movie screens. Sargent hired Steve Binder to direct the shows—an all-star teen music concert—and left the creative decisions in his hands. Binder assembled an astonishing cast for the concerts from the upper reaches of the day's bestselling pop artists, drawing from the English rock and roll that had splashed onto American shores earlier that year, the world of rhythm and blues, and the burgeoning California surf music scene. The resulting film, which spliced together the best performances from the two shows, was called *The T.A.M.I. Show* (Teenage Awards Music International).

Whether he meant to or not, Sargent located the heart of the pop music world in Hollywood. With a theme song out of the Los Angeles surf/car song factory, the film gave California itself a starring role. Since Bobby Roberts of Dunhill Productions also managed director Binder, Roberts suggested Jan and Dean serve as emcees for the concert and offered Steve Barri and Phil Sloan to write the theme song. Sargent didn't care; there was no audition, no testing. Sloan and

Barri were given a list of the acts set to appear, and they fashioned a song, "(Here They Come) From All Over the World."

Binder splashed Southern California across the opening scenes of the film. He shot footage of Jan and Dean weaving through traffic on Honda motorbikes, spinning around a track on go-karts, and skateboarding past the Whisky a Go Go on Sunset Strip. With their new single, "Sidewalk Surfin'," a bald rewrite of the Beach Boys' "Catch a Wave," climbing the charts, Dean executed a perfect slalom for the camera, a quasi-quasimodo down the front of the Santa Monica Civic Auditorium, while Jan crashed into the curb in a fairly spectacular head-over-heels wipeout. They skateboarded onto the stage to start the show, their own Jan and Dean–brand skateboards already on the market.

The twelve acts on the bill captured a perfect time-capsule snapshot of rock and roll at that exact moment in October 1964; from celebrating the music's beginnings with Chuck Berry and drawing the connection to Liverpool with Gerry and the Pacemakers, to generous amounts of prime Motown talent (the Supremes, the Miracles, Marvin Gaye) from Detroit in the country's heartland, and eighteen minutes of heart-stopping, electrifying James Brown and his Famous Flames to represent the rhythm and blues world. The young, savage Rolling Stones brought the mania to the concert finale.

At the center of this extraordinary convergence was California itself. The once-distant outpost of the pop music world looked like the center of the universe. The opening sequence under Jan and Dean's recording of Sloan and Barri's theme song showed the entire cast traveling through the sunny Los Angeles daytime to the Santa Monica Civic, only to be welcomed onstage at the concert by Southern California's Jan and Dean. Of course, the Beach Boys made a triumphant appearance, but the entire house band was all the musicians who had been playing on their records: arranger Jack Nitzsche; session players Hal Blaine, Glen Campbell, Steve Douglas, Tommy Tedesco, Russell Bridges (Leon Russell), the Blossoms, and the others. This was a long way from the University High School boys' locker room.

Nitzsche led the band through two days of rehearsals at Musicians Union Local 47 on Vine Street, followed by an additional two days of rehearsals at the Santa Monica Civic with the acts and cameras. James Brown was the only act to decline a rehearsal. "You'll know what to do when you see me," he told Binder. On October 28 and 29, they shot two shows with full audiences—tickets had been distributed free to local high school students—and a matinee in an empty house. The resulting near-two-hour concert movie was shown in theaters in December, by which time Sargent had sold his entire interest in the project in order to finance the distribution.

The world revolved on *The T.A.M.I. Show*. Mick Jagger learned how to dance watching James Brown from the wings (at first, the Stones refused to follow Brown's incendiary performance, but Binder managed to convince them). Jan and Dean appeared between acts, their antics and goofball *schtick* the glue that held the show together. They played their parts as the clown princes of rock and roll, but if they hoped to capitalize on the theme song, such thoughts were dashed when Screen Gems delayed the release of the single. Jan and Dean finally released their version of "(Here They Come) From All Over the World" three months later, complete with phony crowd noise added. The other side of the single, "Freeway Flyer," was Roger Christian's idea of a protest song—an anti–Highway Patrol diatribe he wrote after getting a speeding ticket on a Hollywood freeway "test-driving" Bobby Darin's $35,000 Rolls Royce. It would be the last car song Jan and Dean recorded, although it was already probably too late for car songs anyway. One month after *The T.A.M.I Show* was released, it was already ancient history, practically oldies-but-goodies.

PART 3

DUSK

If people don't want to see the picture,
nobody can stop them.

— Sam Goldwyn

16

EVE OF DESTRUCTION

Winter 1965

AFTER SIX MONTHS in the Capitol Tower working with Bobby Darin at his TM Music, Terry Melcher returned to Columbia Records. Melcher was riding high and he knew it. He had bragged to Beach Boys collaborator Gary Usher that he and Johnston were so hot, they could get anyone on the charts, so Usher proposed a bet. Darin managed a young singer named Wayne Newton who had been arctic cold since his 1963 hit "Danke Schoen." Usher wagered Melcher $1,000 that he couldn't make a chart record with the kid. Newton showed up at the studio carrying a special lemon-and-honey tea in a thermos, his throat wrapped in a scarf, ready for grand opera, only to discover that Melcher and Johnston had already cut the track and sung all the vocal parts except for about eight bars they left Newton. "Coming On Too Strong" made a respectable showing in the bottom half of the *Billboard* Hot 100, and Usher lost his bet. Melcher and Johnston also worked their Beach Boys impression on — of all people — Pat Boone, giving White Bucks's moribund chart career a brief reprise, swathed in Bruce and Terry surf music harmonies on "Beach Girl."

Staying behind at Columbia, Johnston had continued Melcher's work with Paul Revere and the Raiders, who Melcher had signed to the label after they had a 1963 regional hit long after splitting with Paxton and Fowley. The band covered the old Los Angeles R&B song by Richard Berry, "Louie Louie," for Columbia. The single was a smash on the West Coast but failed to spread, partly because New York A&R chief Mitch Miller hated the record. Another Pacific Northwest group, called the Kingsmen, who happened to record the same song at the same Portland, Oregon, studio a week later, had the big national hit. Melcher tried to capitalize on this success by recording the group's answer record, "Louie — Go Home," and another Richard Berry oldie, "Have Love, Will Travel." Johnston used the customary session players to record the Paul Revere and the Raiders album *Here They Come!*, while the actual band stayed on the road.

The first assignment Melcher drew after coming back to Columbia was a new signing of an unknown Los Angeles–based rock group called The Byrds. On Wednesday morning, January 20, 1965, at Columbia Studios in Hollywood, Jim McGuinn, David Crosby, and Gene Clark of The Byrds looked over the vast expanse of Studio A and couldn't help but feel intimidated and nervous. They knew the carriage-trade label never made the kind of rock music their group played. In fact, Columbia had only committed to one single by the band and signed only the three vocalists to the contract — not the full five-piece band. A bunch of folk musicians inspired by The Beatles and their movie, *A Hard Day's Night*, to pick up electric instruments and play rock music, the five musicians had been together for less than six months, under various names, and had done some experimental recording with a small jazz label called World Pacific at their studios on Santa Monica Boulevard. Bob Dylan had visited the group rehearsing at the studio to listen to their version of his song "Mr. Tambourine Man," which they had learned from a demo that their manager had acquired of Dylan singing the song with Ramblin' Jack Elliott.

Like Paul Revere and the Raiders, the three Byrds found themselves surrounded by musicians they didn't know who were getting ready to play on their record — Hal Blaine on drums, Jerry Cole and Bill Pittman on guitars, Larry Knechtel on bass, Russell Bridges on electric piano. There had been some talk of bringing in Glen Campbell to play twelve-string guitar — he had played twelve-string on Jackie DeShannon's "Needles and Pins," not to mention the Folkswingers' *12 String Guitar!* album — but it was determined that McGuinn could play the part on his Rickenbacker twelve-string. His chiming riff opened the recording of "Mr. Tambourine Man," but it was Knechtel's booming bass line that tied the track together while Blaine's drum part kicked in and set the entire band in motion. McGuinn aimed his lead vocal somewhere between Bob Dylan and John Lennon. Crosby and Clark provided the harmonies they had worked out weeks in advance.

The Byrds had done considerable editing to Dylan's song and worked up their own arrangement, but Melcher wanted them to play the song at a tempo he lifted from the Beach Boys' "Don't Worry Baby." With Melcher, the Beach Boys were always the benchmark. He took the band through twenty-two takes before he was satisfied. A suitable B-side, the Gene Clark song "I Knew I'd Want You," was completed in the three-hour session. Melcher brought as guests his current girlfriend, Claudia Martin, and her younger sister Deana — Dean Martin's girls. He never left Beverly Hills far behind.

Some nights later, Melcher huddled over the track in the studio with his Bruce and Terry collaborator Phil Sloan. Melcher was under pressure to make this Byrds track a hit. The company did not believe in the act and was barely equipped to deal with this kind of music, but Melcher knew The Beatles had wrought changes on the popular music scene that his higher-ups at Columbia didn't yet understand. He had taken a couple of runs at mixing the session already, but he couldn't get the sound he wanted. Melcher and Sloan talked about records they liked and what made them sound the way they did. Sloan reminded Melcher how they got his guitar solo on "Summer Means Fun" to pop by running it through a number of reverb units. Maybe that was an idea worth trying?

The Columbia staff engineers operated by strict rules, both company guidelines and union contracts. They wore neckties and worked three-hour shifts. Producers were not allowed to touch the recording console. Melcher asked the engineer to hook up the echo chambers, which were under the studio, but he told Melcher he didn't have the authority to do so without a requisition. Melcher had to admonish the engineer and remind him of Melcher's special status as the son of one of the label's leading artists (and stockholders). When the engineer went to check with someone about Melcher's request, Melcher and Sloan pushed a chair up against the studio door and went to work. They put triple reverb on McGuinn's guitar, and it popped right out of the speakers. They repeated the treatment to each of the remaining instruments. Melcher dropped out Russell Bridges's piano part and Gene Clark's harmony vocal and had everything in place when the engineer finally resorted to banging on the door and yelling to be let in. They pushed play and sat back to listen.

♪

WHILE THE BAND waited for Columbia to release the single, The Byrds took a residency at Ciro's on Sunset Strip, long past the club's Forties heyday at the height of Hollywood glamor. The current incarnation was called Ciro's Le Disc. The first night, a dozen people showed up. The Byrds, who had never performed in public, started out awkwardly but quickly pulled their act together. By the end of the next week, people were waiting in line around the block and the band was mowing down the capacity crowds. The Byrds at Ciro's in March 1965 became the instant in-spot for the hot crowd, the dance floor alive with wild, free-form dancing. Young Hollywood turned up, often high. Peter Fonda danced with Odetta. Vito and his Freakers, an ad-lib hippie dance troupe, were present, bringing along Kim Fowley, back from England, twisting his long, bent frame into convulsive dance moves, while Vito's wife calmly nursed her baby on the dance floor. The hip, cool, and curious all had to check it out — Sonny and Cher, Mary Travers, Little Richard, Buffy Sainte-Marie. Eventually Bob Dylan showed up and joined The Byrds onstage for a couple of his songs. Terry Melcher took Lou Adler.

Adler watched in fascination as a blonde-haired maniac in white pants and boots, clearly soaring on some mind-altering substance, dancing like a crazy fool, organized other dancers and led a conga line that snaked through the room. Adler asked Melcher who it was. "Barry McGuire," Melcher said. "He can sing, too."

Adler well remembered the gravel-voiced vocalist from "Green, Green" with the New Christy Minstrels. He introduced himself and invited McGuire to come by the office. When McGuire showed up, Adler sent him down the hall to meet with Phil Sloan. Adler had begun his own label, Dunhill Records. The first release was his wife, Shelley Fabares, and the second was an Elvis-like Canadian singer named Terry Black, who had big hits up north with a couple of Barri and Sloan songs. Adler was modeling his operation on the old Brill Building school of pop, but strong undercurrents of change were beginning to swirl through the music world.

Melcher had given Adler an advance copy of the new Dylan album, and he had passed it along to Sloan. "Like a Rolling Stone" changed his life. He pulled on the boots and the fisherman's cap, and he was that guy. In a fit of creativity one night, Sloan pumped out five new songs that reflected the new man he had become. The new man even had a new name: P. F. Sloan. With McGuire in his office, Sloan took out his guitar and played through a batch of his new songs. McGuire thought "Eve of Destruction" was okay, but really liked "What's Exactly the Matter With Me." Adler had heard Sloan's new songs and had been unimpressed. His songwriting partner Steve Barri actively disliked them. They thought he should stick to pop, not polemics.

At Western Recorders a couple of weeks later, with drummer Hal Blaine, bassist Larry Knechtel, and Sloan playing guitar and harmonica, McGuire cut "What's Exactly the Matter With Me" and they took a break to eat some takeout fried chicken. The second song went down with ease and, with twenty minutes left on the three-hour session, Sloan suggested they try "Eve of Destruction." McGuire retrieved the lyric sheet, crumpled and covered with chicken grease, and they ran a take. McGuire messed up some of the lyrics, covering his hesitations with *mmm*'s and *ahhh*'s, but the track entranced everyone in the room. They all marveled at the playback. McGuire wanted to do his vocal again, but Adler said they were out of time and would come back the next week. Nobody thought a song this raw, this radical, this disturbing could ever be played on the radio. They made some acetates and went back to the office, where Adler's promotion man picked up a copy.

Over the weekend, he played the track for the program director of Los Angeles's top radio station, who wanted to hear it over and over and told the Dunhill promo man that if records were in the market, he would start slamming the thing as a pick hit Monday morning. McGuire never got the chance to redo his vocal.

The Hollywood music business was barely beyond the provincial world of surf and car records, but a hit like "Eve of Destruction" by Barry McGuire, which went number one not only in the United States but in another couple of dozen countries around the world, was a jukebox jackpot the size of which Adler had never been associated with before. And he hit the trifecta: he was the producer, publisher, and record label. Meanwhile, "Mr. Tambourine Man" by The Byrds was a new world for Columbia Records, the label's first number one since "Go Away Little Girl" by Steve Lawrence three years before, and the band's album was selling like the good old days of Johnny Mathis. Adler could see Hollywood rock was only beginning to be heard from.

MIKE LOVE PHONED Bruce Johnston to see if he could recommend someone as a last-minute replacement for Glen Campbell, who had taken Brian Wilson's place on the road with the Beach Boys after his breakdown in December. Campbell had other obligations that would make him unavailable for two weeks. Love, who hadn't met Johnston before the Hawaii trip the year before, thought he might know some available session musicians. Johnston called Ed Carter, who he'd known since his University High days, but Carter couldn't take the job. Johnston then called back Love and told him that he didn't play bass—he played keyboards—but he could probably cover

Brian's high parts. On April 8, 1965, the day before the first concert on the tour, Johnston flew down to meet the band in New Orleans, and Carl showed him the tunes.

Johnston was a perfect fit musically, though he had to squeeze into a spare pair of Al Jardine's stage pants, which were about three sizes too small. He began practicing bass in his hotel room. He had never been on tour before. Carl asked him how much he wanted to be paid, and Johnston said $250, thinking he would return home with a nice $500 check and go on about his life. At the end of two weeks, he received his first check for almost $3,000, because Carl thought that he meant $250 a show.

When Campbell returned on bass, they kept Johnston on keyboards, but Campbell didn't stay long. He had been signed to Capitol Records by saxophonist Steve Douglas, who had taken an A&R job at the label, and together they made a version of the Buffy Sainte-Marie protest song "Universal Soldier" that was showing signs of life. Campbell was getting good exposure as a member of the cast of the weekly ABC-TV music show *Shindig!* In May, Campbell moved to opening act on the tour, and Johnston joined the band full-time.

Johnston had joined the Beach Boys during a period of transition. That January, at an emotional meeting, Brian had told the rest of the Beach Boys that he was no longer going to tour with the band but would concentrate instead on songwriting and record production. "I foresee a beautiful future for the Beach Boys," he said.

When Brian heard that Bruce and Terry were doing a cover of the messy version of his song "Help Me, Ronda," which appeared on the new Beach Boys album, *Today!*, he asked Melcher to hold off because he was planning to cut a better version for the band's next single. Melcher shelved their version, and Brian went to work turning the album track into a hit single, adding an *h* to the title along the way:

"Help Me, Rhonda." Brian's parents came by the February session at Western Recorders, and Brian wound up in another screaming match with his father.

Brian was under attack from all sides. He had started smoking pot daily and told his wife that he planned to experiment with LSD next. Marilyn brought down the wrath of the entire band, who searched Brian's house while he was out and confronted him over his drug use when he returned. They demanded Brian stop seeing his new pot-smoking friend Loren Schwartz, who they called his "pusher," something Brian had no intention of doing.

Brian was on his own. Musically, he was so far ahead of the rest of the group, he was beginning to face resistance to his progress. Listening to the slower, ethereal, marijuana-induced productions on the second side of *Today!*, songs like "She Knows Me Too Well" and "In the Back of My Mind," Mike Love had already suggested the songs weren't "Beach Boys enough."

With the band constantly on the road, Brian stayed behind in the studio, composing the grandest, most beautiful music he had ever made. One piece he started writing on the piano in his apartment the day after his first LSD experience. When he began the recording session with his usual group of studio musicians in April, the lavish instrumental introduction seemed to have nothing to do with the body of the work. At that time, the song was titled "We Don't Know." By June, when he moved the session to Columbia's Studio A to take advantage of the state-of-the-art eight-track recorder for the vocal overdubs by the Beach Boys, the song had become "Yeah I Dig the Girls."

Johnston had returned from tour with the rest of the band only a few days before, and he was surprised to be invited along to the studio to sing. He was still officially an employee of Columbia Records and not yet a proper member of the band. He wasn't certain what to do about his job, because he figured Brian could change his mind and come back to the band anytime. He certainly felt comfortable in the Columbia studio, but he didn't expect to be there singing on a Beach Boys session. His falsetto matched Brian's to a surprising degree; the contours of their voices blended like melted butter. Johnston couldn't believe his ears as he and the other Beach Boys laid down three tracks of background vocals over these sumptuous instrumental tracks. He watched as Brian led Mike Love through triple-tracked lead vocals and slowly heard the pieces come together for what would become, finally, "California Girls," Brian's greatest piece of music yet. Johnston gave his notice to Columbia the next day.

BARBARA ANN

AFTER A LATE-NIGHT session spent overdubbing vocals, Nancy Sinatra walked to the parking lot with her record producer, Jimmy Bowen. She reached her car door, turned, and looked up at Bowen. "So, this thing with Keely, is it really serious or what?" she asked.

That caught the twenty-eight-year-old head of Reprise Records A&R completely by surprise. Bowen was engaged to vocalist Keely Smith, but lately he had been entertaining doubts. "Now that you mention it," he said, "no, I guess not."

Bowen was a former rock and roll singer, a professional Texan whose drawl had grown thicker every year he lived in Los Angeles. He had been working at publishing and promotion when he was hired by Reprise to run artist and repertoire and cut hits. Not only did he resuscitate the flat-lined career of Dean Martin with "Everybody Loves Somebody," but he made smashes with the Chairman himself, Frank Sinatra, owner of the label, who hadn't had a big, juicy hit record since the Fifties. Bowen brought in the young studio musicians who had been making all the hits with Phil Spector, the Beach Boys, and everybody else, and used veteran R&B arranger Ernie Freeman

(Sinatra half-jokingly called them "the B Team," which they proudly adopted). Sinatra never liked "Strangers in the Night" or "That's Life," and he certainly didn't perform them in public, but he didn't mind having hits.

Bowen had been teamed with Nancy Sinatra expressly to make a hit record. They worked up a version of Cole Porter's "True Love," with a slow drag rhythm and enough echo it could have passed for a Phil Spector record, that at least sounded like a hit, even if it wasn't. Their affair went bouncing back and forth between Nancy's place at her mother's house in Bel Air and Bowen's bachelor pad in the Hollywood hills. They spent a weekend holed up in one of the bungalows at the Sinatra compound in Palm Springs, but since they never took their personal relationship public, Bowen never knew if her father knew they were seeing one another or not.

He remained engaged to Keely Smith, a formidable woman eight years his senior with two small children from her marriage to band-leader Louis Prima. Smith was pulling down a half million a year by herself working part-time in Vegas. The affair with twenty-five-year-old Nancy Sinatra convinced Bowen to call off the marriage and, blind drunk, he flew off to Las Vegas to tell Smith in person and retrieve the $40,000 engagement ring. He passed out on the plane. The next night, he met with Smith at her hotel suite, but instead of calling off the engagement, ended up marrying her at an all-night wedding chapel with comic Joe E. Lewis and Bowen's assistant as witnesses.

Nancy was stunned and shattered. She came unglued talking to Bowen's man, who called her in Bel Air the next day. She had already heard the news and did not take it well. This put Bowen in an especially ticklish situation at the record company, where he was being pressured to come up with a hit record for the boss's daughter or face dropping her from the label. He went to see Lee Hazlewood.

Bowen and Hazlewood were old friends. Bowen had bought a house next door to Hazlewood in Toluca Lake, near the Warner Brothers studio. A churlish character who was considering retiring from the record business at thirty-eight years old, Hazlewood was the son of an Oklahoma wildcatter and grew up bouncing from one oil field to another before joining the Army and serving in the Korean War. He got into the record business while working as a disc jockey in Phoenix, where he produced a series of cataclysmic rock and roll instrumental hits with guitarist Duane Eddy. He moved to Los Angeles while Eddy was still hot and had been making hits in town ever since.

Hazlewood had been partners in record labels with music publisher Lester Sill, who was a crucial early sponsor of teenage Phil Spector in the record business. Sill sent young Spector to Phoenix to watch Hazlewood record and ask questions, although Hazlewood never particularly cared for the little creep. That was years before Hazlewood went on to produce dozens of records, write songs, and even make records himself. He was a cranky Hollywood cowboy with plenty of money who wanted to sit by his pool, drink Chivas, and tell the record business to go to hell. When Bowen came to see him about Nancy Sinatra, Hazlewood had especially had it with celebrity offspring after spending the previous year making records with teenagers Dino, Desi and Billy — Dean Martin Jr., Desi Arnaz Jr., and their friend Billy Hinsche — who Hazlewood hated but put on the charts with "I'm a Fool." He didn't want anything to do with Nancy Sinatra, but he agreed to take a meeting.

Bowen took Hazlewood and arranger Billy Strange over to the Nimes Road place, where Nancy's father happened to be visiting. While he stretched out with a newspaper in the living room, Nancy and the guys retired to the bar—which was stocked with Chivas, his favorite Scotch, Hazlewood couldn't help but note. They talked songs. Hazlewood took out a guitar and played a few. He wrote songs with attitude; he laced country-flavored chord changes with hard truths and dripping sarcasm. He was surprised to find Nancy Sinatra so smart and engaging. She liked several of the songs, especially one that only had two verses.

"That's not a woman's song," he told her. "I wrote that for myself to sing at parties. It's not even finished."

He told her he would try to write a third verse and that they should meet again. Hazlewood still wasn't certain what to think, but he was more inclined to take her on than he'd thought he would be. When they got to the foyer, her father was waiting to let them out. Sinatra reached out and shook Hazlewood's hand, locking him with those famous blue eyes. "I'm glad you're going to be working with us," he said.

Up to that moment, Hazlewood wasn't certain he was going to, but there was no way he could back out now.

Hazlewood took the woman he came to think of as the "Pope's daughter" into the studio with one of his sneering kiss-off songs. He wasn't buying the coquette act. He knew she had been married and had no reason to sing like she was a virgin. He wanted her to snarl a little, sound a little sultry, maybe even aggressive, but whatever she was he wanted her to sound like an adult. Damn if "So Long Babe," released in October 1965, didn't give Nancy Sinatra her first chart record after four years of trying. It wasn't some monster hit—it slipped on and off the charts in just four weeks—but it meant Nancy Sinatra was not going to be dropped by her father's record company and she would live to make another record.

♪

EASY COME, EASY GO was supposed to be Jan and Dean's *A Hard Day's Night,* a feature film debut at Paramount Pictures for the Laurel and Hardy of rock and roll (Jan and Dean were such fans they met with the aging Stan Laurel a few times at his Ocean Avenue apartment in Santa Monica). The supporting cast for the epic slapstick comedy included Terry-Thomas, Milton Berle, Mel Brooks, Dick Clark, Gene Kelly, Cornel Wilde, Jack Jones (another University High alumnus, who graduated a year ahead of the guys), Bill Dana, Stan Freberg, and somebody in an ape suit. Screenwriter Maurice Richlin, fresh off Blake Edwards's *The Pink Panther,* had won an Oscar for *Pillow Talk* in 1959. Television director Barry Shear would be making his first feature film when filming started in August 1965.

Jan and Dean had to cancel a planned CBS-TV summer replacement series to make the movie, but interest was still running high in the Southern California beach scene. The boys starred in the unaired pilot of the new Dick Clark outdoor music show, *Where the Action Is,* and appeared on the series premiere, which broadcasted from Leo Carrillo Beach north of Malibu in June (nothing signified the growing role of Hollywood in the pop music world more than Dick Clark relocating his *American Bandstand* program from Philadelphia to Los Angeles in 1964). Plans were underway for a weekly Jan and Dean ABC-TV series to begin next fall with producer William Asher (*The Patty Duke Show, Bewitched*).

Jan was finding medical school required more time and actual study than school had in the past. He was still deeply involved in recording, spending an enormous amount of time and effort that spring on recording his own symphonic arrangements of the Jan and Dean songbook. Drawing from Jan's UCLA music theory classes, *Jan & Dean's Pop Symphony No. 1* reimagined "The Little Old Lady" as a Viennese waltz, "Drag City" as a Pied Piper's march, a Wagnerian "Dead Man's Curve." These were not easy listening reductions intended for elevators; string sections or flutes picked up the falsetto vocal parts, and a clarinet and bass clarinet played atonal notes against a tonal background to build suspense in "Dead Man's Curve." Between medical school studies, his music career, and personal life, Jan didn't get much sleep. He kept himself going with brief catnaps and sometimes with diet pills called Eskatrol, made with amphetamines.

After leaving car and surf songs behind, Jan was losing touch, fighting pop obsolescence with Jan and Dean singles like "You Really Know How to Hurt a Guy" — a song Dean hated so much he refused to sing on it — or Sloan and Barri's "I Found a Girl," both of which failed to chart like previous Jan and Dean singles. While Jan pursued his pop symphony conceit, the label insisted on releasing *Golden Hits, Volume 2*, to make sure they had some Jan and Dean product selling.

In April, Jan and Jill Gibson had moved into a brand-new modern home in a development at the top of Mulholland Drive in Bel Air Knolls, above Brentwood. After Jill complained about the frat house atmosphere of living with two other male medical students, they had left Occidental Avenue the year before, but when they moved, Don Altfeld and Vic Amira simply took another apartment in the same building. The new house at the top of the hill would settle that problem once and for all. Jill had become an even more prominent collaborator in Jan's music, often featured as a harmony vocalist on Jan and Dean records. Her song "It's As Easy as 1, 2, 3" began as a Jan and Dean number, but Jan wiped off his vocals and released it as a Jill Gibson single, not that she aspired to a career as a singer in the slightest. Jan always had his own reasons for doing things.

Jill and Jan had an easy familiarity with one another. They called each other "Jilly" and "Janny." Their worst fights always came over Jill's songwriting credits. Jan arbitrarily assigned credits, sometimes to people Jill didn't even know, and would leave her off songs she did help write. She discovered that her name was not included as a songwriter on "A Beginning From an End," and when she saw the song credited to Roger Christian, George Tipton, and KFWB sportscaster Cleve Hermann, she blew up. Jan would frequently dispense songwriting credits as favors, but Jill felt badly betrayed by him in this case. It wasn't the money; what he gave away wasn't his to give. Unlike the compliant Dean, she did not necessarily go along with whatever Jan said.

Jan's driving now scared her enough that when they went out, she would ask to ride with other people, like her friend Elmer Valentine of the Whisky, who drove her to the Jan and Dean show that summer at the Hollywood Bowl. They had barely escaped death one night when Jan whizzed through a red light on Olympic Boulevard, going two or three times the speed limit. He barreled through traffic as fast as he could, zigzagging in and out of lanes, pulling up on other people's bumpers scary fast. Jill could never tell if his aggressive driving came from some gnawing frustration in his life or was a kind of drag-race-of-the-mind game he couldn't stop playing. Jan's inner life could be mysterious.

Jill planted the landscaped gardens of the new home at Park Lane Circle and decorated the enormous house. Carved double doors opened to a marble entryway. A circular fireplace sat in the middle of the giant living room with a sweeping vista from the bay window, an upright piano against the wall. In the back, glass doors opened to the swimming pool. The four-thousand-square-foot Hawaiian Modern home had four bedrooms, four bathrooms, a large dining room, and a kitchen — sixteen rooms altogether — overlooking a proposed golf course and beyond that the San Fernando Valley. Quite the heady aerie for a couple in their early twenties.

And now, Jan and Dean were going to be movie stars. On Thursday, August 5, the limousine picked them up at the crack of dawn at the Paramount studios for the twenty-mile ride to the movie set in Chatsworth for the first day of filming. The day's shoot would be devoted to the ending — Jan and Dean walking alongside a train track, breaking into a run as the train passed, at which point they would be transformed via movie magic into dust that would spell out THE END on the screen.

They arrived at the set, where trucks and trailers were parked; the crew was busy getting ready to shoot, and the sun was already shining. Their job would be to walk down the railroad tracks, breaking into a run as a Southern Pacific locomotive approached from behind, and then jump off the track. All this would be filmed from a flatcar towed by a second locomotive. Jan and Dean finished shooting their part in two takes. The old queen in the makeup trailer working on them was beside himself, ranting about how this TV director didn't know what he was doing and how dangerous it was. After Jan and Dean's shots, they needed to film the train again for the process shot when the boys disappear at the end. Jan and Dean climbed onto the flatcar to watch the filming.

After the second take, when the director signaled for more speed and the trains pulled even closer, Dean thought about the makeup man's warning and decided to get down and take an early lunch break. He turned to Jan. "You can stay on board if you want, but I'm chicken."

Jan helped the film's choreographer off the car and lay down in a prone position on the flatcar to watch the next take. As the locomotive approached, Jan could see it was traveling too fast and jumped off just before the locomotive crashed into the flatcar and drove it down the tracks eight boxcar-lengths before coming to a halt. People flew off the flatcar as the sickening screech of crumpling steel against steel filled the air at ear-splitting volume. Bodies lay strewn like discarded dolls, bloody and broken, scattered across the landscape. Eighteen people from the crew — including the director, the assistant director, and the cameraman — were taken by ambulances to the hospital.

Jan watched in horror as the terrifying scene unfolded before him. He felt lucky to have emerged unscathed, but then looked down and noticed that his foot was pointing in the wrong direction. He pulled up his pants to discover his leg bone protruding from his skin, his pants drenched in blood. He managed to rise off the ground and hop on one foot until a crew member helped him to the highway to flag down a car. He waved at Dean over his shoulder and shouted, "I'm going to a hospital."

An eighteen-year-old department store employee on his way to work in his 1961 Ford Falcon pulled over, and Jan jumped in. The kid pulled away before the crew member could fully close the door. Jan knew enough from his medical studies to pinch off the two arteries that were spurting blood, but he had to let go to reach over and close the car door as the driver swerved around curves at high speed. The car floor flooded with blood before Jan could get his hands back around his leg. At the emergency room, medical student Jan calmly informed the attending physician that his tibia and fibula were broken, but that he still had the anterior artery and tibial nerve. If they blocked the arteries and made sure his foot got a good blood supply, he told the doctor, everything should be all right. When he heard the word "amputation," Jan turned apoplectic, fiercely resistant, insisting nothing be done until his own orthopedic surgeon, Dr. Robert Graves, one of his professors at the California College of Medicine, arrived on the scene. When Dr. Graves did get to the hospital to examine Jan and assured him there would be no amputation, Jan finally passed out. By the time Jill arrived, he was already sitting up and wearing a leg cast up to his thigh.

♪

THESE WERE TURBULENT times for Brian Wilson. He faced an overwhelming struggle to express himself with his music. He stayed up late nights at the piano in his new home on Laurel Way, a large, handsome house at the top of the Bel Air hills. He installed a sandbox in the living room for his piano and curtained off the rest of the room. The curtain was made of material that depicted toddlers playing with their buckets in the sand. Brian could pull the curtain and disappear into his own world.

He was driven to create greater and greater work, tormented by inner demons he could not ignore. People around him were leery about him killing the golden goose. He experimented with orchestration on the new Beach Boys album *Summer Days (And Summer Nights!!)*, on a track titled "Let Him Run Wild," and the startling departure from formula was not greeted with universal acclaim by all members of the group.

Constantly trapped between his own desires and the demands of his family and business, Brian was continually negotiating between his brothers and the other Beach Boys, his parents, his record company, and his teenage wife. He could be incredibly joyful, funny, and playful, but he was never deeply happy or comfortable with himself. And nothing was getting better; the pressure kept building, outside and within.

Still, Brian was searching for a bigger, richer, more CinemaScope sound for the Beach Boys. He took a baker's dozen of Hollywood's finest from his usual crew into Western Recorders in July 1965 to lay down basic tracks for a sumptuous, densely layered version of the old Kingston Trio number "Sloop John B," a song Al Jardine had long lobbied for Brian to adapt. Guitarist Billy Strange was brought in to play a twelve-string guitar part, but he didn't own a twelve-string. A suitable guitar and amplifier were purchased at nearby Wallichs Music City at Sunset and Vine. Strange cut his solo in one take, and Brian gave him the guitar and amplifier to take home as a gift. The session was an anomaly; there was no album underway. Brian was experimenting with sound. He was determined that the next Beach Boys album would be a grand statement.

But Capitol Records couldn't wait for inspiration to strike. The label wanted an album before Christmas. Brian came up with the idea of recording a bunch of old rock and roll songs like they were playing at a party, using acoustic guitars and bongos. Such an album could be recorded in a matter of days. While a few of the guys found the proposition odd, even coming from Brian, for four days in September, the Beach Boys went into Western Recorders, Studio Two, to record an album they would call *Party!*

On one hand, this was simply a stopgap measure to quickly and easily produce another album while Brian could concentrate on more serious recordings. On the other hand, the album captured another California-of-the-mind scene, a kind of faux beach party (what other kind of party would the Beach Boys throw?) that teens across the country could bring into their own bedrooms and join.

The Beach Boys brought their wives and girlfriends and plenty of beer to the session. They sang songs that they all remembered, including "Alley Oop" by the Hollywood Argyles, "Papa-Oom-Mow-Mow" by the Rivingtons, and a Phil Spector number written for the Crystals, then goofed around with some classic Beach Boys tunes, a little Beatles, and even a touch of Bob Dylan. There was a lot of singing, laughing, and joking around, and the convivial mood of the sessions was captured by the recordings.

Down the hall in another room at Western, Jan and Dean were having a screaming match. They were recording a piece Dean couldn't stand, "A Beginning From an End," a turgid potboiler of a song about a man whose wife dies during childbirth and who is reminded of the dead woman by their daughter—a long way from *bust yer buns*. Intricately arranged and elaborately orchestrated, the instrumental tracks had long been recorded; Jan and Dean were there to do the vocals. Jan was sitting on a stool with his leg in a cast and starting to record his lead vocal when Dean finally boiled over about the song.

Jan had lost his bearings. He didn't know what Jan and Dean were supposed to do in this new world of British beat groups and Hollywood folk-rock that was quickly making surf and car songs obsolete. He could feel the pop zeitgeist slipping away from him, slowly, inexorably; the more he reached for it, the more it eluded his grasp. He couldn't admit his fears, and he felt the shadow of panic slowly seeping into his mind.

For someone accustomed to having his own way, Jan was having to deal with the struggles and disappointments of the past year. Paramount Pictures had quickly abandoned the movie after the train crash. His injuries caused Jan to withdraw from medical school for the semester. The pop symphony had been a pointless indulgence. Their latest singles weren't hits. As he tried to summon the confidence and inner resources so readily available as recently as a year before, his creeping desperation began to show. He became even more autocratic, dismissive, even contemptuous of Dean.

Dean, who customarily repressed his resentments capably, knew Jan was floundering. No further evidence needed to be found than this awful, morbid song. It was so obvious to Dean, he felt compelled to make his point of view known, and Jan did not take kindly to rebukes. The situation descended into angry yelling, and Dean stormed out of Studio Three as Jan adjusted his headphones and turned to lay down his vocal.

She looks like you in every way...

When Dean pushed open the door to Studio Two, it was like walking into a different world. Dean found the Beach Boys party in full swing. They were halfway through their fourth day of sessions for this crazy album. Everybody was drunk. Dean was fully welcomed. He popped a beer, ate a couple of potato chips. Simply walking into the session was a modest act of rebellion by Dean. The Beach Boys had invited Jan and Dean to join the sessions long before they started, but Liberty Records adamantly refused to allow it.

After almost four days, the Beach Boys had largely exhausted the ready supply of songs they knew well enough to sing. When Dean showed up, they were in a slightly intoxicated quandary about what to do next. They asked Dean for suggestions, and without giving it much thought, he said they should do "Barbara Ann." They all knew the song from the album *Jan & Dean's Golden Hits*, which was collected at a point in their career when they did not actually have enough golden hits to fill an entire album. Jan and Dean had learned the song from a group called the Regents, whose 1961 original was about a year old at the time.

The Beach Boys attacked "Barbara Ann" with inebriated gusto, Dean and Brian matching falsettos on the lead vocal, Dean's wobbly, casual falsetto blending effortlessly with Brian's pinpoint precision, lending a California cool to the entire performance that couldn't be rehearsed. They ran the song three times. Dean drank a second beer. They joked around a little and then Dean left. "Thanks, Dean," shouted Carl Wilson. Dean had been gone maybe half an hour.

Down the hall, Dean pushed open the control room door and looked through the glass into the studio. Jan was still struggling with his vocal to "A Beginning From an End," taking it from the top. The engineer hit "record."

She looks like you in every way...

18

CALIFORNIA DREAMIN'

KIM FOWLEY HAD been back from England only a few weeks in February 1965 when he went to see The Byrds, who were rehearsing before an audience of freaks at Vito Paulekas's dance studio on Laurel Avenue in Hollywood, headquarters for this free-thinking, free-loving, free-form dancing communal troupe. Having marinated in the fashion-conscious British rock scene for most of the past year, Fowley instantly understood this scene, even though he couldn't at first envision what his exact role would be.

In London, he had looked up another Hollywood expatriate who Fowley last knew in California as Jett Powers, but who was now known as P. J. Proby, doing fairly well as a kind of baby Elvis for the English market. Fowley moved into the spare room of Proby's Knightsbridge mews flat, along with Viv Prince of the Pretty Things downstairs and early Rolling Stones crony James Phelge on the ground floor. He went to work as emcee for Proby's live shows and made his way around the nascent London record business, flogging his "Alley Oop" credentials because the Murmaids record had not been a hit in the U.K.

He and Rolling Stones manager Andrew Loog Oldham rewrote "The House of the Rising Sun" as "The Rise of the Brighton Surf," about the epic Bank Holiday riot between the Mods and the Rockers, by Bo and Peep, which Oldham produced for English Decca (Mick Jagger sang the Tab Hunter oldie "Young Love" on the other side). Fowley found a British band called the Kossacks and cut his song "Surfers Rule," the first surf record made in England, which he shipped off to Arwin Records for release in the U.S. by the Rituals, a group whose name Arwin controlled.

Fowley loved England. He found a steady procession traipsing through Proby's flat of naked women, criminal masterminds, and rock and roll geniuses. He went bar-hopping with a drunken Judy Garland after they met at an engagement party for one of the Pretty Things, who was marrying Douglas Fairbanks Jr.'s debutante daughter. He caught a new rock band called the Yardbirds in one of their first performances, at the Richmond Athletic Ground. He grew his hair into a flowing pageboy and polished his eccentricities; Fowley figured he had at least two dozen distinct personalities and practiced them all extravagantly in England. But as November turned to December and the British winter came calling, twenty-four-year-old Kim Fowley headed home to Southern California.

Back in town, Fowley tried to gauge the temperature of the scene. He was an ever-present specter lurking in the corners of Sunset Strip nightclubs and outside on the sidewalks. Fowley was flailing around, looking for traction, not finding any purchase. He tried his hand at solo singles — "The American Dream" was a Sonny and Cher knockoff; "The Trip" had an impressive introduction that he nicked from a Swedish record he heard in England — and he had his fingers in dozens of other nowhere records on nothing labels. He signed up a folk act, James Hendricks & Vanessa, that he produced doing a Byrdsian folk-rock riff on Pete Seeger's "The Bells of Rhymney" straight out of the band's stage shows at Ciro's.

Hendricks, who lived with his girlfriend in a small, squalid apartment in the Hollywood hills, had only recently moved to Los Angeles after several years in the Greenwich Village folk scene as the member of a group called the Mugwumps. Fowley was around frequently. When Hendricks's ex-wife—and singing partner from the Mugwumps—turned up sleeping on his floor, she told Fowley about her friends from the Virgin Islands who sang together so well. When they arrived, she phoned Fowley, who was the best contact with the record business she had been able to find since hitting town, and told him those Virgin Islands friends had arrived and he should come over and hear them.

When he got there, Fowley found three ragged hippies: John Phillips; his young, beautiful, blonde wife, Michelle; and their singing partner Dennis Doherty. They sang him three of John Phillips's songs: "California Dreamin'," "Monday, Monday," and "Straight Shooter." Fowley immediately contacted his longtime associate Nik Venet, who had shortened the spelling of his first name by one letter. Venet was long gone from A&R at Capitol Records, where he had shepherded the Beach Boys through their first two albums and made some fine records with Bobby Darin. He was hot at the moment with "Hey Joe" by the Leaves on Mira Records and looking for talent. He told Fowley that he could be the publisher and Venet would produce; they should come over and sing for him.

The three hippies had arrived in town just days before with the city in flames. The Watts Riots that August had all of Los Angeles in turmoil. They were broke, starving, and crammed on the floor of Hendricks's place, where the gas had been turned off. They only managed to make food by taking the electric heater off the wall and cooking over the toilet. Only Cass Elliot, Hendricks's ex-wife, had a car, so she drove the other three to the audition at Venet's house. Elliot had long wanted to be part of their group and knew all the songs from having lived with the others in the Virgin Islands, but John Phillips was strongly resistant to the idea. When they rang the door at Venet's and he looked out and saw all four of them, he was sold in a heartbeat. He loved their look, the combination of types, the oddball assortment. Cass demurred that she was only the driver. "Do you sing?" Venet asked and she nodded. "Then you're in the group."

He told Phillips he didn't even want to know what the three of them sounded like without her. They sang the songs Fowley had heard earlier, and Venet wanted to make a deal. He asked the four of them to come to the Mira Records offices the following afternoon and play for the head of the label. Phillips wanted money, and Venet gave him what he had, $150. They agreed to meet at three o'clock the next day in Hollywood.

When Phillips and the group returned to Hendricks's place, another old friend from Greenwich Village was visiting: Barry McGuire, who they all knew from his days with the New Christy Minstrels. "Eve of Destruction" was happening, and McGuire arrived on a brand-new Royal Enfield motorcycle, wearing new clothes and boots. He suggested they come down tomorrow morning to meet his producer, Lou Adler, at Western Recorders where they were working on McGuire's new album.

The session was set up in Studio Three, so Adler, engineer "Bones" Howe, and McGuire took the four friends down the hall into the big room at the back of the building. Phillips started playing the twelve-string, and in this acoustic environment, his guitar sounded like an entire orchestra. When they joined their voices and started to sing, they sounded like a choir. He played "California Dreamin'."

Before the song ended, Adler leaned over to McGuire. "So whose song is it, and who's fucking the blonde?"

Adler immediately thought the song could be the next Barry McGuire single. He asked Phillips who they'd been talking to about their music. When Phillips described the sticky matter of Nik Venet and Mira Records and the name Kim Fowley came up, Adler leveled his gaze at Phillips. "I'll give you what you want; just don't see anybody else," he said.

"What I want is a steady stream of money from your office to my house," said Phillips.

Later that afternoon, Venet phoned Fowley to report that Phillips and his group hadn't shown up for the scheduled audition. "Where are they?" he asked. "Maybe somebody else grabbed them."

♪

LEE HAZLEWOOD WROTE that third verse to the song that Nancy Sinatra had admired. Her father had overheard the tunes from the living room. "I like that boots song best," he told her after Hazlewood and the others had left Nimes Road that afternoon, but Hazlewood was not convinced. He wrote another song specifically for Nancy, "The City Never Sleeps at Night," that he was certain would be her breakthrough hit. Hazlewood saw Nancy for who she could be.

Nancy had been a typecast innocent ingenue in motion pictures like *Get Yourself a College Girl*, where she was added as teen bait to the cast but left the music to the Dave Clark Five and the Animals, not that anybody noticed her in her few scenes, her hair still mousy brown, skirts below her knees. But her career in show business was little more than generational entitlement on her part; her public appeal nothing but curiosity. She was a twenty-five-year-old rich kid living at home after a divorce who wouldn't have a job if it wasn't for her last name.

Hazlewood saw something more. He treated her less reverentially than she was accustomed to; his working nickname for her was "Nasty." He was a crusty contrarian who carefully maintained his outsider status even after years in Hollywood. In Hazlewood, Nancy Sinatra finally found someone in her life who could see her as separate and distinct from her father. It was not that he wasn't impressed by who her father was. He simply didn't care.

It was arranger Billy Strange who thought of adding the descending quarter tones leading into the verses. For the November 19 session at Western Recorders, Hazlewood hired Chuck Berghofer to play double bass—he was bassist in the house band at the Hollywood jazz club Shelly's Manne-Hole, owned by drummer Shelly Manne—as well as Carol Kaye, a more familiar presence at rock and roll sessions, on Fender bass. He also booked seven additional guitarists for the session, drummer Hal Blaine, and the rest of the gang. The first time they ran the tune and heard the bass break on the track, everybody in the room knew they were on to something special.

"These Boots Are Made for Walkin'" wasn't meant to be sung as much as sneered. The message was all in the attitude. Nancy Sinatra had never been asked to inhabit such a commanding role in any of her past performances. But Hazlewood was determined to make a woman out of her. He would tell her to think sexy, and she would wonder what that meant. "Bite the lyric," Hazlewood told her. "Don't sing it like a child." Hazlewood knew what he wanted. "Sing it like you're a sixteen-year-old girl who fucks truck drivers," he said.

Nancy got the picture. What followed "These Boots Are Made for Walkin'" for Nancy Sinatra was nothing less than a complete reinvention, starting with golden blonde hair. She had always underplayed herself; being her father's daughter was more than enough. She compensated by blending in, being accessible, cheerful, undemanding. At University High, she worked hard to be popular. Married to Tommy Sands, she struggled to meet her husband's expectations. She had never been encouraged to be herself. She wouldn't have known what to do if anyone had. Being known as someone's daughter tended to infantilize her. She needed to draw a mustache on that Mona Lisa and break out of the trap.

Nancy adopted the wardrobe of a go-go dancer and posed for her album cover prone in textured stockings, striped shirt, and miniskirt, with the camera looking straight up her skirt and her looking back with an insouciant stare. The single caught on out of the gate. "Miss Sinatra has top of the chart potential with this fine folk-rock material from the pen of Lee Hazlewood," wrote *Billboard*. "Her vocal performance and the Billy Strange driving dance beat should move this one rapidly up the chart."

Also reviewed on the same page was "California Dreamin'," the new single by Lou Adler's latest signing on Dunhill Records, now calling themselves the Mama's and the Papa's, who ended up doing the song instead of Barry McGuire. John Phillips's song, of course, was the Brian Wilson view of the California paradise turned inside out, but the message was the same. Even as he invoked the falling leaves and cold winds of the New York winter, his song was really selling the same California fantasy as the Beach Boys records, only viewed through an East Coast lens. Brian had introduced California as a pop concept, more a state of mind than a state of the union.

♪

THE PHONE RANG on the desk of Tony Asher, a twenty-seven-year-old junior account executive at Carson/Roberts advertising agency in Hollywood. "This is Brian Wilson," the voice on the other end said. Yeah, right, Asher thought, suspecting one of the guys in the office was fooling around. But Brian was able to convince him that he was indeed who he said he was. He wanted to know if they could get together.

Brian was in a tough spot. Capitol Records was exerting maximum pressure on him to produce a new Beach Boys album, going so far as to threaten to sue him. After Brian's last Beach Boys single, "The Little Girl I Once Knew," with its dense orchestration and stop breaks in the chorus, failed to break into the Top Twenty, a cunning Capitol Records executive edited a version from the *Party!* album of "Barbara Ann"—with Dean Torrence on vocals—into a single without the Beach Boys' knowledge, and the record skyrocketed to the top of the charts, the group's biggest hit single yet.

In December 1965, Brian heard The Beatles' album *Rubber Soul* and, his mind blown, immediately decided the next Beach Boys album needed to be a statement, an album as great as *Rubber Soul*. He was caught between his own grand ambitions and the demands of the record company and his group, who made Brian's life miserable whenever they came off the road. Their mutual friend Loren Schwartz, the same man who introduced Brian to pot and LSD, recommended he call Asher.

Brian and Asher had met briefly in the past, but Asher was beyond surprised to get this phone call. Brian wanted Asher to help him write songs for the next Beach Boys album. Asher was well positioned in a growing firm that represented clients such as Mattel toys and Max Factor cosmetics, a jinglesmith and copywriter whose Gallo wine commercial drew praise around the office. He had long dabbled in songwriting and was quite aware of the royalty opportunity he was being offered. He went straight to his boss to plead for an immediate three-week vacation and arrived the next day around noon at Brian's Laurel Way home.

Brian played Asher the nearly completed "Sloop John B" and a lush, imaginative instrumental track that had been a song called "In My Childhood" before Brian wiped off the vocals (it was still decorated with bike horns and tricycle bells, though). Asher was impressed. He recognized the brilliance of the music and couldn't believe the absurdity of the situation — being called to work with someone who knew nothing of his abilities or had ever heard his lyrics. The Laurel Way place was a madhouse and Brian was a mess: unkempt, ungainly, and often intellectually vacuous and naive, especially to Asher who was a straight-arrow kind of guy.

Brian had pieces of material and ideas about what he wanted to do, but the songwriting sessions could be tortuous — endless inane discussions of books Brian was reading, his fascination with his sister-in-law Diane, anything but what they were there to do. When they did get down to writing, Asher found Brian to be thinking on many levels about his songs, especially keeping in mind the youth of his audience. The first song they worked up, "Wouldn't It Be Nice," another too-young-to-get-married song, was inspired in part by Brian's obsession with his wife's sister, who also worked as Brian's secretary. Brian negotiated a rocky path with his wife, Marilyn, who was yet another source of pressure on him.

The sessions were conducted entirely with studio musicians who Brian had come to know so well that they were embedded in his music. He knew that combining the Danelectro bass of Lyle Ritz with Carol Kaye's Fender bass produced a broader tone spectrum that he specifically wrote parts for. He learned that if he combined two instruments, such as a banjo and harpsichord, he could create a third, wholly different tone. The music was rich with luscious chord combinations and fluid tempo shifts, strong dynamics and eccentric but evocative harmonics. Brian and the dozen or so session players were making pop music like nobody had ever heard. They eagerly followed his lead and collaborated where they could, in awe of the idiot savant in the striped T-shirt conducting the experiments. But he was off on his own.

As the rest of the Beach Boys heard the works-in-progress over the phone while on tour in Japan in January, there was some doubt, uncertainty, and grumbling about Brian's new direction. By the time the group returned to California in February, Brian had laid down most of the tracks. When he brought the group into the studio to record their first vocals, on a song called "Hang On to Your Ego," there was outright revolt. Brian backed down and rewrote the song. Still, Brian's drive for perfection could frustrate the less exacting musicians in the group. Often, he would be the only one in the room who heard something wrong, and he could bark out orders like a drill sergeant. Disagreements could be loud and animated.

The other Beach Boys were becoming increasingly less important to Brian's music. He would cut and recut vocals with different members and end up singing the song himself, often singing background vocals too. In the middle of the sessions, he released one of the tracks as a single under his own name: "Caroline, No" by Brian Wilson was a gorgeous, plaintive cry of lost innocence — poignant, personal, and vulnerable — set against a mellifluous stream of instruments including ukulele, harpsichord, and vibraphone. The solo single was apparently released with the approval and cooperation of the other members, who taped promotional messages for radio stations on behalf of it, but the modest reception did nothing to stave off the criticism and discontent within the group over the new music.

Mike Love, all money and business, worried about evolving away from the Beach Boys' trademark sound ("Don't fuck with the formula," he told Brian). Al Jardine and Carl Wilson were also vocal about their doubts. Dennis Wilson loved everything his brother did but wasn't around the sessions that much anyway. Bruce Johnston, who had not been in the group a full year, acted like a cheerful guest. He was enjoying his newfound status as a Beach Boy bachelor around town. But on the night he brought a date to visit the session at Western Recorders and heard the tracking for "God Only Knows," Johnston realized this was anything but just another Beach Boys record.

Johnston was not only an outsider in the group, he was also the most highly trained and experienced musician among them. He may not have been as invested in the group's sun-and-fun image, but he was overwhelmed by the sheer beauty and magnitude of what Brian was doing. Johnston knew better than the others what realms Brian was exploring. He was transformed by the experience and took new, intense interest in the sessions. The Beach Boys became an obsession for Johnston. He was still making Bruce and Terry records with Melcher, but the lines were blurring; he brought Melcher to the Beach Boys sessions to sing on "God Only Knows."

When Brian finished the album, which would be titled *Pet Sounds*, he brought an acetate home. He and his wife Marilyn lay in their iron-and-brass bed, turned the lights down low, smoked a joint, and listened to the record in its entirety. By the end, they were huddled together weeping.

19

RIVER DEEP — MOUNTAIN HIGH

NOTHING REFLECTED THE shift of power in the record business
from New York to Hollywood more than Phil Spector moving back to
Los Angeles in October 1965. He left behind a Manhattan penthouse
and a wife—a loose end still to be tied—and opened his record
company offices on Sunset Strip. At the same time, he leased a baro-
nial Beverly Hills mansion that had once been the Woolworth estate.

As Hollywood and London eclipsed New York as the new polar
axis of rock music, the reins of the industry passed into younger, more
sympathetic hands. In the two years since The Beatles upended the
pop system, the entire record business had exploded, but the sales
surpassed the understanding of many longtime executives. California
was a youth culture, more fluid and informal, without the rigidly
established hierarchies of Manhattan, and the music they made out
West reflected that mentality—fresh, vital, unbeholden to convention, open to invention. The West Coast was where the action was,
and Spector knew it.

After "He's a Rebel," he stopped recording in New York, choosing
to cut his massive string of hits in Hollywood at Gold Star Studios

on Santa Monica Boulevard, where the trademark echo chambers had become as much a part of Spector's sound as the wallop of Hal Blaine's drums. The landmark records he made in Hollywood contributed immensely to the town's growth as a serious pop music center. Spector commuted back and forth across the country for four years, making hit after hit, building to the biggest record of his career earlier that year, the Righteous Brothers' "You've Lost That Lovin' Feelin'."

He arrived back in Hollywood no longer the short, pasty-faced drip who wasn't going to get the girl, but a celebrity pop music aristocrat in tinted glasses, luxuriant wigs, custom-made ruffled shirts, and velvet Edwardian suits, teetering on his lifts, driven around in a white Rolls-Royce, surrounded by a retinue of sycophants and bodyguards. Spector was ready for his close-up.

The Righteous Brothers had imploded after their massive success dissolved into a miasma of disagreements, negotiations, and ultimately lawsuits. Spector was suffering something of a crisis of confidence with his other big act, the Ronettes, whose lead singer, the Spanish Harlem teen dream Veronica Bennett, he'd fallen in love with. Spector flew her in and out of Los Angeles for recording sessions at Gold Star and romantic retreats to the gothic opulence of his twenty-one-room mansion, which was filled with antique furniture and nineteenth-century art, at 1200 La Collina Drive. The Ronettes had all but disappeared from the charts, while Spector fretted endlessly over unreleased sessions with some of their best songs that he could never quite bring himself to release.

Spector missed out on signing two up-and-coming rock groups, the Young Rascals and the Lovin' Spoonful, but had started working with a group of Southern California musicians called the Modern Folk Quartet in an effort to update his scene, maybe incorporate some folk-rock into his repertoire. They eventually cut "This Could Be the

Night," a remarkable blend of Spector, Beach Boys, and The Byrds that, again, Spector could never bring himself to release.

Spector knew something was happening. He spent a lot of time with comedian Lenny Bruce, who had been beaten down and abused by the criminal justice system into a bitter, angry, and lonely man with few remaining supporters. Spector not only befriended the brilliant, maligned comic, but produced an album for him, *Lenny Bruce Is Out Again,* and financed a three-week run at the Music Box Theatre on Hollywood Boulevard, which played to largely empty houses that October.

Spector signed up as musical director for *The Big T.N.T. Show,* the follow-up to the previous year's *The T.A.M.I. Show,* to be filmed over two nights at Hollywood's Moulin Rouge Theater on Sunset Boulevard in November. The program prominently featured The Byrds, the Lovin' Spoonful, Donovan, Joan Baez — who Spector incongruously put up to singing "You've Lost That Lovin' Feelin'" while he accompanied her on piano — strains of folk music and folk-rock that were entirely absent from the previous year's edition. Petula Clark ("Downtown") represented British pop. Roger Miller sang his quirky country songs. Spector's own teen queens, the Ronettes, sang his epic "Be My Baby" and a rousing version of "Shout," a song the girls had performed since their early days doing the Twist on the rail at the Peppermint Lounge. Producers rounded out the bill with established rhythm and blues stars Bo Diddley, Ray Charles, and Ike & Tina Turner.

It was Ike & Tina Turner who fascinated Spector most. He had gone to see the act at a club called the Galaxy up the block from the Whisky on Sunset Boulevard, and when Spector introduced himself backstage to Ike and Tina, she had no idea who he was. They burned up *The Big T.N.T. Show,* laying waste to the mostly white teen audience. The Ike & Tina Turner Revue, featuring the Ikettes, background vocalists, and dancers wearing dangerously short skirts, was one of the leading attractions on the rhythm and blues circuit, in its own way as explosive a live show as the histrionic James Brown. Ike Turner himself was one of the music's founding fathers. Leading a band out of St. Louis called the Kings of Rhythm in 1951, Turner cut what came to be considered one of the first rock and roll records, "Rocket 88" by the Kings of Rhythm vocalist Jackie Brenston. Turner went on to talent-scout the South for Northern record labels, which is how he ended up playing piano on the first records by bluesman B. B. King in Memphis.

Turner met eighteen-year-old Anna Mae Bullock in a St. Louis nightclub, married her in a Tijuana wedding parlor (without dissolving any previous bonds of matrimony he may have entered into), renamed her Tina, and fashioned her into one of the most striking R&B stylists of the era on records like "It's Gonna Work Out Fine" and "A Fool in Love." Her scorching rasp, instantly identifiable on anything she sang, made her a perfect candidate for Spector. He paid a princely $20,000 to lease their record contract from Loma Records, the rhythm and blues subsidiary of Warner Brothers, and signed a deal with Ike for Spector to produce Tina Turner for his Philles Records, on the condition that Ike not be allowed in the studio. Spector did not want Tina's husband looking over his shoulder. Ike didn't mind. As long as his name was on the record, he didn't care what Spector did.

To make the monumental record he intended, Spector turned to the songwriters who had written his earliest hits with him, the husband-and-wife team of Jeff Barry and Ellie Greenwich. Spector had no idea the couple had, only a month before, gone through an agonizing divorce, a rupture they agreed to keep secret for professional reasons. For Greenwich, the breakup was especially painful; Barry had been seeing another woman. Spector flew to New York City to work with the pair for a week at Barry's Seventy-Second Street apartment. The air was thick with tension and anxiety. Greenwich felt that instead of authentic collaborations, the songs were like patchworks pieced together from bits of music each of the songwriters brought with them. At the end of the week, Spector emerged with three songs, including the promising "River Deep — Mountain High."

Ike allowed Tina to take the black Lincoln and drive herself to La Collina Drive and rehearse the song with Spector. He sat at the piano and went over the song with her endlessly, insisting she sing the melody and not resort to any of those tricks and stunts Ike had taught her and that she had come to rely on. It was a foreign process to her; she couldn't even sing the song to Ike when she came home.

In late February 1966 at Gold Star, Spector called together two dozen musicians and singers, and over the course of two nights they laid out the floorplan for the record. Spector took those tapes home and subjected them to his most thorough scrutiny before returning to Gold Star on March 7 to cut the final master track. Arranger Jack Nitzsche and Spector, at the peak of their collaboration, crammed into the room four guitars, four basses, three keyboards, drums, additional percussion, and a monster brass and reed section, and kept them playing all day and deep into the night.

By the time Tina Turner arrived, another half dozen background singers had joined the crew and the control room was stuffed with more than fifty onlookers and hangers-on. Nitzsche, who was also recording with the Rolling Stones at RCA Studios, brought Mick Jagger, who sat on an equipment case in the corner. Rodney Bingenheimer, the teen scenester of the Sunset Strip, brought Brian Wilson. Dennis Hopper took photographs. Spector presided over the madness with the authority of an old-time movie director on a film set. Tina was too intimidated by the atmosphere of great expectations and grand illusions. The session ended earlier than planned.

A week later, Tina returned to sing her vocal and brought Ike, who sat against the wall in the control room, overwhelmed by what he was hearing. He may have been hostile when he walked into the studio, but he knew what he heard was not something he could have done. He stayed in the corner—for once in his life, speechless.

Spector worked over Tina in the studio, making her sing and sing again, dozens of takes. Nobody had ever made her work like this in a recording studio. As the session ran past midnight with no end in sight, Tina asked for the lights in the studio to be lowered. She stripped off her blouse and stood there in her brassiere, dripping with perspiration, belting the song into the darkened room. When she was done and left the studio at the end of a session where she'd sang for hours, Tina still didn't know if she had given Spector what he wanted.

In truth, neither did Spector. There were additional sessions to overdub strings and mixing, including ample use of the Gold Star echo chambers. Spector spent an astronomical $22,000 on the record; enough to make four or five *albums*, not merely one single. When they were done, Spector and Nitzsche looked at each other and smiled. They knew they had wrung the greatest possible glory out of the sound they had been chasing. It had been an incredible run. But after this, they both knew, there was nowhere left to go.

♪

FRED MANNING INGRATIATED himself into Jan Berry's life at the hospital in Chatsworth following the train crash, by bringing bags of cheeseburgers and french fries. Jan hated hospital food. When Jan went home, Fred followed him. He was a helicopter pilot who had inherited a lot of money, although the settlement was held up in the courts, he explained. Jan and Jill cruised the Hollywood canyons with Fred, spying from above Doris Day's house, Brian Wilson's place, all the highpoints of Beverly Hills.

Jan and Fred made plans to buy a helicopter and start a service. Fred planned to fly Jan to medical school, where they had a helipad, a ten-minute flight from his Park Lane Circle home. Fred negotiated with the developer to buy the house next door and was close enough to taking possession to have ordered landscaping. He was going to finance J&D Records, which Jan planned to start when the Liberty Records deal with Jan and Dean expired in early 1966.

Having his leg in a cast didn't slow down Jan Berry. He did withdraw from medical school for the time being but plunged ahead on many other fronts. In November 1965, he and Dean began filming the pilot for an ABC-TV series planned for broadcast the next fall. Envisioned as a kind of *Route 66* meets *A Hard Day's Night*, the show was based on their real lives, two college students who travel around the country on weekends to play rock and roll. The pilot caught the boys (with sidekick Hal Blaine, no less) at the San Diego Zoo, the Smithsonian Institution, and other exotic locales. Producer William Asher already had one hit TV series on the air, *Bewitched*, starring his wife, Elizabeth Montgomery, and had directed the Frankie Avalon–Annette Funicello feature *Beach Party*, among other surf 'n' sand cinema epics.

Jan was still feuding with his publishers and record label; at the same time, he was cutting tracks for a new album. Jan misunderstood the pop moment. For someone whose unerring instincts had so far served him so well, Jan felt quiet panic building inside as he tried to connect with the rapidly changing times and his slipping chart positions. "The Universal Coward" was a right-wing spoof of the anti-war song by Buffy Sainte-Marie—not only a nasty piece of work on its own but, as Dean pointed out, a questionable screed coming from someone who was holding a student deferment from the draft. Dean didn't want anything to do with the song.

Dean had entered USC graduate school that fall and was growing ever more skeptical about a career in pop music. The television pilot had been daunting: hard work, long hours, and lines to learn. He also clearly didn't figure in Jan's plans for the record company. He would be a salaried employee of J&D Records and receive a higher royalty rate than anybody else would pay him, but Jan and Fred Manning, who would be financing the venture, would own the label, which Jan expected to be distributed by Lou Adler's Dunhill Records. There was talk of licensing Dean's name in the event he needed to be replaced. Dean concentrated on designing the record label.

At Park Lane Circle, Jan suffered occasional bouts of insomnia, so Jill was not surprised to wake up one night in December to find herself in an empty bed. Their bedroom was at the far end of the large house, and she sleepily rose to wander out and see where Jan was. She could see light in the front of the house and hear noises, which she could make out as voices as she padded down the hall. When Jill walked into the room, she could tell that was Jan but who was he with? It wasn't clear and then...it was.

There were two women with Jan. They were rubbing up against him, hugging him, their voices purring. They weren't having sex, but they were about to. A short, startled gasp escaped Jill's throat, and her mind went blank. She couldn't move. The world stopped turning. She always knew that Jan might be with other women while he was touring or even around Hollywood, the way that town was. She did not dwell on that. She never gave it a second thought. On some level, she understood that he was probably screwing around, but it wasn't like he was seeing someone who mattered. In her mind, she and Jan were forever. They had already spent lifetimes together. But she never expected to have her face planted in it so flagrantly. In her own home, while she was sleeping in the other room.

Jan had never shared his feelings easily. What passed for intimacy between them was more like shared experiences. They had shared so much, it certainly seemed intimate. But Jan kept his life compartmentalized, and Jill was accustomed to living in an interior world of her own making. Jill and Jan were classic artistic-temperament types, and their relationship would never change that. They were young and foolish. Confronted with this savage scene, Jill short-circuited.

She went catatonic. She couldn't stay. She couldn't go. She wanted to die. She retreated to bed, where she took a handful of sleeping pills. Later, she woke up and realized she hadn't taken enough. She took some more. Jan's groundskeeper and University High pal Buzz Hernandez found Jill the next morning. He brought her around, and as she came to consciousness Jill knew she wanted to live and that she needed to see a therapist. She also knew she would leave Jan and never come back.

AFTER JILL LEFT, Dean Torrence finally moved out of his parents' home and bunked up with Jan at Park Lane Circle. Jan was crushed and had appealed to Jill to reconsider. They met and talked a couple of times, but that flame had been extinguished for her. Jill moved into an apartment on Glendon Avenue in Westwood with her best friend from University High School, Nancy Golden. Jill went back to work at her father's travel agency.

Park Lane Circle took on a frat house atmosphere. Dean's collection of framed artwork and antiques cluttered the once-spare house. Jan threw weekly Batman Night parties to watch the hit new ABC-TV program (Jan and Dean's version of the theme song, "Batman," was his latest bid for relevance). Jan's brother Brian, working as a delivery boy for Harold's Liquor at Westwood and Santa Monica Boulevards, would bring Jan's order and hang out to watch the TV show and look at the girls. After *Batman,* Jan liked to run the old Laurel and Hardy movies. Jan's policemen friends showed up frequently. Hal Blaine, in between marriages, was a regular. Although his broken leg kept him from playing, Jan still dreamed up plays and rooted from the sidelines for the flag football league team that Dean managed, Jan and Dean's Bel Air Bandits. Before they went to school in the morning, he and Dean would meet by the pool to eat jelly doughnuts.

The walls started to close in on Jan before they left for tour in March 1966. The draft board reclassified him 1-A since he had withdrawn from medical school until September. He applied to UCLA to see if he could take some classes in the meantime. He informed the draft board that he had a severe leg injury and would be returning to school; he requested an appearance before the board.

At the same time, Jan kept up a running beef with Liberty Records over the new Jan and Dean albums (he tried to work comedy material into the albums; they wanted music) and other music business matters. He was also trying to produce a new Jan and Dean single to be ready as soon as they were free of Liberty at the end of March. In making plans to start his own label, Jan and Don Altfeld had a bitter fight over credits, royalties, and the plans for J&D Records. They stopped speaking. Then Jan's new best friend, the helicopter pilot Fred Manning, disappeared.

Fred Manning wasn't even his real name, it turned out. By the time Jan discovered the masquerade, Manning had not only promised to finance the record label, he had borrowed considerable money from Jan while waiting for his inheritance to come through, and run up bills at clothing stores on Jan's credit card. His helicopters were borrowed from companies that thought he was a potential buyer, and he never paid for the landscaping he ordered on the house next door. Manning simply vanished. Something of a con artist himself, Jan did not like being taken.

Jan and Dean returned home for a Hollywood Bowl benefit concert for KHJ Radio on April 2, the day before Jan's twenty-fifth birthday, and some quick sessions for the new Jan and Dean single — another ghastly right-wing, pro–Vietnam War song called "Only a Boy" — then headed back out for a week of dates ending in Oklahoma City, where the lads taped an appearance on a local WKY-TV show called *The Scene.* In town for a Batman-themed concert with the Marketts (who had the instrumental hit of the TV theme), Jan wore one of the black-and-yellow Batman pendants Dean had designed over a white mesh T-shirt and Hawaiian shirt. For the first time in five months, he no longer sported a cast on his leg.

In high schtick, Dean, wearing an untucked red-and-blue striped T-shirt with a sweater tied around his neck, pranced around behind Jan, strumming a toy mandolin and feigning bass licks on a mop, while Jan lip-synched through his laughter. Despite everything, it could still be fun to be Jan and Dean. They went home, with Jan set to unravel the Gordian knot of the draft.

After spending the next night in the studio, Jan left around seven-thirty in the morning on April 12 for his appointment across town with the draft board. Appearing before the board in Westwood, he explained his leg had still not completely healed, that there was the prospect of subsequent skin graft operations and that, with his injured leg, he likely couldn't pass the draft physical examination. He added that he expected to be enrolled in medical school in the fall and was taking classes at UCLA in the meantime. His arguments went nowhere. The board refused to reclassify him. His draft status remained 1-A.

Jan stormed out of the meeting. He was furious and frustrated. His sense of injustice inflamed his rage. The draft seemed intractable, but it was not the only obstacle Jan was facing. Ever since the train crash ended their movie careers, Jan had been reeling from one adversity to another. He was not accustomed to not having his way. He had always been able to bend the rules, go around the side, cut the class, do whatever he wanted and not have to pay the price. But there was so much pressing down on him—the new record label, his failed romance, the chart numbers for "Batman"—even before the draft issue exploded. Jan was told he could expect to be called for a physical within ninety days. He roared up the hill to Park Lane Circle in his latest new Stingray. He was bleary-eyed from a lack of sleep and flushed with anger.

Jan didn't stay long. He had a meeting scheduled at the Beverly Hilton with Bud Dain of Liberty Records, who he hoped to hire to run J&D Records. It was shortly before noon when he left Park Lane Circle. He tore back down the hill, whipping around sharp turns he knew well. He reached Sunset Boulevard and headed east, negotiating the twists above the UCLA campus he had immortalized in "Dead Man's Curve," moving through traffic, changing lanes, and driving aggressively, maybe even more than usual. Jan turned right off Sunset onto North Whittier, a wealthy, tree-lined residential street about a mile long that ended at Wilshire Boulevard across from the Beverly Hilton. He gunned his engine and accelerated down the wide, empty street.

Gardener Mitsuru Ondo was trimming the front lawn of one of the houses on this quiet side street. His pickup truck was parked across the street. All the houses sat far apart and back from the road with spacious, manicured front yards. Tall, leafy trees shaded the sidewalks, and the bright orange Southern California sun warmed the peaceful morning. Los Angeles was paradise on days like this. The roar of a sports car motor punctured the sylvan silence, and Ondo looked up.

A green flash screamed down the street. There were no other cars parked where the road bowed slightly toward Wilshire. The sports car was driving extremely fast. He saw the car waver slightly and strike the curb with its right rear wheel. The car flew out of control down the street until it smashed into the back of Ondo's truck and, as the sound of breaking glass and screeching metal tore through the air, shoved the truck another seventy feet down before coming to a rest. Jan's Stingray was crushed underneath the rear of Ondo's pickup. Jan had smashed into the truck at something like eighty miles per hour.

The fiberglass body of the Stingray exploded. Chips scattered all over the street. Smoke poured out of the engine. Ondo rushed to the crash. The teenage son of TV actor Gene Barry heard the squealing tires and busting glass and came running. A near-hysterical housewife neighbor was standing on the sidewalk screaming. Neither of the men could get Jan out of the car. The door was jammed closed and the top peeled back. The broken windshield was wrapped around Jan's face. The Beverly Hills Fire Department ambulance arrived. Young Barry pulled back the windshield while the ambulance attendants lifted Jan's body out of the wreck. Jan's head was split like a coconut. They took him to the emergency room at the UCLA Medical Center, where the admitting nurse thought he was dead.

Jill received a phone call at the travel agency from Jan's mother. Jill had been rebuilding her life. She was seeing the photographer Ralph Gibson. In fact, her roommate and now former best friend Nancy Golden had moved out of their apartment in a fury over Jill dating the man she considered to be her boyfriend. Photographer Gibson had worked with Dorothea Lange, and Jill was studying photography under his tutelage. She had become fascinated with the art form and staged a ritual burning of her model's portfolio as a symbol of her dedication to a new life. Four months later, she was slowly recovering from her traumatic breakup with Jan, but everything came crashing back like a thunderstorm with that phone call from Jan's mother. Jill was so distraught, her mother had to drive her to the hospital.

PET SOUNDS

KIM FOWLEY RETURNED to England in the spring of 1966 by scamming another older Hollywood woman. This one wanted her daughter to marry British nobility. Fowley took the daughter (and her boyfriend) to England to search for appropriate suitors on her mother's dime. By the time the mother joined the party in London, the whole nutty project had predictably gone to hell and Fowley was out on the street.

He hustled his way into songwriting work with a London music publisher, where he co-wrote the B-side of the first single by a young singer calling himself Cat Stevens. He produced a few rock groups, including a couple of fellows who used to be in the Irish rock group Them, now in a band named the Belfast Gypsies. He covered the U.S. novelty hit by Napoleon XIV, "They're Coming to Take Me Away, Ha-Haaa!" Anything for a quid or a giggle. Fowley was ensconced at the Bayswater Hotel when he received a handwritten letter on Holiday Inn stationery from his old Uni High friend Bruce Johnston telling him he was coming to London.

The Beach Boys had hired a Los Angeles–based publicist named Derek Taylor, a former Fleet Streeter and the original British press agent for The Beatles, who had relocated to Hollywood and taken on clients such as Paul Revere and the Raiders and The Byrds. Taylor decided it would be a good idea to dispatch Johnston as ambassador to Great Britain on the occasion of the release of the new Beach Boys album, *Pet Sounds*. The single, "Sloop John B," was already a hit in the British charts ahead of the album's release. After a round of East Coast dates, Johnston flew out of Chicago to London and checked into a suite at the Waldorf, the grand Edwardian hotel on the Strand, on May 16. At age twenty-three, Bruce Johnston had never left the country (other than a couple of drunken excursions to Tijuana with Sandy Nelson). He brought with him two advance copies of *Pet Sounds*, an album that he unreservedly loved. Derek Taylor had set forth in a detailed memo his instructions for courting the British music press.

Fowley met Johnston at his hotel and walked him through Taylor's memo. Johnston had a unique relationship with Fowley, who never tried to hustle him. Whatever airs Fowley affected as he became more and more of a caricature, Johnston knew the real guy. Unlike almost everybody else, Johnston liked Fowley. He was relieved and happy to have him as his guide, as he had no idea what to expect from the procession of London music press and scene-makers that started snaking through Johnston's suite the next morning.

Johnston treated the music press to highlights of the *Pet Sounds* album and they went away starry-eyed — "nothing short of sensational," wrote Keith Altham of *New Musical Express*.

"I think our records have improved almost one hundred per cent in the last year, mainly due to Brian being able to concentrate on records without being involved in the exhausting business of personal appearances," Johnston told Altham. "He has written every number on our new LP, *The Beach Boys Pet Animals* [*sic*], and it's the best we have ever done."

Andrew Loog Oldham brought along Mick Jagger. "You're the one who goes 'Do-wah,'" said Jagger.

"No," said Johnston. "I'm the one who goes 'Wah-do.'"

Bruce Johnston's Waldorf suite with the advance copies of *Pet Sounds* was the place to be that week in swinging London. Fowley brought them in—drummer Dave Clark of the Dave Clark Five, Marianne Faithfull, a couple of the fellows from the Merseys, who were high on the British charts that week with "Sorrow." Keith Moon of The Who turned out to be a major surf music fan and was not only overjoyed to make the acquaintance of an actual Beach Boy, but knew all of Johnston's car and surf work as well. Moon was responsible for adding songs like "Barbara Ann" and "Bucket T" to The Who's songbook.

Moon took Johnston to see Tony Rivers and the Castaways play at a Catholic school in Essex. They were coaxed onto the bandstand, where Johnston was handed a bass—they didn't have a piano—which he regarded with some uncertainty as the band launched into "The Little Girl I Once Knew," which they had rehearsed in preparation for the occasion. With Moon thrashing around on drums and Johnston fumbling the bass, they murdered a couple of Beach Boys songs and beat a retreat. But not before the promoter announced the audience would have to pay an extra fee for this additional talent, which would be collected upon exiting at the door.

When Johnston strolled back into the Waldorf lobby near midnight, he found a highly agitated Kim Fowley waiting for him, ready to drag him upstairs back to the suite. Sitting around a table playing canasta quite properly were two young ladies, members of the Beach Boys British fan club, and two of The Beatles, John Lennon and Paul McCartney. They had come to hear the new Beach Boys album. Johnston made a grand entrance, looking every bit the quintessential

Beach Boy, shining like the California sun in white suit, white tie, and white shoes.

Fowley served the guests rum and Coca-Cola. McCartney asked everybody to please not talk while they listened to the record. Johnston dropped the needle on the plastic portable record player, and Barney Kessel's crystalline guitar lines announced the beginning of "Wouldn't It Be Nice." The two Beatles sat rapt as they heard "God Only Knows" for the first time. When the record was done, McCartney asked if they could hear it again. After the second listening, Lennon and McCartney sat together at the portable piano and tinkled on the keys. They signed one of the playing cards to Bruce and headed off to McCartney's Wimpole Street lodgings, where in the wee hours they put the finishing touches on a song called "Here, There and Everywhere," a piece for their new album, *Revolver*, currently under production, with an introductory flourish that sounded more than a little like *Pet Sounds*.

This Olympian interlude completed a psychic cycle. After Brian had heard *Rubber Soul*, he swung into an unspoken competition with The Beatles. *Pet Sounds* had been his formidable reply. Under no circumstances could the four Beatles match the kind of intricate arrangements and orchestrations found on *Pet Sounds*, let alone some of the complex instrumental parts played by professional studio musicians, Brian's hired assassins. They couldn't handle much more than a piano overdub without running screaming to George Martin. *Pet Sounds* was a gauntlet thrown down. Johnston wasn't even one of the Wilson brothers, but here he was, delivering the news from California to John and Paul.

The next night, Johnston's new best friend, Keith Moon, took him as his surprise guest on the weekly British TV pop program *Ready Steady Go!*, where host Cathy McGowan interviewed Johnston about the new album and a possible U.K. tour by the Beach Boys. Johnston went with Moon and Who bassist John Entwistle, who first stayed behind at the TV show to have a few drinks and pop a couple of pills, to The Who's gig at the Ricky Tick Club in Newbury, where they were surprised to find bandmates Roger Daltrey and Pete Townshend, tired of waiting for them, already playing the show using the rhythm section from the opening band. Entwistle and Moon took their places on the stage, but the tension eventually erupted on the "My Generation" finale when Moon kicked his drum set apart and sent the cymbal stand flying at Townshend, who swung his guitar at the speaker stack but missed and hit Moon's head instead. The bandstand exploded in violence and the show ended suddenly. Backstage, Johnston was waiting to ride back to his hotel with Moon, who was sporting a bloody slash across his face and a black eye. Johnston was impressed; Beach Boys gigs were not blood sport. He flew back to Southern California the next morning.

♪

AFTER BRAIN SURGERY at UCLA Medical Center, Jan was left in a deep coma, wrapped in bandages like a mummy and frankly not expected to survive. Jill's life collapsed. Although they were broken up when the accident happened, Jill discovered she was still attached to Jan in a profound, primal way. Her feelings overcame her. She joined his parents, Bill and Clara Berry, in daily vigils at his hospital room, Jan strapped to his bed, connected to the outside world by wires, tubes, and nozzles.

He was unconscious for two weeks. Then, one afternoon, Jan sat up and looked at his mother. "Hi, mom," he said. "How ya doin'?" Before she could reply, his eyes closed again and he slumped down, returning to the dark silence. When he finally came out of the coma, he came out swinging. He was violent and out of control. He would snarl and growl through the bars on the side of his bed like a caged animal. He could not speak, his right side was paralyzed, but he could pull out his tracheostomy tube. The doctors gave him powerful tranquilizers. He was not a pretty sight. Dean stopped coming after a couple of visits. Jill and Jan's parents spent every day at the hospital.

The doctors encouraged his visitors to talk to Jan, thinking it was possible he could receive the communication through his subconscious. A window in his hospital room looked out on the bright blue Southern California sky. Lou Adler brought a movie projector and showed Laurel and Hardy films on the opposite wall. Hal Blaine chattered away about the various sessions he was playing and, when he was leaving, leaned over the bed to say goodbye. Jan reached up to his neck and pulled Hal closer. Hal burst out of Jan's room, breathlessly reported the breakthrough, and broke down in tears.

Jill gave up her life. The hospital visits took over to the point where she broke off with Ralph Gibson. Her therapist warned her against it, but there was no way she couldn't do this. She isolated herself from the outside world, walking like a zombie through the antiseptic hallways and impenetrable gloom. She started smoking cigarettes again her first day at the hospital when Dean's girlfriend, Sonnie Morrow, offered her one. As Jan slowly recovered, he couldn't speak in more than spurts, like a three-year-old. He had lost all his knowledge and memories. He only recognized his mother and Jill. He had no recollection of their having broken up. To his parents, he could be cruelly indifferent, even rejecting them in favor of the medical staff. In private moments, he would plead with Jill to take him out of there, his eyes filled with panic and uncertainty.

The Berrys had already lost two children; another son had died in a mountain climbing accident, and their infant daughter drowned in their swimming pool. They patiently tended to their son, stoic and devoted. At first, Jill had been invisible to them, but as the circumstances developed, they could see her usefulness and encouraged it. Their world had shrunk to this small hospital room and the adjacent corridors.

Adler spent a surprising amount of time at the hospital. He was genuinely concerned, even though he had a lot going on. His world, in fact, was exploding. While Jan was lying in his hospital bed, Adler had the number one record in the nation, "Monday, Monday" by the Mama's and the Papa's. If that wasn't enough, Adler and his partners had sold their company that month to ABC, a scant thirteen months after releasing their first record. The deal made Adler a millionaire. Somehow, he handled his business and still managed to show up almost every day at Jan's hospital room.

Adler's pal Elmer Valentine, owner of the Whisky a Go Go, became something of a support system for Jill Gibson, taking her to lunch and inviting her for the weekend to his place in Palm Springs. It was at Valentine's weekend home in the desert that Jill began her affair with Adler. They had been spending time close together at the hospital; with Jan comatose, it often felt like they were the only people in the room. Jill was touched by Adler's feeling for Jan; his heart was showing. There was a growing intimacy between them. He was warm, funny, attractive, a safe harbor in a turbulent sea that Jill needed badly.

Jan was distracted by a twenty-one-year-old psychiatric technician named Sandy Ward, who started work with Jan on speech and aphasia therapy at the hospital. She had an uncanny knack for intuiting his barely comprehensible speech. Jan's brain injuries left much of his thought processes intact, but the most badly damaged part translated thought into action. He experienced immense frustration. Sandy's ability to communicate with Jan helped. Her curves didn't hurt either.

Jill and Adler kept their relationship secret. Along with everything else, Adler was still married and living with his wife in Bel Air. These circumstances did not make Jill comfortable. She had never cheated on her boyfriends. Plus, she liked Shelley; everybody did. Jan and Jill had often double-dated with Adler and Shelley, frequently dining out and retiring to one or the other's home to play charades. Jill and Adler continued to spend hours together in Jan's hospital room. Jill maintained her daily vigils. Adler kept running the Laurel and Hardy films. Don Altfeld stopped by one evening after he had been screening the films and thought Jan had enjoyed them. Jill barely noticed them.

Jan's recovery traveled a slow, tortuous path. The difficulty and frustration of trying to make himself understood with his garbled bursts could send him into paroxysms of anger. He could exchange a few words with doctors, but only with great effort. Jan would act out his frustrations violently. Doctors administered the powerful tranquilizer Thorazine to facilitate handling him. When Bill Berry discovered that his son was being tranquilized not for his own benefit but for the convenience of the staff, he complained to hospital officials.

The Berrys were diligent advocates for their son's care. Bill Berry kept careful, detailed notes on Jan's condition and treatment. This grueling ordeal spared caretakers like the Berrys and Jill nothing. As difficult as it was for Jan, he was receiving treatment and care. The people around him were left to fend for themselves. They also had to struggle with Jill's indeterminate role. Jan's parents knew that he and Jill had broken up, but Jan didn't. His bond with Jill remained strong, and his parents were not above exploiting her position with their son.

One day, they took Jill out to the hallway, and both stood with her while Jan's father suggested that Jill take care of Jan's "needs." She immediately understood him to mean sexually. Jill couldn't believe what she was hearing; she was appalled and disgusted by the suggestion. It finished her. Jill knew she could never return to the hospital. There was no other possible response. She walked out of the UCLA Med Center that day and never came back.

♪

THE MAMA'S AND the Papa's may have been one of the hottest new rock groups in the world, but their lives had quickly devolved into the kind of tawdry soap opera that people write pop songs about. John Phillips and Michelle had split up after he discovered her affair with Denny Doherty, the other male singer in the group. To further complicate matters, Cass Elliot was crazy in love with Doherty, who deeply disappointed her by treating her like a jolly uncle. These were tumultuous times for the group members, who had arrived in Hollywood penniless hippies a mere eight months before. One million-selling album and two hit singles later, they had joined Hollywood's *nouveau riche* with fancy cars, expensive clothes, houses in the hills, and all the necessary accoutrements for the young, hip, and rich. But their lives were disasters.

Since Michelle and John had separated, Michelle had been quietly seeing Gene Clark of The Byrds, a neighbor of hers in Laurel Canyon. She arranged for him to attend the concert by the Mama's and the Papa's on Saturday, June 4, at Melodyland Theater in Anaheim, a theater-in-the-round across the street from Disneyland. It was Michelle's twenty-second birthday, and she was planning on celebrating after the show with friends in the Canyon.

When she took the stage, Michelle was shocked to see Gene Clark sitting in the front row wearing a bright red shirt, vivid scarlet, impossible to miss. Michelle grabbed Cass, who knew about the secret romance, and they stationed themselves in front of where he was sitting, hoping to block him from the view of her husband. Michelle was anxious. Even though John's date was also sitting in the audience, close enough that Michelle could see her short green dress, she knew John would be enraged if he figured out what was going on between her and Clark. The subterfuge worked, and by the end of the routine, after the two women performed practically the entire show to Clark, Michelle was blowing him kisses from the stage. Singing happily, she heard John's voice thunder out of the speakers: "Get the fuck over here."

Michelle's stomach dropped. She and Cass quickly changed sides of the stage and finished the show. Michelle scampered off stage, fearing her husband's wrath. She collected her gear backstage and scooted. Outside in the parking lot, Michelle was throwing her stuff into her baby-blue XKE when John caught up to her, grabbing her by the arm. "You're fired," he screamed, as exiting patrons walked past.

The remaining Melodyland shows were cancelled. John Phillips spoke to the other two group members the next day and told them he could not continue working with Michelle. Either they agreed to fire her, or he would quit. Him or her. They chose him. Three weeks later, Michelle received a letter from their attorneys officially firing her from the Mama's and the Papa's. Although this posed significant problems for the group, a replacement hovered in the wings.

With production already underway on a much-anticipated second album, and a great deal of money at stake, Adler suggested his girlfriend, Jill Gibson, could step in. Indeed, Jill was tall, slim, and blonde, like Michelle, and Adler knew she wrote music and sang with Jan. They had already broken up once in the few weeks they had been seeing each other, but after Adler left his wife, he and Jill were back together. He broached the issue, but it was John Phillips who convinced Jill to take the part. They sat on a bed in an empty hotel room in New York, talking over the prospect. Phillips assured her that even if he repaired his marriage with Michelle, she would never sing with the group again. Jill loved the music of the Mama's and the Papa's, and she loved singing harmonies, but she was wary of coming between a married couple. Still, the position held a certain appeal to her introverted self; she didn't have to be the star, merely a harmony vocalist, and it wasn't her music. She was being offered a place in one of the hottest new groups in pop, about to record their surefire hit second album — a once-in-a-lifetime opportunity.

The Mama's and the Papa's decamped with Jill to London, partly to get away from Michelle in Hollywood. Adler came along, as did his pal Terry Melcher. Denny Doherty told *New Musical Express* that Michelle was in Mexico visiting family. The plan was for the group to rehearse. They spent days singing together and working Jill into the act. They rented half a house in Berkeley Square and made an immediate splash on the rock partying circuit, hobnobbing with various Rolling Stones and Beatles, who were all keen to meet this fabulous new group from the exotic West Coast. Lennon and McCartney came by the Berkeley Square place after an evening at the clubs. Lennon wanted to meet Mama Cass, who had gone home early and taken something to sleep. He leaned over her bed and kissed her cheek. She woke, saw who it was, and jumped into his arms. As the party wound down near dawn, Jill sat looking out the window as a stray cat prowled the empty street and Paul McCartney picked out a melody on an out-of-tune harpsichord, coming to an end just as the cat finally found his place and curled up to sleep. A couple of days later, they went to George Harrison's house for dinner and sat around on the floor, passing joints and listening to records.

In July, Adler and the group returned to Western Recorders to work with Jill on the second Mama's and the Papa's album. They re-recorded some songs on which Michelle already sang and cut a bunch of other pieces fresh with Jill. Her photo was stripped into the cover shot. Michelle stormed into the sessions one afternoon, confronting Adler in the control booth while the group was on the other side of the glass in the studio. She had come to demand a formal release, on the advice of her attorney. Adler was uncomfortable, but John Phillips was openly hostile. Michelle tried to involve Denny Doherty, her former lover, and he stared at his shoes. She boiled over, smacked Doherty hard enough to knock him off his stool, and stalked out of the studio.

A handful of dates had been postponed, and the group booked a Learjet to make the five concerts. At the first show in Dallas, Phillips introduced Mama Jill and awkwardly explained that Mama Michelle was taking a vacation in Mexico. The audience was restless but raised no objection. The abbreviated, forty-minute set included one song, "I Saw Her Again," from the forthcoming album. By the time the group appeared at the Forest Hills Music Festival in Queens, New York—before a sellout crowd of fourteen thousand, where the opening act, Simon and Garfunkel, cleaned their clock with an hour-long, precision performance—audience sentiment had grown more vocal. Cries from the crowd of "Where's Michelle?" dotted the short, perfunctory set.

The chemistry in the group had been crucially altered, and everybody knew it. Jill could sing and certainly looked great, but Adler kept her separated from the others, so she never had the chance to develop the kind of natural relationship that could have built rapport. The original four had known each other for years. Jill also couldn't keep up with the debauchery. She had only started dabbling in smoking pot after leaving Jan (Terry Melcher first turned her on). Denny Doherty was a drunk, his purple sack of Crown Royal always handy. Phillips insisted Jill get high with them and gave her uppers to take before performing, promising it would make her feel better and improve her performance. In Phoenix, the Eskatrol she took did anything but, and she struggled to make her way through the show. Jill was being asked to make a massive transition on a dime; she went practically straight from Jan's hospital room to hanging out with The Beatles. She was a traumatized gentle soul walking through her own life like a ghost.

Of course, Michelle came back — to both the group and her husband. She returned to the studio on August 23 — two months after receiving the termination letter from the group's lawyers — sang in the studio on the last two songs of the album, and went home with John that night. Adler told Jill, who was too numb to have a strong reaction. She did want to be paid her royalties, though. Adler walked her right up to the office door of his partner Bobby Roberts and stood in the doorway encouraging her to settle everything with Roberts herself. Jill knew nothing about business matters, and she certainly had no idea what a conflict of interest was. She trusted Adler and believed he had her best interests at heart. He gave her arm a reassuring squeeze, turned, and walked out of the office down the hall. Bobby Roberts told her she would have to sue John Phillips for her royalties, and the best she could hope for was to get the advance money she was originally promised — but never paid — for joining the group in the first place. She believed him.

2 1

GOOD VIBRATIONS

BY THE SUMMER of 1966, Phil Spector was cowering in seclusion in his twenty-one-room Italian mansion, surrounded by more than an acre of land, tucked away on a quiet side street up above the Sunset Strip. Behind the gates was a slate driveway and patio with a marble fountain and towering Italian cypresses flanking the front door of the faux-Tuscan villa. The regal entrance hall greeted visitors with a Louis XV credenza in carved gilt wood and a green marbletop table. The baroque mansion was cluttered with authentic French antiques and whimsical kitsch like the life-size blackamoors that lined the hallway and a giant oil painting of Muhammad Ali. The grand living room with twenty-foot ceilings and gable archways was stuffed full of nineteenth-century armchairs and sofas, oil paintings of Louis XIV and Queen Marie-Thérèse in large gilt frames hanging on the wall, a Napoleon round table decorated with medallions, bronze candelabra, a French clock on the mantel. An ebony Steinway grand piano sat at the center of the room.

Spector would no longer go to the recording studio or nightclubs. He wouldn't even go to his beloved Canter's for takeout deli.

He sulked in the rental palace that had once belonged to tobacco heiress Doris Duke. He closed himself off in his study during the days, talking on the telephone, and hid away at night in the billiards room with the giant sound system he had the Gold Star Studios staff install, shooting pool and listening to Wagner's "Ride of the Valkyries" over and over again.

Pool was a recent obsession. Spector had invited famous professionals like Minnesota Fats and Willie Mosconi to shoot with him, betting $10,000 a game. Now he closed the door, turned up the stereo, and stayed awake all night playing by himself and brooding.

The utter failure of his masterpiece—"River Deep—Mountain High" by Ike & Tina Turner—had sent him into seclusion. In May, when the record was released, it rose no higher than number eighty-eight on the charts and fell off entirely before the month was over. He knew it was the greatest record he ever made, the pinnacle of his career, the ultimate fulfillment of his artistic vision, and he was crushed by the public's rejection of his creation. It validated his worst fears and insecurities. Spector's confidence gave way to dark, paranoid moods and smoldering anger and resentments.

Of course, even paranoids have real enemies, and Spector had been arrogant, obnoxious, and haughty enough to piss off people throughout the radio and record business, people only too happy to ignore the Ike & Tina record. Top Forty radio stations considered Ike & Tina a rhythm and blues act, while rhythm and blues stations thought the record was pop. Spector already felt the breath of his adversaries on his neck; the week he was in the studio recording Ike & Tina, the Righteous Brothers had their first number one hit without Spector, "(You're My) Soul and Inspiration." The twerp he fired as his promotion man, Sonny Bono, had gotten together with one of Spector's old background vocalists, and Sonny & Cher were now one of the biggest new rock acts of the year. These people mocked Spector from their places above him in the charts.

Part of him worried that he was washed up, that there was no longer any place for him in today's pop world. At twenty-six, Spector was already out of date and past his prime. Of course, he couldn't believe that about himself, but doubt flooded his mind. It had always been Phil versus the world, with the rest of the world waiting for him to fail. He closed the Philles Records offices and started talking about retirement. He made plans to go into the movie business, optioning a script from his friend, actor Dennis Hopper, and gave an interview to the *New York Times* where he claimed he had "lost interest" in the record business. "Art is a game," he said. "If you win that game too regularly it tends to lessen your motivation."

In England, "River Deep—Mountain High" reached number two on the charts. As his parting shot to the record business, Spector took out full-page advertisements in the trade magazines that simply said BENEDICT ARNOLD WAS RIGHT.

Spector kept his girlfriend, Ronnie Bennett, trapped inside La Collina with him. She was not allowed to leave or have friends visit. He would shut himself away from her all day and night. When The Beatles asked the Ronettes to open the group's U.S. tour in August, Spector insisted that her cousin replace Ronnie in the live show and that she stay home. When Lenny Bruce died of a heroin overdose at his Hollywood hills home that same month, Spector locked himself in his study for hours with police photos of Bruce's sordid death scene, sobbing and shaking, obsessively playing Bruce's albums. He was living on vampire hours and never leaving the house. His hostage girlfriend heard the pool balls clicking down the hall long into the night.

♪

ON AUGUST 11, Carl Wilson returned to his hotel room after a sold-out concert before more than four thousand fans at the Civic Memorial Auditorium in Fargo, North Dakota. The Beach Boys had stirred up considerable excitement in the landlocked Dakotas; more than fifteen hundred fans had greeted their plane at Hector Airport that afternoon. The phone rang. It was a long-distance call from his brother Brian, who was phoning from Western Recorders, where he had spent the last three days editing and mixing a piece of music he had been working on since February—music that none of the Beach Boys had yet heard. Brian held up the phone for Carl to hear as the instrumental track roared out of the studio monitors.

"That's really bizarre-sounding music," he told Brian when he got back on the phone.

"Huh?" mumbled Brian. "What do you mean?"

"I mean bizarre," said Carl. "It sounds bizarre."

The commercial failure of his masterpiece *Pet Sounds* not only left Brian personally shattered, deeply discouraged, and artistically uncertain, but also freshly vulnerable to criticism and skepticism from the other members of the group and the record label. Despite its glowing reception from fellow musicians, *Pet Sounds* didn't even earn a gold record. Capitol Records buried the album by releasing *The Best of the Beach Boys* two months later. The group teetered on the brink of irrelevancy in their striped shirts and suddenly outmoded values. The contemporary pop scene had moved forward. Brian was seeking new ground for the Beach Boys and nobody, including Brian, felt all that confident. With the rest of the group spending the year non-stop touring, Brian had immersed himself in the studio, devoting most of the first part of the year to producing *Pet Sounds*.

Brian had first composed this new piece of music that he now played for Carl on his third LSD trip, an ecstatic and enlightening spiritual experience for Brian. As a child, their mother had told Brian that dogs could pick up vibrations, a thought he always found scary—animals transmitting invisible feelings through the air. This song would be about only good vibrations, although on the session log for February 17, when Brian first rehearsed the song during the afternoon with his session players at Western Recorders, it was simply titled "#1-Untitled."

"Hold it, please," shouted Brian after the second take. "Let me hear the organ... perfect! We'll go with that... Organ, Fender bass, and piccolo."

Later that night, down the street at Gold Star Studios, Brian and the thirteen musicians ran through twenty-six takes. A lot of time was devoted to properly embedding into the huge sound of the band an electro-theremin, an obscure radio-controlled instrument usually associated with low-budget Fifties science fiction film soundtracks. The next day, Brian led the band through another twenty-eight takes at Gold Star and even added scratch vocals using lyrics from his *Pet Sounds* collaborator Tony Asher. He spent another couple of days at Western the following week, recording inserts from various instruments and changing some of the arrangement, before deciding the track would not fit comfortably with the other material he was developing for the *Pet Sounds* album. For the time being, he set aside the track, now titled "Good Vibrations."

Brian envisioned the piece as his greatest work, a self-conscious masterpiece. The song was written in three pieces, more a mini-suite than the pocket symphony Brian called it. The instrumental tracks sounded like parts of different songs, floating around each other in different keys, like nothing Brian had ever asked the musicians to do before, like nothing anybody had ever asked them to do before. "Who-ee, Brian, what were you smoking when you wrote this?" asked session guitarist Glen Campbell after the first run-through.

One month after the first three Western sessions, Brian took another crack at cutting the instrumental track at Columbia Studios. Sixteen days later, he booked another tracking session at Gold Star, before the rest of the Beach Boys returned to town the next week to do the final vocal overdubs on *Pet Sounds*. Four weeks later, the sixth session produced a complete live track, a rhythm and blues–style version with Tony Asher's lyrics.

The other Beach Boys were beginning to lose patience with Brian's seemingly endless work on the track. Brian himself was growing dubious about the piece. He wondered if the song was as good as he thought it was. He was keenly aware of the tragic fate of Phil Spector's "River Deep—Mountain High," and the devastating effect its failure had on his idol Spector. Brian started to lose interest in the project; he had met a new collaborator and was already dreaming up a significant new work with him.

Brian was introduced to Van Dyke Parks at a party at Terry Melcher's place on Cielo Drive in Bel Air. They stood on Melcher's manicured front lawn and talked. Parks was a gnomish, erudite Southerner with a picturesque vocabulary, razor wit, and a penchant for puns and wordplay that bordered on compulsive. The first time he arrived at Brian's house to work, he was accompanied by a police officer who didn't think someone as disreputable-looking as Parks riding his dinky Yamaha motorbike had any good reason to be in the neighborhood, and didn't believe his story. Once Brian identified him and gave the policeman an autograph for his sister—a big Beach Boys fan with a crush on Dennis—all was forgiven, and the cop went on his way.

Brian was shocked to learn that Parks couldn't afford a car and asked how much a car would cost. Parks reckoned he could buy a decent used Volvo for five thousand dollars, and Brian immediately called his accountant and ordered a check. Parks was stunned; he and his wife were living in severe penury at the time, in the corner of a garage without a bathroom. He and Brian went to work.

Brian played him a melody that Parks said reminded him of a Marty Robbins song, and Brian was excited. He envisioned a western epic and already had a title, "Heroes and Villains." Parks asked him to play the melody again. And again. He noted the cadences, the little rhythmic turns in the melody. Parks closed his eyes to collect his thoughts and then spat out an opening line: *I've been in this town so long that back in the city I've been taken for lost and gone and unknown for a long, long time...* They finished the song that night. Brian cut a demo five days before the release of *Pet Sounds* in May.

One week later, when Brian reconvened the session crew to again tackle "Good Vibrations," he had decided against trying to record the basic track in one piece. At Sunset Sound, he focused on the second section, which now had a few lyrics (*gotta keep those good...*). After two nights at Sunset and another daytime session two days later at Western, Brian came back for five more sessions over the next week at Western. At the end of the June 18 session, Brian pronounced himself happy with the recording; it was ready to be the next Beach Boys single. But by the next morning, after listening over and over to the record, Brian had changed his mind. Demoralized, bewildered, and depressed, Brian put "Good Vibrations" on the shelf and turned his attention to his new friend.

Parks declined Brian's invitation to work up lyrics for "Good Vibrations" in favor of fresh collaborations. All through that summer, Brian and Parks squirreled away with enormous amounts of hashish and a steady supply of Desbutal to keep them going through the night, and produced a flurry of extravagantly eloquent material. Brian planned an ambitious album titled *Dumb Angel* that would be just as much a departure for the Beach Boys as *Pet Sounds*. Brian didn't return to the studio for another six weeks, until August, when he started recording the new material that he and Parks had been compiling at Western.

At the same time, David Anderle, a former record company executive and a close friend, revived Brian's interest in "Good Vibrations." During a visit to Brian's Laurel Way home, Brian played Anderle the work-in-progress "Good Vibrations." Brian said he was thinking of selling the song to Warner Brothers for a rhythm and blues group. Blown away by what he heard and astonished at Brian's professed indifference, Anderle called back the next day and asked Brian if he could have the song for an artist that he managed named Danny Hutton. Brian decided he should finish the record for himself.

That week, Lou Adler invited Brian to RCA Victor Studios in Hollywood to visit a Rolling Stones recording session. Adler gave him a potent joint, and Wilson felt like he was transported to another world. In contrast to his solemn, businesslike sessions, the Stones were throwing a party. They were recording a song, "My Obsession," with a powerful, propulsive rhythm track and carefully layered guitar parts. There were drugs and girls everywhere, and a table full of food and drinks. Compared to this, Brian's sessions were like going to church. He mentioned as much to Stones vocalist Mick Jagger. "This works for us," Jagger replied.

Brian spent the next three days painstakingly mixing, editing, and rearranging "Good Vibrations." Finally, he reached a point where he felt confident enough to play the track over the long-distance phone call to Carl. His brother's underwhelming response was hardly encouraging. Within the Beach Boys, dissension in the ranks was a way of life, but Brian and the rest of the group were living in two different worlds now.

Two weeks later, with the Beach Boys back in town, Brian had them singing the a cappella "Our Prayer" for the *Dumb Angel* project at Columbia Studios, and two nights later, August 24, he moved the session back to Sunset Sound, where Brian liked the vocal sound (Brian was using the different studios as elements in his composition). He had given Mike Love an acetate of "Good Vibrations" and asked him to write new lyrics. Love, who thrived on pressure, shoved the disc into the automatic record player in his canary-yellow Jaguar XKE as he pulled out of his in-laws' place in the San Fernando Valley with his pregnant wife, Suzanne, and headed into Hollywood for the session. While his wife took dictation, Love tossed off two verses, finishing up as he cruised down the Hollywood Freeway. He showed up to the session late, but he had the lyrics.

Brian drove the vocal recordings relentlessly. He wanted more than harmony; he was looking to match timbre, shading, overtones. He put the Boys through their paces, working over small pieces of music dozens of times. But hours later he still had not heard what he wanted. Carl and Dennis would return to complete the vocal over-dubs with Brian, who would spend another day at Western preparing an intensely detailed final mix.

A week later, in a paroxysm of self-doubt, Brian hastily went back into the studio to recut the entire track. Unhappy with the results, he blew up at the session musicians ("I'm going to play all the instruments myself!"). He finally accepted that the recording he had scrupulously edited the week before was the best he could do, then went into a panic when the tapes went missing for two days before mysteriously turning up at his Laurel Way house.

In a marathon eight-hour session at Columbia, Brian finished the vocals, touched up the electro-theremin part, and mixed until three in the morning. When he sat back to listen, he felt the music fall down on him from the studio monitors like a warm rain. The next day he played the finished version for the rest of the Beach Boys, who didn't know what to think. They knew it was different; they had never heard anything like it. An uncomfortable silence loomed. Finally, Bruce Johnston spoke up.

"Either we're going to have the biggest hit in the world or the Beach Boys' career is over," he said.

After more than seven months, twenty-two sessions, and somewhere between six and ten finished versions of the song, Brian had spent more than $50,000 on the record, more than any single ever. Released on October 10, 1966, "Good Vibrations" sold more than one hundred thousand copies a day during the first week; it was the biggest hit the Beach Boys ever had. Brian's dream of a masterpiece had come true.

But when Brian got word that the band planned to debut "Good Vibrations" on the road, he grew frantic about their ability to play the song live. He and an assistant flew to Chicago and then drove to Ann Arbor, Michigan, where the Beach Boys were playing two shows in the University of Michigan gym. Brian ran the band through a rigorous rehearsal, stopping every few bars to make a correction, but the song came off flawlessly at both shows. At the end of the second show, the guys dragged Brian onstage with them. Reluctant at first, Brian loosened up as the crowd showered him with a standing ovation and the band launched into "Barbara Ann."

On the way back to the Chicago airport, Brian got stoned. He caused problems in first class by ordering all three entrees on the menu, and when the stewardess said he couldn't do that he raised enough fuss that she brought him all three entrees anyway. He stopped the stewardess later and told her he needed to make an emergency phone call to his wife. She told him that wasn't possible, but after Brian displayed enough anxiety, she agreed to give the pilot a message to radio and have it relayed to her by telephone. Brian told Marilyn to gather all his friends and bring a photographer to meet him at the airport when his plane landed.

After all the months in the wilderness, the confirmation of Brian's vision of "Good Vibrations" did not ease the yawning maw of insecurity and doubt the failure of *Pet Sounds* had enflamed. He was already lost in his *Dumb Angel* project with Van Dyke Parks, his vision sprawling out of control. Surrounded by a tight-knit family group that criticized, undermined, and second-guessed him all the way, Brian carried the weight of the entire enterprise on his back. Now he needed some reassurance. He sought connection. He wanted to feel the love.

At the TWA terminal of Los Angeles International Airport, Marilyn assembled nearly two dozen of Brian's friends to pose with him under the colorful, childlike mural of airplanes taking off and landing, while photographer Guy Webster snapped away. Van Dyke Parks and his wife were there, as were David Anderle and his wife; Brian's driver; Marilyn and her two sisters; Carl's wife; musicians Dean Torrence, Mark Volman of the Turtles, and Danny Hutton; in addition to a handful of cousins and other friends. In the center, wearing his crooked "look what I've done" smile, Brian peeked out from under a brush of hair with a feigned confidence he surely did not feel. Standing next to his wife, he confessed to feeling confused, and she asked why. "Isn't this what you wanted?"

"Yeah," said Brian. "The problem is I don't know whether I should be saying hello to everyone or whether it's time to say goodbye."

♪

AFTER TWO MONTHS at the UCLA Med Center, Jan moved to a rehabilitation unit at Cedars-Sinai Hospital in Hollywood. Jan insisted on returning to his own home and taking care of himself, even though he was still in bad shape. He couldn't speak well enough to make himself understood; he was relearning how to use his tongue to form words. His right side remained useless. He could barely dress himself. He was angry and confused, not sure what was happening much of the time. Who could tell what he knew and what he remembered? He couldn't say, but he didn't show signs of recalling much of anything.

The Berrys hired Sandy Ward to move into the Park Lane Circle house with Jan and provide him with full-time care. Sandy and Jan had bonded at the UCLA Medical Center, where she displayed a unique ability to anticipate Jan's needs and interpret his mostly inarticulate grunts and gargles. Jan was being treated by an aphasia specialist, the same speech therapist who guided actress Patricia Neal back from her stroke, and he had made impressive progress, but the brain damage was extensive. Anyone with any less will and determination than Jan Berry would have surrendered to life as a vegetable.

Adonis no more, Jan looked beat up, his face swollen, his eyes dark, a tracheostomy scar across his neck. He'd put on weight and shuffled when he walked, dragging his right side. The fake seizures weren't fake anymore; Randy was real. Sandy Ward enforced a daily therapy routine and managed to negotiate Jan's manipulative wiles. He could be a spoiled brat about food. He insisted on having his hamburgers brought from Bel Air Market and eating two or three of them in a sitting. He did not like being confined to a wheelchair. He hated not being able to do things for himself, and he was constantly frustrated by his speech and not being able to say what he wanted. He fought his therapy every step of the way.

But Ward was clever. She knew that Jan wouldn't get into the pool for his physical therapy if she didn't wear a bikini. She used that. She would wear a white one-piece until he did the therapy. After he finished, then she would change into her bikini.

Ward argued with him that he needed to do as much as he could to recover now because the longer he put off doing the hard work, the less ability he would have to do it. She used everything she could to encourage him and keep him on track. Jan was demanding and thankless but could also be charming and lovable. Ward worked closely with the speech therapist, who Jan visited three times a week, although it could sometimes be hard to see much progress.

Bill Berry called Dick Clark and asked him to come see Jan and show him some old television appearances. The TV host brought a stack of kinescopes up to Park Lane Circle one afternoon that summer. They sat together in the darkened living room watching old Jan and Dean performances on *American Bandstand* and *Where the Action Is.* The flickering black-and-white images showed young Jan, healthy and handsome, lip-synching to "Honolulu Lulu" and other hits, wearing those striped rugby shirts, impossibly confident and comfortable at the top of the world—a sharp contrast with the broken man now hunched in a wheelchair in his living room. Clark searched his face for signs of recognition, as Jan stared deadpan into the TV set. Clark thought he detected a distant light in his eyes, but Jan said nothing.

If you can't remember something, did it really happen? What is a life other than memories and the air that you breathed? A person's life is so often summed up by their deeds—what do you have if you lose those? When simply getting your right foot to point in the direction you want is a struggle, nobody gets too philosophical. But still, somewhere in the deep recesses of his brain, Jan remembered. How could he not? But why would he want to remember? There was nothing left.

Ward took Jan to regular outpatient appointments. It could take considerable time and energy to prepare Jan and get him to the doctors. As difficult as they could be, these outings were good for Jan's spirit and developed his abilities, which Ward thought was a good idea. Although she had no evidence, Ward suspected there were stirrings deep inside Jan that had not yet bobbed to the surface. Taking him out of the house and into ordinary activity seemed like a good way for him to return to something resembling a normal life. They often ate lunch after his appointments at a nearby Westwood diner.

Joe Lubin and his wife, Paulette, were seated at a booth across the room. It was Paulette the costume designer who recognized Jan. "That looks like Jan Berry over there," she said. At a table on the other side of the room was indeed someone who looked like a weather-worn Jan Berry sitting with a beautiful young woman. Lubin, who had started everything rolling eight years before with "Jennie Lee," hadn't seen Jan in years. He knew Jan had been injured in a car crash but had no idea how serious it had been. Lubin walked over to where they were sitting and sat down next to the girl.

"Hello, Jan," he said.

Jan looked him straight in the eye, without displaying the slightest emotion.

"Hello, Joe," Jan said.

Sandy Ward caught her breath, then instantly excused herself. This was the first time Jan had recognized anyone. She rushed to find a pay phone and call the doctor, who had asked to be alerted if anything like this happened. It was odd to see it now, as Jan sat calmly in his seat acting as if he had seen Joe only last week, no sign he knew what an important moment it was. Lubin had no idea what was going on. He called his wife over. "You remember Paulette?" Lubin asked.

Jan nodded.

PLAYLIST

Jan and Arnie / "Jennie Lee"
Kip Tyler and the Flips / "Jungle Hop"
The Teddy Bears / "To Know Him Is to Love Him"
The Teddy Bears / "Don't You Worry My Little Pet"
Kip Tyler and the Flips / "She's My Witch"
Jan and Arnie / "Gas Money"
Bruce and Jerry / "I Saw Her First"
Sam Cooke / "Wonderful World"
Jan and Dean / "Baby Talk"
The Renegades / "Geronimo"
The Renegades / "Charge"
Sandy Nelson / "Teen Beat"
Tommy Sands / "That's Love"
Skip and Flip / "It Was I"
Hollywood Argyles / "Alley Oop"
Dante and the Evergreens / "Alley Oop"
Richie Allen / "Stranger from Durango"
The Innocents / "Honest I Do"

Jan and Dean / "Heart and Soul"

Dick Dale and the Del-Tones / "Let's Go Trippin'"

The Belairs / "Mr. Moto"

Bruce Johnston / "Do the Surfer Stomp"

Sandy Nelson / "Let There Be Drums"

Dick and Dee Dee / "The Mountain's High"

Nancy Sinatra / "Cuff Links and a Tie Clip"

Nancy Sinatra / "Like I Do"

Tijuana Brass with Herb Alpert / "The Lonely Bull"

The Crystals / "He's a Rebel"

Beach Boys / "Surfin'"

Beach Boys / "Surfin' Safari"

Beach Boys / "Surfin' USA"

Jan and Dean / "Surf City"

Hot Doggers / "The Original Surfer's Stomp"

Hot Doggers / "Balboa Blue"

The Murmaids / "Popsicles and Icicles"

Johnny Rivers / "Memphis"

Rip Chords / "Here I Stand"

Bruce Johnston / "Surfin' Round the World"

Beach Boys / "Be True to Your School"

Beach Boys / "In My Room"

Beach Boys / "Warmth of the Sun"

Rip Chords / "Gone"

Rip Chords / "Hey Little Cobra"

Jan and Dean / "Honolulu Lulu"

Beach Boys / "Fun, Fun, Fun"

Jan and Dean / "Drag City"

Jan and Dean / "Dead Man's Curve"

Jan and Dean / "The New Girl in School"

Bruce and Terry / "Custom Machine"
Bruce and Terry / "Summer Means Fun"
Beach Boys / "I Get Around"
Beach Boys / "Don't Worry Baby"
Fantastic Baggys / "Tell 'Em I'm Surfing"
Beach Boys / "When I Grow Up (To Be A Man)"
Jan and Dean / "Ride the Wild Surf"
Sandy Nelson / "Teen Beat '65"
Jan and Dean / "Little Old Lady (From Pasadena)"
Jan and Dean / "(Here They Come) From All Over the World"
Jan and Dean / "Freeway Flyer"
Wayne Newton / "Coming On Too Strong"
Pat Boone / "Beach Girl"
Beach Boys / "Help Me, Rhonda"
Beach Boys / "She Knows Me Too Well"
Beach Boys / "In the Back of My Mind"
Beach Boys / "California Girls"
The Byrds / "Mr. Tambourine Man"
Barry McGuire / "Eve of Destruction"
Nancy Sinatra / "So Long Babe"
Jan and Dean / "You Really Know How to Hurt a Guy"
Jan and Dean / "I Found a Girl"
Jan and Dean / "A Beginning From an End"
Beach Boys / "Let Him Run Wild"
Beach Boys / "Barbara Ann"
Beach Boys / "Sloop John B"
The Mamas and the Papas / "California Dreamin'"
The Mamas and the Papas / "Straight Shooter"
The Mamas and the Papas / "Monday, Monday"
Nancy Sinatra / "These Boots Are Made for Walkin'"

Beach Boys / "Caroline, No"
Beach Boys / "Wouldn't It Be Nice"
Beach Boys / "God Only Knows"
Modern Folk Quartet / "This Could Be the Night"
Ike & Tina Turner / "River Deep — Mountain High"
Jan and Dean / "The Universal Coward"
Jan and Dean / "Batman"
The Mamas and the Papas / "I Saw Her Again"
Beach Boys / "Good Vibrations"

ACKNOWLEDGMENTS

MY FIRST VISIT to Los Angeles at age ten left me with a lifelong romantic notion of Hollywood in the late Fifties and early Sixties, a scene I first explored in a biography of Ricky Nelson. It was still a small town then, where anything could happen. Southern California was a world unto itself, its own little corner of the earth remote in those pre–jet-travel days from the centers of power and the traditions of age. California was freedom—freedom from convention, freedom from restriction, freedom to dream and be who you dream.

The characters in *Hollywood Eden* did not come to California. They are the sons and daughters of the Golden State, and they accepted all that they were given without question. They are like the people in New York City who never look up at the tall buildings. The wonder, the majesty, the beauty of where they lived simply blended into the background for them, even as it fundamentally shaped their lives and endeavors. This story is so thoroughly embedded in Southern California; it couldn't have happened anywhere else.

Many previous authors have researched this history and written about it with passion and power, but my enduring interest in the role of community in creating culture led me to this specific approach. The yearbook collection of my friend and correspondent Kevin P. Walsh led me to University High. Although many Los Angeles high schools have distinguished histories and illustrious alumni, the University High class of '58 stood out as especially archetypical, a convergence of time, place, and people that sparked the beginnings of rock and roll in Los Angeles.

Many people went above and beyond to help. Jill Gibson spent hours delving into a past she rarely contemplates. Bruce Johnston couldn't have been more supportive. Lou Adler spent an afternoon at his beautiful Malibu home, recalling his early days. Kathy Kohner Zimmerman — the one and only Gidget — went from dubious to enthusiastic. Sandy Nelson was a constant source of entertainment and information. Herb Alpert and Dean Torrence offered their encouragement.

Dee Dee Phelps recalled her Dick and Dee Dee days (she has written her own excellent account, *Vinyl Highway*). Judith Lovejoy became a friend and proved to be a portal to other valuable connections like Ann Marshall (the girl in the short green dress), another remarkable gal. Denny Bruce — the Zelig of Hollywood rock — can always be counted on to be Denny Bruce. Likewise, the redoubtable Billy James is always a reliable source. And there is nothing to be said about Don Drowty other than he is a blessing to all who know him.

Thanks to Dave Shostac, Jane Johnson, and Nancy Golden for their time and memories. Also, much appreciation to Oscar Arslanian, Bob Marx, Carolyn Kreisman, Andrew Loog Oldham, Fabian Forte, Denny Tedesco, and anyone else who picked up a call or answered an email. Thanks to Art Fein of Hollywood and Mark Battermans of Studio City for the accommodations and inspiration. Also inspiring, Bob Merlis.

Many of my fellow journalists contributed. Gene Sculatti gave the project a lot of thought and a few books. Surf music scholar John Blair, a friend since college days, was helpful and encouraging. Harvey Kubernik, Domenic Priore, Barney Hoskyns, William McKeen—who have all written persuasive books of their own on the subject—were all gracious and generous. Alec Palao, king of CD reissue liner notes, also gladly shared his research.

And many big thanks to the Vagabonds of University High School '58 who gave me a hand: Ron Chase, Eugene Gierson, Elizabeth Ansley, Val Romoff Sherman, Maxine Trimble, Lynn Crumpler, and Dave Stevens.

My friend Steve Douglas died more than a quarter century ago, but rarely a day goes by that I don't think of him. Our many conversations helped deeply inform this book, and I would be remiss not to make note of his contributions.

Charlie Winton also edited and published my 2014 biography of Bert Berns, *Here Comes the Night: The Dark Soul of Bert Berns and the Dirty Business of Rhythm and Blues*, and has been involved in this book from its conception. Given that Charlie has been editing books longer than I've been writing them, he is a partner of incalculable gifts. Doug Richmond at House of Anansi supplied thoughtful and penetrating editorial direction. This book has been doubly blessed by two outstanding editors.

House of Anansi gives the Lower 48 another great reason to love Canada. In addition to editor Richmond, thanks go to superb copyeditor Peter Norman, always the unsung hero to any manuscript, brilliant designer Alysia Shewchuk, publicist Curtis Samuel, utility infielder Joshua Greenspon, and managing editor Maria Golikova. Cheers to both departed chief Sarah MacLachlan, who introduced us, and arriving majordomo Bruce Walsh, who greeted us.

Counselor Brian Rohan Esq. has provided ample encouragement and inspiration to this project. Dennis McNally was, as always, the sage first reader. Susana Millman helped with the photos. Sam Hoffman and Ward Long of LightSource SF did the scans. Carol Mastick typed some transcripts. My deep personal thanks go to Frank Weimann of Folio Literary Group, my dear friend Pamela Turley, and my darling daughter, Carla Selvin.

A couple of additional notes: in this book, the remarkable batch of studio musicians who played on these records is never referred to as the Wrecking Crew, even though this loose-knit group of virtuosos came to be known by that name long after the fact. Denny Tedesco even made an excellent documentary about them titled *The Wrecking Crew*. But it was a term that was never used at the time; Hal Blaine invented the name sometime around the publication of his memoirs in the Eighties. It was a rewriting of history that annoyed Steve Douglas to his dying day.

Also, the term "doo wop" to describe the vocal group rhythm and blues records of the early Fifties was not contemporaneous nomenclature. Such distinctions were only begun to be made in the early Sixties, around the time "oldies but goodies" emerged to imply that rock and roll was developing its own literature and culture. But that music has always been a strong part of Los Angeles music. The El Monte Legion Stadium lives.

BIBLIOGRAPHY

BOOKS

Abbott, Kingsley, ed. *Back to the Beach: A Brian Wilson and The Beach Boys Reader*. Helter Skelter, 1999.

Badman, Keith. *The Beach Boys: The Definitive Diary of America's Greatest Band on Stage and in the Studio*. Backbeat Books, 2004.

Barrett, Don. *Los Angeles Radio People*. Vol. 2, *1957–1997*. db Marketing, 1997.

Blaine, Hal, with Goggin, David. *Hal Blaine and the Wrecking Crew: The Story of the World's Most Recorded Musician*. MixBooks, 1990.

Blair, John. *The Illustrated Discography of Surf Music, 1961–1965*. Popular Culture Ink, 2008.

———. *Southern California Surf Music, 1960–1966*. Arcadia Publishing, 2015.

Bono, Sonny. *And the Beat Goes On*. Simon and Schuster, 1991.

Bowen, Jimmy, and Jerome, Jim. *Rough Mix: An Unapologetic Look at the Music Business and How It Got That Way.* Simon and Schuster, 1997.

Braun, Eric. *Doris Day.* Orion Books, 1991.

Brennan, Joe. *Duke of Hawaii.* Ballantine Books, 1968.

Bronson, Fred. *The Billboard Book of Number One Hits.* Billboard Books, 1997.

Broven, John. *Record Makers and Breakers: Voices of the Independent Rock 'N' Roll Pioneers.* University of Illinois Press, 2009.

Brown, Mick. *Tearing Down the Wall of Sound: The Rise and Fall of Phil Spector.* Alfred A. Knopf, 2007.

Brown, Peter Harry, and Broeske, Pat H. *Down at the End of Lonely Street: The Life and Death of Elvis Presley.* Dutton, 1997.

Carlin, Peter Ames. *Catch a Wave: The Rise, Fall, and Redemption of the Beach Boys' Brian Wilson.* Rodale, 2006.

Cogan, Jim, and Clark, William. *Temples of Sound: Inside the Great Recording Studios.* Chronicle Books, 2003.

Collis, John. *Ike Turner: King of Rhythm.* Do-Not, 2003.

Cornyn, Stan, with Scanlon, Paul. *Exploding: The Highs, Hits, Hype, Heroes, and Hustlers of the Warner Music Group.* Harper Entertainment, 2002.

Crosby, David, with Gottleib, Carl. *Long Time Gone: The Autobiography of David Crosby.* Doubleday, 1988.

Darin, Dodd, and Paetro, Maxine. *Dream Lovers: The Magnificent Shattered Lives of Bobby Darin and Sandra Dee — by Their Son.* Warner Books, 1994.

Des Barres, Pamela. *Rock Bottom: Dark Moments in Music Babylon.* St. Martin's, 1996.

Dolphin, Jamelle Baruck. *Recorded in Hollywood: The John Dolphin Story*. CreateSpace, 2011.

Einarson, John. *Mr. Tambourine Man: The Life and Legacy of the Byrds' Gene Clark*. Backbeat Books, 2005.

Elliott, Brad. *Surf's Up! The Beach Boys on Record 1961–1981*. Pierian, 1982.

Emerson, Ken. *Always Magic in the Air: The Bomp and Brilliance of the Brill Building Era*. Viking, 2005.

Fiegel, Eddi. *Dream a Little Dream of Me: The Life of Cass Elliot*. Chicago Review, 2005.

Finnis, Rob, and Dixon, John P. *Duane Eddy*. Bear Family Records, 1994.

Fowley, Kim. *Lord of Garbage*. Kicks Books, 2012.

Funicello, Annette, with Romanowski, Patricia. *A Dream Is a Wish Your Heart Makes: My Story*. Hyperion, 1994.

Gaines, Steven. *Heroes and Villains: The True Story of the Beach Boys*. New American Library, 1986.

Gold, Jeffrey, ed. *A&M Records: The First 25 Years*. A&M Records, 1987.

Greenwald, Matthew. *Go Where You Wanna Go: The Oral History of The Mamas and The Papas*. Cooper Square, 2002.

Guralnick, Peter. *Careless Love: The Unmaking of Elvis Presley*. Little, Brown, 1999.

———. *Dream Boogie: The Triumph of Sam Cooke*. Little, Brown, 2005.

Guralnick, Peter, and Jorgensen, Ernst. *Elvis Day By Day: The Definitive Record of His Life and Music*. Ballantine Books, 1999.

Hardy, Ed, with Selvin, Joel. *Wear Your Dreams: My Life in Tattoos*. Thomas Dunne Books, 2013.

Harris, Michael. *Westside Stories: Recollections and Reflections on Life in West Los Angeles from the 1940s to the 1960s*. The Americas Group, 2017.

Hartman, Kent. *The Wrecking Crew: The Inside Story of Rock and Roll's Best-Kept Secret*. Thomas Dunne Books, 2012.

Hjort, Christopher. *So You Want To Be a Rock 'N' Roll Star: The Byrds Day-By-Day, 1965–1973*. Jawbone Books, 2008.

Hoskyns, Barney. *Waiting for the Sun: Strange Days, Weird Scenes, and the Sound of Los Angeles*. St. Martin's, 1996.

Hotchner, A. E. *Doris Day: Her Own Story*. William Morrow, 1975.

Jackson, John A. *Big Beat Heat: Alan Freed and the Early Years of Rock & Roll*. Schirmer Books, 1991.

Love, Darlene, with Hoerburger, Rob. *My Name Is Love: The Darlene Love Story*. William Morrow, 1998.

Kaplan, James. *Frank: The Voice*. Doubleday, 2010.

———. *Sinatra: The Chairman*. Doubleday, 2015.

Kaufman, David. *Doris Day: The Untold Story of the Girl Next Door*. Virgin Books, 2008.

Kelley, Kitty. *His Way: The Unauthorized Biography of Frank Sinatra*. Bantam Books, 1986.

Kelly, Michael "Doc Rock." *Liberty Records: A History of the Recording Company and Its Stars 1955–1971*, vols. 1 & 2. McFarland, 1991.

Kent, Nick. *The Dark Stuff: Selected Writings on Rock Music, 1972–1995*. Da Capo, 1995.

Kohner, Frederick. *Gidget: The Little Girl with Big Ideas*. Michael Joseph, 1958.

Kubernik, Harvey. *Hollywood Shack Job: Rock Music in Film and on Your Screen*. University of New Mexico Press, 2006.

————. *Turn Up the Radio! Rock, Pop, and Roll in Los Angeles, 1956–1972.* Santa Monica Press, 2014.

Love, Mike, with Hirsch, James S. *Good Vibrations: My Life as a Beach Boy.* Blue Rider, 2016.

Martin, Deana, with Holden, Wendy. *Memories Are Made of This: Dean Martin Through His Daughter's Eyes.* Harmony Books, 2004.

McKeen, William. *Everybody Had an Ocean: Music and Mayhem in 1960s Los Angeles.* Chicago Review, 2017.

McParland, Stephen J. *California Confidential: A Small Taste of California Dreamin' and California Schemin': In Conversation with Kim Fowley, 2000 and 1985.* CMusic Books, 2001.

————. *The Grand High Potentates of California Rock Jan & Dean "In Perspective" 1958–1968,* vols. 1 & 2. CMusic Books, 2000.

————. *In the Studio with Brian Wilson and the Beach Boys: Our Favorite Recording Sessions.* CMusic Books, 2000.

————. *Inception and Conception: The Beach Boys, 1961–1963: From Hite Morgan to Nick Venet.* CMusic Books, 2016.

————. *Sound Waves and Traction: Surf and Hot-Rod Studio Groups of the '60s.* CMusic Publishing, 2002.

Moore, Mark. *The Jan & Dean Record: A Chronology of Studio Sessions, Live Performances and Chart Positions.* McFarland, 2016.

Murphy, James B. *Becoming the Beach Boys, 1961–1963.* McFarland, 2015.

Nash, Alanna. *The Colonel: The Extraordinary Story of Colonel Tom Parker and Elvis Presley.* Simon and Schuster, 2003.

Nash, Alanna, with Smith, Billy; Lacker, Marty; and Fike, Lamar. *Elvis Aaron Presley: Revelations from the Memphis Mafia.* HarperCollins, 1995.

Oldham, Andrew Loog. *Stoned: A Memoir of London in the 1960s.* St. Martin's, 2000.

O'Rourke, Steve. *The Herb Alpert File.* Lulu Books, 2008.

Passmore, Mark Thomas. *Dead Man's Curve and Back: The Jan & Dean Story.* 1st Books Library, 2003.

Phelps, Dee Dee. *Vinyl Highway: Singing as "Dick and Dee Dee."* Altergate Publishing, 2007.

Phillips, John, with Jerome, Jim. *Papa John: A Music Legend's Shattering Journey Through Sex, Drugs, and Rock 'n' Roll.* Dolphin Books, 1986.

Phillips, Michelle. *California Dreamin': The True Story of The Mamas and The Papas.* Warner Books, 1986.

Podolsky, Rich. *Don Kirshner: The Man with the Golden Ear — How He Changed the Face of Rock and Roll.* Hal Leonard Books, 2012.

Port, Ian S. *The Birth of Loud: Leo Fender, Les Paul and the Guitar-Pioneering Rivalry that Shaped Rock 'n' Roll.* Scribner, 2019.

Priore, Domenic. *Riot on Sunset Strip; Rock 'n' Roll's Last Stand in Hollywood.* Jawbone Books, 2007.

Reed, Tom. *The Black Music History of Los Angeles — Its Roots.* Black Accent on L.A., 1994.

Ribowsky, Mark. *He's a Rebel: The Truth About Phil Spector — Rock and Roll's Legendary Madman.* E. P. Dutton, 1989.

Rogan, Johnny. *The Byrds: Timeless Flight Revisited: The Sequel.* Rogan House, 1997.

Scherman, Tony. *Backbeat: Earl Palmer's Story.* Smithsonian Institution, 1999.

Selvin, Joel. *Here Comes the Night: The Dark Soul of Bert Berns and the Dirty Business of Rhythm and Blues.* Counterpoint, 2014.

————. *Ricky Nelson: Idol for a Generation*. Contemporary Books, 1990.

Sinatra, Nancy. *Frank Sinatra: My Father*. Doubleday, 1985.

Sinatra, Tina, with Coplon, Jeff. *My Father's Daughter: A Memoir*. Simon and Schuster, 2000.

Sloan, P. F., and Feinberg, S. E. *What's Exactly the Matter with Me? Memoirs of a Life in Music*. Jawbone Books, 2014.

Spector, Ronnie, with Waldron, Vince. *Be My Baby: How I Survived Mascara, Miniskirts, and Madness, or My Life as a Fabulous Ronette*. Harmony Books, 1990.

Starr, Michael Seth. *Bobby Darin: A Life*. Taylor Trade Publishing, 2004.

Stebbins, Jon. *Dennis Wilson: The Real Beach Boy*. ECW, 1999.

Stebbins, Jon, with Marks, David. *The Lost Beach Boy*. Virgin Books, 2007.

Taylor, Derek. *As Times Goes By: Living in the Sixties*. Straight Arrow Books, 1973.

Torrence, Dean. *Surf City: The Jan & Dean Story*. Select Books, 2016.

Turner, Ike, with Cawthorne, Nigel. *Takin' Back My Name: The Confessions of Ike Turner*. Virgin Books, 1999.

Turner, Tina, with Loder, Kurt. *I, Tina: My Life Story*. William Morrow, 1986.

Wallace, Wyndham. *Lee, Myself & I: Inside the Very Special World of Lee Hazlewood*. Jawbone Books, 2015.

Warner, Jay. *The Billboard Book of American Singing Groups: A History, 1940–1990*. Billboard Books, 1992.

Warshaw, Matt. *A Brief History of Surfing*. Chronicle Books, 2017.

Whitburn, Joel. *Joel Whitburn's Top Pop Albums, 1955–1985*. Record Research, 1985.

———. *Top Pop Records, 1955–1972*. Record Research, 1973.

White, Timothy. *The Nearest Faraway Place: Brian Wilson, the Beach Boys, and the Southern California Experience*. Henry Holt, 1994.

Wilson, Brian, with Gold, Todd. *Wouldn't It Be Nice: My Own Story*. HarperCollins, 1991.

Wolff, Daniel, with Crain, S. E.; White, Clifton; and Tenenbaum, G. David. *You Send Me: The Life & Times of Sam Cooke*. William Morrow, 1995.

Wolfe, Tom. *The Kandy-Kolored-Tangerine-Flake Streamline Baby*. Farrar, Strauss & Giroux, 1965.

SELECTED ARTICLES, LINER NOTES, AND INTERVIEWS

Altham, Keith. "The Beach Boys: Complex and Intricate," *New Musical Express,* May 20, 1966.

———. "The Mamas and the Papas: The Morning After the Beatles' Night Before," *New Musical Express,* June 24, 1966.

Beard, David M. *Jan & Dean: Complete Liberty Singles* CD liner notes, EMI Special Markets, 2008.

Christy, George. "Frankie's Kids," *Good Housekeeping,* June 1964.

Douglas, Steve. "Money Honey: True Stories of Rock and Roll in the '50s." Unpublished manuscript, 1991.

Drowty, Don. *Dante: Evergreens & Friends* CD liner notes, Clifton Music, 1998.

Everett, Todd. *Boots: Nancy Sinatra's All-Time Hits,* album liner notes, Rhino Records, 1986.

Gilliland, John. Herb Alpert interview, unpublished transcript, *Pop Chronicles,* May 21, 1968.

————. Lou Adler interview, unpublished transcript, *Pop Chronicles*, January 5, 1968.

Gilstrap, Peter. "Barry Keenan: Snatching Sinatra," *Washington Post*, March 8, 1998.

Hopkins, Jerry. "Lou Adler: California Dreamin'," *Rolling Stone*, December 21, 1968.

Hoskyns, Barney. Kim Fowley interview, Rock's Backpages Audio, 1993.

Kelly, Michael "Doc Rock." *Jan &Dean* CD liner notes, Dominion Entertainment, 1996.

Kendall, Elliot. *Jan & Dean: Teen Suite 1958–1962* CD liner notes, Varèse Sarabande, 1995.

Kolanjian, Steve. *Jan & Dean All the Hits—From Surf City to Drag City* CD liner notes, EMI Records, 1996.

————. *The Rivingtons: The Liberty Years* CD liner notes, EMI Records, 1991.

Kubernik, Harvey. "Prod. by Terry Melcher Arr. & Cond. Jack Nitzsche," Spectropop.com 2004.

————. *Kim Fowley: Underground Animal* CD liner notes, Bacchus Archives, 1999.

Leaf, David. "The Making of Pet Sounds" CD booklet, *The Pet Sounds Sessions*, Capitol Records, 1996.

————. *Smiley Smile / Wild Honey* CD liner notes, Capitol Records, 1990.

Marsh, Dave. *Jan & Dean Anthology Album* album liner notes, Legendary Masters Series vol. 3, United Artists Records, 1971.

McParland, Stephen J. *The Hot Doggers: Surfin' USA* CD liner notes, Sundazed Records, 2006.

Morantz, Paul. "The Road Back from Dead Man's Curve: The Tragic Life of Jan Berry with & without Dean Torrence," *Rolling Stone*, September 13, 1974.

Mugsy. *Johnny Rivers: Totally Live at the Whisky a Go Go* CD liner notes, EMI Records, 1995.

Nolan, Tom. "Surf's Up! Melcher's Nightmare Is Over," *Rolling Stone*, May 8, 1974.

———. "The Beach Boys; A California Saga. Part One: Mr. Everything. Part Two: Tales of Hawthorne," *Rolling Stone*, October 28– November 11, 1971.

———. "Terry Melcher: A Beach Veteran Looks Back," *Phonograph Record Magazine*, September 1974.

Priore, Domenic. "Steve Douglas: The Last Word, All Summer Long," *Dumb Angel Gazette* no. 4, Neptune's Kingdom, 2004.

Quaglieri, Al. *The Best of Bruce & Terry* CD liner notes, Sundazed Records, 1998.

———. *Bruce Johnston; Surfin' 'Round the World* CD liner notes, Sundazed Records, 1997.

Shelley, Michael. Steve Barri interview, WFMU, June 23, 2018.

Sims, Judith. "Two Lonely Bulls & How They Grew," *Rolling Stone*, October 12, 1972.

Sinatra, Nancy. *Boots* CD liner notes, Sundazed Records, 1995.

Smith, Joe. Off-the-record interview with Herb Alpert, February 12, 1987, Library of Congress.

———. Off-the-record interview with Lou Adler, February 25, 1986, Library of Congress.

Stax, Mike. "Kim Fowley: Sins & Secrets of the Silver Screen," *Ugly Things* no. 19, 2001.

Teicholz, Tom. "Lou Adler: Low-key, Lucky and Very Cool," *Jewish Journal,* November 28, 2013.

Waller, Don. *The T.A.M.I. Show* DVD liner notes, Shout Factory, 2009.

White, Timothy. Brian Wilson interview, *Crawdaddy,* June 1976.

———. "Please Don't Wake Me: Producer Russ Titelman Recalls 35 Years in the Service of a California Dream," *Billboard,* June 22, 1996.

INDEX

Note: The "The" is not included in group names.

Author photograph: Author's collection

JOEL SELVIN is an award-winning journalist and music critic who covered pop music for the *San Francisco Chronicle* for more than thirty-five years. His writing has appeared in *Rolling Stone*, the *Los Angeles Times*, *Billboard*, and *Melody Maker*, and he has contributed liner notes to dozens of recorded albums. Selvin is also the bestselling author of more than twenty books about pop music, including *Fare Thee Well: The Final Chapter of the Grateful Dead's Long, Strange Trip*; *Altamont: The Rolling Stones, the Hells Angels, and the Inside Story of Rock's Darkest Day*; and *Here Comes the Night: The Dark Soul of Bert Berns and the Dirty Business of Rhythm and Blues*. He lives in San Francisco.